The story of .

Bernard Capes

Alpha Editions

This edition published in 2024

ISBN : 9789362924674

Design and Setting By
Alpha Editions
www.alphaedis.com
Email - info@alphaedis.com

Contents

CHAPTER I

I ALWAYS come back to Paris or to London as to a rich feast after abstinence. There are the reserves of perfect health to draw upon for its enjoyment; and I enjoy it while the reserves last. But, on the first sign of their depletion, I return to my lentils and spring water, which can stand my happiness in quite as good stead as young partridges and Montrachet.

So the New Zealand shepherd, come once in a while to town, dissipates in a week of glorious debauch the accumulated earnings of a year or so spent in the comfortable solitudes. I don't blame him: on the contrary. What is the sense of storing up health and vigour for no other purpose than, like a miser, to hoard them? I use *my* physical energy to serve every ounce of me, brain, nerves and organs. A man in health is a man in happiness, whether he be dining at Voisin's, or on ripe figs on the hot rocks of les Baux. And I am a man in health; thank my good stars for that.

Of all the great cities, I have sojourned in Paris more than in any other. I have not, like Byron, shaken the dust of my native land off my shoes; but I came so early abroad, that English ways have grown foreign to me. I did not in fact ever fit into their social scheme, though somewhere in my heart a respect survives for it. But the little island is too small for me; or I am too big for it. There is not my peer there in the art of modelling; not a piece of native sculpture that I should like to acknowledge for my own.

For some years now I have rented a little flat in the Rue de Fleurus. It is the topmost suite in a high building, and troublesome of access to short-winded visitors, on whom the interminable succession of bare stone flights with their iron railings acts as a veritable treadmill. But the eyrie, once reached, is remote, and the view from its windows superb, including on the right the fathomless green sea of the Luxembourg gardens, on the left, like a golden buoy in the transparent mists, the dome of the Invalides. Here I possess three rooms at no great rent; and it suits me to retain them, as a conventional refuge, for use when I make my periodic returns from the wilderness.

I had been in repossession of them but three or four days when the story of Fifine began for me. It opened with a visit from Marion.

Marion, my step-sister, is the daughter of the Vicar: I am the son of the Vicar's second wife, whose first husband was a barrister. In most tales the step-mother indulges her own offspring at the expense of her spouse's; in mine the custom was reversed. Marion had ruled at Neverston, and Marion continued to rule. She ruled my mother consecrate, and myself unregenerate, and we both accepted her finding—with unnatural consequences for me. At the age of twenty-one I carried my Pariahship abroad for good, and my visits to Neverston since have been few and unexhilarating.

On one of these I discovered, to my amazement, that Marion herself had gone to Paris—that actually, without my knowledge, she had been living there for over a year. She was a woman of really surpassing energy, which, in course of time, I suppose, had craved a wider scope than that afforded by the narrow bounds of a country parish. And she had wanted to improve her French, for Marion was always wanting to improve something or somebody. So she had accepted a position, au pair, in the household of a penurious French Marquis—recently made a widower, and possessing one child, a daughter—where she had established herself in the true Marionesque spirit, ruling and dogmatising. I wrote to her, on my next visit to the Capital, and she came to see me once or twice, and always, as the more experienced Parisian, with some condescending pity for my easy capacity to be led astray through my ignorance of the world. *She* had seen enough in her short time to qualify her for a very Mentor to the gullible. But it was not to be supposed that, with my record, I should come to do other than perish in my own conceit. So she accused and judged me without a particle of evidence; but I had a small amused liking for her, all the same. She was so sturdily insular, from her contempt for temperament to her tailor-made dress, which she persisted in wearing in defiance of all continental fopperies.

On this September evening in question I had been dining in one of those exiguous Cafés in the Boulevard S. Michel, which cater largely for students of the Sorbonne and their little chère-amies. I have never much to say against the custom of such connexions, save for the hardship they entail upon certain of the girls—mostly shop or factory hands—when a necessary period is put to them. In other respects they serve to solve, and to solve cleanly, a problem which English prudery cannot bring itself to face. Yet better surely the informal comrade than the bagnio; and, after all, those who consent accept with their eyes open, and with a full knowledge of the impermanent nature of the relations.

I returned to the flat about eight o'clock, to find the wife of the Concierge already peering for me behind the closed iron gates of the lodge, which led out of a courtyard reached through an archway.

"Why closed?" I said.

"Ah!" returned Madame Crussol, snapping viciously at the lock: "Why indeed, but to oblige the laudable sister of a good-for-nothing, who is never so little to be found as when respectability calls. Likely this is one of your pranks, for which you are to be taken to task. You will find Madame upstairs."

She swung open the gate, and locked it behind me again as I entered. I accepted the enigma with a laugh, and a little pat on the good wife's ample shoulder. I am never eager about solving riddles which left alone will unravel of themselves. It is a good rule for ensuring serenity of mind.

As I turned to the stairs, I noticed a figure seated dimly in the porter's lodge. It was shrouded and obscure, but I believed it was that of a young girl, whose white face, picked out by the lamp-light, blossomed from the shadows with an oddly Rembrandtesque effect. It seemed, as I passed, to be projected in sudden interest or curiosity, and then, like a face seen from a train at night, to vanish instantly.

I found, on entering my principal room, the electric light turned on and the curtains drawn close. Marion, her hands clasped behind her back, was striding restlessly up and down; but, I observed, with a stealthy motion, as though she feared the sound of her own footsteps. She stopped, on the instant of my entrance, and faced on me, her lips compressed. I thought she looked unusually grim, and that her constitutionally dead complexion betrayed a livider pallor.

"At last!" she said. "Shut the door, Felix Dane. I want to speak to you."

"I have only been dining, Marion. Quite respectably, believe me. Had you any reason for drawing to the curtains this warm night?"

"I never do anything without a reason. I was afraid of being followed and the light betraying me."

Marion the subject of an adventure! I begged her to be seated, with the urbanity of a doctor introduced to a remarkable case.

"No," she said: "I cannot keep still."

She walked, in fact, as she spoke, her gaunt figure jerked by some odd emotion. She was struggling to meet me on equal terms. Though she was my senior by two years, you must understand that mine numbered full thirty-five, and that I had had quite a little experience of the world. But it would never have done for me to presume on that pretence with her. Presently she made up her mind, and gave forth, still tramping:—

"You know my opinion of you, Felix Dane?" She commonly addressed me by my full name, as if to remind me of my untitled place in the family connexion.

"Quite," I answered. "It is summed up in one word—wastrel."

"Not a very flattering opinion."

"Not in any way otherwise, Marion. It means merely to be natural."

"Natural in the irresponsible and squandering sense."

"Why, of course. That is the very essence of Nature—to show a blind trust in a bountiful Providence. Look at animals feeding—birds, beasts and fishes. They take the best of what is offered to them, and trample or spill abroad the ninety per cent. residue. You kept a parrot once, and ought to know. I am really, if you look at it rightly, the more religious of us two!"

She did not answer me, but continued her spasmodic march, while I observed her curiously. Suddenly she flounced to a stop before me, a suggestion of queer defiance in her expression.

"I should not have come to you," she said, "in a very difficult situation, if I had believed your character really summed up in that word. Perhaps I can do you more justice than you do yourself, Felix."

"That I can't tell, Marion, until I know what it is you ask of me."

"Courage, Felix Dane," she answered, looking me straight in the face; "and self-restraint."

A short silence ensued. Then, "I am waiting," I said.

She took yet a quick turn or two, and came back as before.

"You know something of my position here," she said, "and of its responsibilities? Well, those have suddenly assumed a very grave and menacing aspect. There have been discoveries and revelations of late, more than enough."

I saw that, for all her self-repression, she was distressed and agitated, and the man in me, no less, perhaps, than the curiosity, was moved.

"Well, take my better qualities for granted," I said.

She squeezed her lips with her hand, still staring at me; then broke out:—

"I will—I must. I have a claim upon them, after all, and a right to urge it. Felix, if you will swear to keep my confidence———"

"I will swear to nothing. Tell me or not, as you like."

She canvassed me a little before deciding. I would not have accused her of guile, though I fancied I knew something of women. And at last she spoke:—

"I have got the Comtesse de Beaurepaire hidden away in the Conciergerie below, and I want you to take charge of her, to conceal and protect her, until such time as I can redeem her from your hands."

She gave a gasp, having got it all quickly out, and stepped back, to observe the effect on me. It was startling enough; but, somehow, I was tickled rather than prostrated.

"The Comtesse—your young pupil—the little au pair?" I asked. "What on earth has the bad child been doing?"

"Her father is a madman," said my step-sister, with more passion than I should have thought possible to her—"a morphiomaniac, who has suffered, as I know now, from toxic delirium. Some weeks ago he discovered, among his dead wife's papers, compromising documents which made him doubt his daughter's legitimacy. Since then he is like a rabid animal; he has always been an unnatural parent; and now the girl's life is not safe in his hands. It came to this at last, that to rescue her from his brutality, she must be smuggled away into hiding. Arrangements were made to convey her this day after dark to the school of Les Loges, which is twelve miles distant. We started, she and I, in a hired fiacre; but had not reached the barriers, when a note was thrown into our carriage from an overtaking automobile informing me that our escape had been discovered, and that emissaries of the Marquis were even then on the way out to waylay and dispose of us. Panic seized me: I was in despair. To return would be to submit my charge, perhaps, to an unspeakable fate; to go on would be to invite some nameless catastrophe. I ordered the coachman to turn; and in the act a thought came to me. To forestall the chase, and, by doubling, be lost to it in the intricacies of the City! It was then the idea of you occurred to me, and we drove straight for the Rue de Fleurus, alighted short of it, and hurried the rest of the way on foot. Madame Crussol, in response to my entreaties, shut the gates upon us, and—there it stands."

I sat up stiff, I ruffled my hair, I laughed aloud.

"My dear Marion! This wild melodrama in the midst of modern Paris! Have you not been testing some of his lordship's drugs?"

She stood looking at me steadily.

"I should have thought," she said, "that even for you by this time the criminal possibilities in a great capital could have no surprises."

"But the position of the parties—a confessed morphiomaniac—his, as I understand you, hardly-veiled threats! You had only to go to the police."

She regarded me with grey tolerance.

"There is such a thing as scandal; there is such a thing as despotic influence, even amongst this supposed discredited noblesse. The Marquis, for all his domestic parsimony, is a man of immense political power. And he is rich; he can command what instruments he pleases. Besides, you are not to suppose that he habitually reveals himself in his conduct. That is not at all the way with such aliénés. He can be suavity itself—most convincingly, most alluringly. You have much to learn, Felix Dane."

"I have, indeed. This is not Paris, but mediæval Rome. Has the young lady no relatives, great or small, to whom to appeal?"

"Not one, who is not subject in some way to his tyranny or dislike. He is a strange unnatural character, and greatly feared."

"Well, I think, if you are not dreaming, that I must be. My step-sister Marion, from Neverston Vicarage, and implicated in a transpontine mystery of abduction and murder! The young Countess is here, you say—in pledge to me until redeemed by you. And what do *you* propose doing?"

"I propose going back to the Hôtel Beaurepaire."

"Going back? To invite the reprisals of that monster?"

"I have no fear of him for myself—if for no other reason than that in me lives the only clue to this poor unhappy child's whereabouts."

Marion had courage. I had never doubted that; but this manifestation of it, whatever ludicrous fancy it might be based on, surprised while it interested me. She had never been wont to sentimental attachments. But I had thought of late that in many ways she was an altered woman, broader-minded, more humanly worldly than of old.

"You could be trusted not to betray it, I will swear," I said. "But how about others? There was the coachman who drove you, for instance."

"We dropped him near the Mont de Piété, pretending it was our destination."

"Admirable strategist! But you say you were warned of pursuit. That seems to speak some knowledge of your movements."

"I am afraid so! We can only hope that it will prove knowledge misled."

"Afraid so—afraid so!" I got to my feet, more inclined to laugh than protest, for all my perplexity. "Then I am to take it—provided I accept this amazing trust—that, if this maniac succeeds in penetrating our secret, the young lady will be in danger?"

My step-sister, it seemed to me, hesitated momentarily, with a queer down-glance, before answering my question.

"In the gravest danger, Felix—I am forced to admit it."

"And—incidentally—I, perhaps?"

Again she appeared to hesitate, before facing me with a bold challenge:—

"I do you the justice that, for all our differences, I should never have denied you. You will not take personal peril into account in the matter of protecting an unhappy young woman against her persecutors."

"Thank you," I said shortly.

"It is possible," continued Marion, "that the place of her retreat *may* be discovered. God forbid it should be so; but it may be. In that case we can only pray that the worst may not happen."

I crowed. "Well, pray," I said, "with all your heart; you had better begin at once. As a Vicar's daughter you should know the ropes. But for me this is a very practical matter, it seems."

She failed to protest, after her custom, over my profanity; and I paced a turn or two in sheer desperation.

"Well," I said at last, "you have appealed to our relationship, and to the knowledge it gives you of me, and, for the sake of my own credit, I must not be found wanting. I tell you candidly that I believe this all to be some wild hallucination of your brain; but I am ready to humour it, if that will satisfy you. Trot up the young victim—but wait a minute. She is to live, pour le moment, you say, under my protection. As what?"

She looked at me very oddly.

"You are a gentleman, Felix Dane," she said.

"I may be the incomparable Bayard himself, Marion; but jealousy has denied me his reputation."

"'As thy days, so shall thy strength be,' Felix" (it was her only concession to the old Marion). "For the rest, she must not be known, of course, for whom she is. Call her simply Fifine."

"And Madame Crussol and the others?"

"What does it matter? When she leaves you, it will be to resume herself—to disappear from all imaginary associations."

This from Marion! I stared in amazement. Surely she had travelled a long way from Neverston.

"When she leaves me?" I said. "And at what date am I to look for that happy release?"

"I cannot tell you yet," answered my step-sister hurriedly. "We must be guided by events. Only I beg you in the meantime, for your own sake and hers, to keep her close, to whisper no word about her to your friends, never to let her leave your chambers, and to make her lock herself into them when alone."

"My chambers!" I looked desperately round the ill-furnished room. "I never thought of that. What accommodation have I for Countesses, what knowledge of their needs and caprices?"

"You make my task too difficult, Felix," said Marion fretfully; "and I want to escape—every moment is important. Even now I may be tracked and watched for."

"Heaven forbid! Why not take possession of my rooms, you and she, and leave me to find another lodging?"

"Impossible—it is impossible. I cannot stop now to explain why. Will you do it, Felix, or will you not? I am quite at the end of my resources."

I stepped aside.

"It is lunar madness—but call her up. You will come again soon? You will communicate with me, at least?"

"The very moment it is safe."

She was going, but turned at the door, as if in an afterthought.

"She is only nineteen, Felix—a child. You will bear that in mind?"

"And I am thirty-five, Marion. I had better come down with you now, in case——"

"No. Well, perhaps, if you like——"

We descended to the Conciergerie. Madame Crussol, severe but curious, awaited us in the doorway.

"Fifine," said my step-sister, whispering into the room, "you are to go upstairs to your cousin's apartments. He is prepared to grant you asylum until such time as the right authorities can be found and appealed to."

She had run away from school and the religious life: that, I perceived, was to be the fiction. My cousin! I blushed, if Marion did not. There was a little rustle in the room, as of some one rising. Marion begged the porteress to open the gate for her without more ado. I accompanied her into the street. It appeared empty, and void, of course, of any lurking shadow of suspicion. Strenuously combating my offer of escort, Marion bade me back into the glooms, and, herself turning into the Rue de Luxembourg, disappeared abruptly from sight.

At the gates Madame Crussol met me returning.

"Where is my errant young cousin gone?" I asked.

"Where do you suppose?" said the good lady drily. "She is very obedient to her instructions, that. She is high up by now. That is a good school of hers to end in such promotion. But I daresay your sister knows you better than I do."

From which I perceived very clearly that my difficult time was beginning.

CHAPTER II

I COMPILE these notes, these memoirs of a past episode, from what motive? I do not know. From vain unhappiness, perhaps: perhaps from an ineradicable instinct to deliver myself, in some concrete form, of a haunting vision. I do not seek the world's opinion on them; I should care nothing for it, whichever way pronounced. If anything, they are in the nature of an appeal to the one spirit that could appreciate them, a grave self-analysis, a considered defence, offered to the clear judgment of the disembodied. If there is any moral weakness in them, let me abide by that judgment. I plead nothing in extenuation but sentiment, which in heaven, I think, is still allowed more place than in this modern world of ours, where it has come to be regarded as a contemptible thing, to be rigorously eschewed in art, in education, and, save in its most hypocritically clap-trap form, in the gamble called politics. Yet by sentiment, I think, we humanise, and without it retrograde. When there is no more, we shall have returned to the primal anarchy.

Looks are a powerful influence in the shaping of one's destiny. The really good-looking man, having the confidence of his parts, finds himself easily equipped for the conquests for which souls less naturally endowed must suffer a severe handicap. He is a laggard if he allows himself to be overtaken; and so I have often found it. My excuse lies—my salvation, perhaps—in my inborn faculty for creating things of beauty far beyond the material reach of the senses. To carve divinity out of stone is ever a higher joy to me than to beget its fleshly image. Wherefore I can assert truly that personal coxcombry is as remote from my nature as the pride of the craftsman is near and holy. That may be believed or not: it may concern others to dispute what it does not concern me to defend.

I put this to myself, and to one other, if not as a justification, as a plea. I have sinned, if I have sinned, not from vanity at all. A thousand times I would rather have suffered that longest handicap than have basely used a favour due to no merit, but merely to inheritance. I did not so use it. It was the traffic of souls, not of bodies, that made the real joy and misery. It would have been the same in the end, though I had possessed the features of a Caliban. And with that I will leave it.

It seems appropriate here to interpolate a note, descriptive of the writer in his late thirties, from the pen of Monsieur C., professor of the Ecole des Beaux-Arts in Paris and himself a distinguished sculptor—who knew intimately, and was an ardent admirer of, the erratic genius self-portrayed in these pages. Monsieur C. writes:—

"Le Danois is very amusing, very clever, very suffisant. He will be here one moment and nowhere the next; and so with his work, his opinions, his enthusiasms. No one must doubt him, even when to-morrow he advocates the cause or the theory which to-day he denounces. And no one, I am sure, will think of doing so—for the moment: his personal magnetism, his unvexed effrontery see to it. His clothes—a hardy Englishman's compromise with the French habit—are generally patched and mended: his manners show no bad places at all. He commonly wears what they call a Norfolk suit, but without lapels; knickerbockers, a white handkerchief round his neck in lieu of collar, and white canvas boots with string soles. And in these he will appear unembarrassed in drawing-rooms—to make ladies in love with vagabondism. I think I have never known in another the true gentleman and the true Bohemian so naturally blended. There is not a shadow of pose about him: his belief in himself is too simply unaffected for it. In person he is tall, somewhat lean, and muscular, with the thews of a mountaineer and the eyes of a jay. His hair, thick and brushed forward like a thatch, is coloured a warm brown, and his strong brows, moustache, and short beard au poinçon, are of the same satisfying tone. His face is very agreeably formed, with a look of power and self-confidence in it; and yet he is a disappointed man, one whose expectations have run well ahead of his achievements. He is interested in too many things, that is the fact. In his youth he was bred for the Bar, but soon abandoned its attractions for those of the free life and the pursuit of beauty. An artist, with an irresistible penchant for metaphysics, music, and mechanical science, and an insatiable curiosity about everything, he has never quite succeeded in realising himself or convincing others. Yet some magnificent fragments exist to his credit—a noble head or so, a torso worthy of Praxiteles. I suspect he is too impatient of practice to make perfect. It is a danger, after all, to be too deft with one's fingers. Things picked up quickly quickly lose their interest; and there are so many fine things in the world to be picked up. Will our friend ever learn to concentrate? I fear. And, by the by, where is he just now? Nobody knows, of course. B. C."

With a smile for Madame Crussol [continues the narrator], I went up the stairs leisurely. I found my "cousin" standing outside my door, and she turned to look at me as I arrived. I saw question but no embarrassment in her eyes. She held wrapped about her, more for concealment than warmth, I supposed, one of those heavy military capotes of stone blue which have become fashionable with ladies of late; and a black velvet hat, of Tudor shape and with a small white feather, surmounted her head coquettishly.

"You have been a long time coming, Monsieur," she said; and her voice was soft to sleepiness.

"Ah, true!" I answered. "I have cause for deliberation."

The door was ajar; I motioned her in and closed it behind us. It shut with a snap, delivering us to complete privacy. Preceding her, I went through the little passage into the salle-à-manger, whence on one side opened the tiny kitchen, on the other my large sitting-room, leading into the single bed-chamber beyond, which together comprised my whole domain. She had followed me, and stopped, as I did, in the main apartment.

"So far so good," I said. "And now, if you please, what next?"

Her eyes, I could see, were busy with her surroundings, and I took the word from them:—

"Yes, it is all very plain and ungarnished, the quarters of an unstable vagabond quite unused to entertaining countesses. But for what they are worth, they are entirely at your disposition."

Her eyes came round to me, impassive but wondering.

"You are not to call me that," she said.

"To call you what? O, yes! I understand. But there is still the question of the moral inference. Am I to defer to what I may not specify—your rank— or to disregard it altogether?"

The eyes seemed to expand momentarily.

"Would there not be danger in the first?" she asked.

"No," I answered gravely; "I believe not, if we are careful."

"Then I think I should like it," she said, with the tiniest sigh as of relief.

I bowed. "The only difficulty lies in my ignorance of the forms, the ceremonial. But I am adaptable, and learn quickly. It occurs to me that, having placed all that I own at your disposal, it is meet for me to retire to the kitchen, while you take stock of the premises. An inventory will not fatigue you. I ask your permission to withdraw."

I left her standing mute—appraising me, it seemed, with those solemn enigmatic eyes.

"This is petrifying," I said, apostrophising the saucepan on my little electric stove. There were the cold remains of a curry in it, an excellent curry concocted by myself; but it was not to that I alluded. "I am to be kept in my place, it seems; to esteem at its worth the honour of this condescension, and not to think of presuming upon it. I look for some sign

- 12 -

of the stress and tragedy which brought a fugitive to my door. I might as well look for blood in a statue. But it is all very amusing, and I am going thoroughly to enjoy myself."

It occurred to me that, what with the hour and the exercise, my cousin might be hungry. Anyhow, to prepare and produce a meal would serve to give her time for her exploration, and perhaps to thaw the ice. Wherefore I set to work and cut some sandwiches, knocked up an omelette aux confitures, brewed some chocolate, and, when all was ready, carried in the whole on a tray.

She was standing where, but not as, I had left her. The cloak was doffed and the hat. I saw her clearly for the first time, a placid self-possessed young figure, and with nothing but her rank to signal her out from the majority. Comely if you like: if you like, a thought more Southern in suggestion than Parisian. There was the complexion of warm ivory, deepening to a glow under the eyes, which were of a hot velvet brown; there was the short straight nose, the smooth rather round cheek and ripe babyish mouth. But all was impassive, unperturbed, and seemingly imperturbable. She was dressed in black, very plain and showing the full of the neck, which was certainly a shapely feature. I had seen many girls of her pattern south of Valence, "*où le midi commence*," and she was neither better nor worse than the pick of them—just a proud-fleshed young animal.

"Will you?" I said. "After this stress and fatigue you must need refreshment."

I fancied her eyes glistened a little at the sight. I pulled a small table towards a chair, set out my feast, and asked her to be seated. She glanced at me a little doubtfully before complying.

"I understood that Monsieur's ménage——"

"Was summed up in Monsieur himself? That is quite right. I am my own portier, my own garçon-de-chambre, my own cook—all of the best character. I do not believe in doing things by halves. What I take up I master. 'Well meant' is not enough for me: it must be 'well done.'"

"I will tell you that," she said, "when I have eaten."

The calm insolence of it! I banged the chair down on my own foot, as I set it in place for her. She hesitated a moment before seating herself. There was a perplexed look in her eyes, between condescension and reluctance.

"No, thank you," I said: "I couldn't dream of it. I shall have my supper presently among the cinders."

She ate with evident enjoyment, and in complete self-possession. Indeed I have never known a Frenchwoman, though the cynosure of a score of eyes surrounding her, show embarrassment over a solitary meal. At the end she wiped her lips and her fingers, and, putting down her napkin, leaned back.

"It was very nice," she said. "I liked it all."

I came from the background, to which I had considerately withdrawn, pretending to read a book.

"I am reassured," I answered, preparing to remove the tray. "I hope the rest of my establishment is as much to your taste?"

She glanced up at me, with an indolent question:——

"Where will you sleep yourself?"

Of course: it was a reasonable query, yet it took my breath away.

"O! don't trouble about me," I said, "I am a seasoned vagrant. A rug, and the kitchen table, will serve my needs. When we have disposed your baggage——"

"I have no baggage."

The shock of the retort! And yet I might have foreseen.

"It was all decided in such a hurry," she said—"and at the last moment. There was no time to prepare anything."

"Then——" I stood fairly petrified. "It all turns upon the resources of my wardrobe—*mine*."

"If you please," she said. "To-morrow we can arrange things better."

"You must excuse me," I answered. "You will understand that you find me as ill-prepared as yourself. If you will take a book—or a cigarette—I will go and see what can be done."

She took a cigarette, impassively content, and I disappeared into the bedroom. There were her hat and cloak placed on a chair, and it gave me an odd turn to encounter those signs of feminine usurpation.

I could find sheets and linen; I could dispose my other effects, appropriately and with resignation. And then I paused, before producing from a drawer my smartest pair of clean pyjamas. I looked at the length, and shook my head; I turned up the cuffs and the end of each leg, folded and lay the things gently on the pillow, and returned to my visitor.

"I have done my best," I said. "When it pleases you to retire——"

She rose at once, yawning slightly.

"I am ready, Monsieur. I can hardly, as it is, keep my eyes open"—and she went, and the door was shut between us.

I stood gazing a moment; then switched off the light, turned into the salle-à-manger, closed the door, took a chair, filled and lit my pipe, and sat drawing at it and grinning to myself, like a blissful sucking infant half-hypnotised by the enormous novelty of things. Was it constitutional or "serenical," in the exalted Highness sense, this impassibility in the face of shocks, this unquestioning acceptance of services as a favour not so much received as bestowed? This girl, this serene infant, had just, if I were to credit my step-sister, passed through a crisis, the consummation of a long ordeal of hate and tyranny, enough to try the stoutest nerves; yet she had shown no more agitation, no more embarrassment over the turn of events than if she had gone out for a drive and been belated in a country inn. The flight by night, the pursuit, the sudden immurement and isolation in strange quarters, appeared to have left her wholly unperturbed. What traditions of command and self-will lay at the back of such assurance, what arrogance of blood and class insolence! and she no more than a grown child, whose contact hitherto with the world must have been of the slightest. It was a new experience for me, this calm overriding of a man's intelligence and independence by sheer virtue of aristocracy—a new, and I will own, a rather piquant one. I foresaw plentiful amusement for myself in the situation—if I could only accept it on its merits.

I could not, nevertheless, quite do that at once. The thing appeared too wildly fantastical for sober belief. There must be some mystification somewhere, whether unconscious or deliberate, in the story—enough, at least, in my suspicions, to make a farce of my tragic undertaking. Still I had given my word and must play out the farce—conceal what nobody, perhaps, wanted to discover, watch and ward what nobody, perhaps, wanted to injure. Only I hoped devoutly it would not last for long. I was no sybarite, but—

I slept out the night in my chair.

CHAPTER III

THE unexpected is the salt of life—enough or too much as the case may be. The Chef who arranges this mortal mess of ours is not always to be trusted in the matter of seasoning—or, indeed, of seasonableness: perhaps he has too many conflicting tastes to consider. Still, one would rather chance encountering the unexpected in excess than be without it altogether. Let me start and shudder in an occasional briny spasm, if saltless insipidity is to be the sole alternative. I would sooner be a man and fear shadows than be a god and command them. Think of the boredom of an existence beyond the reach of thrills!

Toutes choses peut on suffrir qu'aise. Well, the Fates were kind to me as a rule in the respect of too much ease; and here was a rare new instance of their favouritism. I hoped to prove myself worthy of it.

I was up early, getting ready the rolls and coffee. The baker left the former at my door; the latter was my particular province. I had no plans for the day beyond the present plan of breakfast; but I was prepared for anything, in reason or out of it.

I was laying the table leisurely in the salle-à-manger, when, to my surprise, my visitor walked in on me. I had not for a moment supposed her risen, or indeed even aware that such an hour as seven o'clock in the morning existed outside dreams; but it was evident that my estimate of the haute monde needed some readjustment. Perhaps there *was* a faintest suggestion of shamefacedness on the smooth cheeks, of apology in the eyes.

"I was so hungry," she said, "and I couldn't wait any longer."

So she had waited, implying a yet earlier toilette! I could only assume that the martinet of the Hôtel Beaurepaire, including a deprivation of sleep in his scheme of tortures, had habituated this poor victim of his to a premature wakefulness. Yet the languor that remained to her eyes appeared rather their indelible characteristic than the dust of slumber.

"No need to in the world," I said. "Your will is my law. If I forgot to mention it, I entreat you to understand now that in placing all that is mine at your disposal I meant to include the least of my possessions, myself."

"I do not think you mean that," she said.

"Mean what?"

"To estimate so low such a sum of perfections. What has become of the universal genius who masters all he touches?"

It was uttered quite impassively. I opened my eyes. So the badinage was not to be all mine. There was something here unsuspected, a hint of activities hardly suggested by that soft indolence of look and gesture. Was this to prove a smouldering fire, only damped down, as they say, by circumstance? I was warned, at least, to look out for my fingers.

"He is here all the same," I said. "Only he counts as his great possessions the work of his own hands. He did not make himself, you see, or he might think better of the result."

"Well," she said, "the great work of his hands that concerns me just now is breakfast."

She sat down at the table, and I served her with an elaborated respect, the pleasant irony of which seemed quite thrown away upon her. She dipped her roll and ate her brioche entirely unembarrassed, and at the end turned to me with calm enquiring eyes.

"We had better talk together now, had we not?"

"I daresay I shall not be the worse for postponing my own breakfast," I said, with futile sarcasm. "Will you go and make yourself comfortable in the other room. The *Matin* and the *Petit Journal* should be on the mat outside. I will get them for you."

She was ensconced in the only comfortable chair by the window when I returned.

"You have a very sweet view, Monsieur," she said. "It is like being a sparrow up here among the tree-tops."

"Or a swallow under the eaves," I said. "I am of the migratory order, Cousin."

She lifted her eyebrows a little, at that.

"Pardon me," I said, leaning back against the piano—for I possessed an indifferent instrument: "but I think we must be consistent. It should be either the whole fiction or none at all. You know I told you I didn't favour half measures; and if we are to feign familiarity we should use its terms."

"You said," she answered, "that there was no danger."

"I did," I said frankly; "but that was before I had had an opportunity of studying you."

"Yes—and now?"—the eyebrows went up again.

"Now—the instincts of class are so strong in you—I think to avoid the risk of self-betrayal, you had better let me appear your cousin in fact."

"You mean, you are not to defer to me, not to show any knowledge of— of my rank? But, when we are alone——"

"It is the question of the habit. Once acquired, accident might surprise one into a blunder before witnesses."

"Why should there be any?"

"There shall not be, if I can help it. But it is best to guard against contingencies."

She yielded the point reluctantly, and with evident disappointment.

"Very well," she said. "Call me Cousin, if you must."

"The truth remains to our hearts," I said. "Subconsciously, you shall still be Countess, and I your faithful commoner. It is really a compromise, if you would know. My step-sister's directions to me were to call you Fifine."

She bit at her little round lower lip, as if in a sudden flush of resentment.

"I will not be Fifine to you," she said. "That is positive."

"You will be to me what I find in you," I answered—"just that and no more. It may be anything or nothing; but you will not know, whatever name I call you by. Still, 'cousin' is a good workaday title, and we will agree to compromise on that."

She rounded her eyes at me.

"You are very rude and very peremptory all of a sudden."

"No. Only wise in my trust, Cousin. When I accepted it, I accepted it on its professed merits. Perhaps you might, if you would, put a different complexion on those. You must remember that until yesterday I had hardly known of your existence, save in an abstract way; and then suddenly this business was exploded on me. I should like, now we have settled down to it, some confirmation of its details from your lips—as, for instance, the fact of your personal peril. Do you *really* go in fear for your life?"

She had dropped her eyes, and sat silently, sullenly perhaps, wreathing her fingers together.

"I should like an answer," I said.

She looked up quickly—defiantly, I thought.

"Yes," she said—"your tone, I know perfectly well, is full of mockery and derision; but he would have me killed if he knew where I was."

I drew in my breath a little, still, I am afraid, incredulous.

"Very well," I said. "Whatever my tone may be, your belief shall be my law. But then comes in another question. Any port, we know, in a storm; hence this descent on the Rue de Fleurus. But, now we have had time to breathe and look around——"

She broke out passionately:—

"You are afraid; you want to get rid of me. Very well, I will go."

Actually she rose; but I stopped her.

"Where to?"

"Anywhere—I do not know—only away from a coward."

"Now, is that consistent?" I said. "You first accuse me of incredulity, and then of fearing a bogey I don't believe in. I gave my promise to Marion, to hold you in pledge until redeemed, and I have no intention of breaking my promise. You might know of safer quarters—some friend's, say—where I could still continue my trust—that was my sole meaning. You do not? Very well. Now sit down again. It is only of your reputation I am thinking. If you are ready to confide it to me——"

Her bosom heaved heavily once or twice. She looked me in the face.

"Why not?" she said.

"That is for you to say," I answered. "I know no reason, on my honour. Is that enough?"

She seemed to think awhile, frowning and pouting her lips.

"It is enough for me," she said suddenly, with a resolved challenge in her eyes.

"Bon!" I nodded, and signed to her to be seated, a direction which, after a moment, she obeyed. "Then we have only to think of your temporary needs here."

"I have plenty of money," she said. "I do not ask to be your debtor for anything."

"Then you shall not be," I responded, "unless, perhaps, for the one thing you cannot help."

"What is that?"

"Can you not guess? Then it shall remain my secret. And now about the material commodities. Am I to buy them for you—or what?"

She thought awhile, then looked up.

"Can I trust you?"

"With the money?"

"No; with the choice."

"What is it you require?"

She gave a little deprecating laugh, with a tiny protest of the shoulders.

"Not, at least, what I found on my pillow last night."

"What—Ah, very true! I was afraid they were too large."

"They smelt of tobacco—pouf!"—she made a wry face.

"I swear they were clean from the wash."

"I daresay. But there was a coat where they had lain—an old coat—*for I looked.*"

"Well, you had carte-blanche. And—now I remember: I had lost that coat, an old, old friend that I valued."

"He must have died, I think, of senile decay. I would let his memory rest."

"That is not my way of honouring old friends."

"What would you, then? Set him up in a field for the crows to reverence? At least remove him from my room."

My room! But this young woman was beginning to interest me.

"It shall be done," I said. "In fact I will empty out my whole wardrobe for yours to take its place. If you will only tell me what to get."

She stood up.

"You know very well for one thing, Monsieur. For its quality, and that of all the rest, you will be guided, if you please, by your knowledge of my position."

I bowed, with profound gravity.

"It is necessary, I suppose," I said, "first to take your measurements. I should guess your height at five foot six, and your waist at twenty-two inches."

She looked surprised. "That is very accurate. How do you know?"

"I am a sculptor, Cousin, and, I pray God, an artist. My eyes have had to train themselves to a nice perception of proportions."

"C'est la?" She exclaimed it, with the pretty understanding of French lips, and stuck out her foot. "What size for that, then?"

"If I fail to fit it," I said, "call me an impostor."

But dismay was in my heart. What did all this suggested elaborate outfit, from shoes to nightgear, portend? Surely something more than a flying visit. "Perhaps you had better write me out a list," I said weakly.

She frowned a little; then proceeded to comply. It was a shorter list, when finished, than I had dared to hope.

"Now," I said, with the thing in my hand, "I will pay for these articles, and bring you the bills, and you can settle with me. I shall lock you in, you understand, and leave word with the Concierge that nobody is to be sent up; and if, in spite of that, accident should bring a knock to my door, you are not to answer it—not to respond to any voice, unless by chance it should be my step-sister's."

She nodded. "The important thing is, I hope your choice will justify your claim to be thought an artist. But we shall see."

To be *thought* an artist! I ran down the stairs like an infuriated lamplighter.

CHAPTER IV

I HAD Fifine's figure in my mind's eye as I made my purchases. The practice of mentally revisualising things once seen left me in no doubt as to its proportions. It was somewhat developed for a girl of nineteen, but I had reason to believe that a certain precosity was not suggested in her shape alone. There was a hint also of mental ripeness beyond her years, oddly irreconcilable with the passive front she maintained—a readiness of retort which I had found exhilarating, and hoped yet to provoke to my greater confusion and diversion.

The young ladies of the Magasin du Louvre made themselves very merry over my commission. I thought it best to confide one section of Fifine's list to the expert judgment of the lingerie department, with directions only that the articles specified were to be of the best. The dresses, the stockings and the shoes, with some small fanciful accessories, I made it my own business to select. After all, a Frenchman would do these things unabashed, so why should I demur.

A sweet young sylph—libelled, as I have since learned, under the name of "mannequin"—offered, for my behoof, to exhibit on her own jimp and faultless figure the one or two frocks I preferred for consideration. Nothing loth, since I was agent for a Countess, I stood and thrilled to see this vision of grace pose in beauty before me, while I considered her points with all the fastidious brutality of an Oriental slave-buyer. She stood as undisturbed as Fifine herself, a little arch challenge on her lips, and I had to summon up all my resolution in order to resist, in the face of that pretty allurement, the conquest of my individual taste and judgment.

"But is it not perfect!" (this from the showwoman): "Monsieur is very certainly ravished by the divine cunning of a creation at once so simple and so elaborate in its simplicity."

"Truly, Madame, if I am ravished I cannot help myself. But my transports, I find, do not amount to that. If I might suggest an improvement——"

"But surely, Monsieur, if Monsieur can find the heart."

Monsieur found the heart, and also the deft fingers, while the warm palpitating little mannequin stood, smiling, to be manipulated. A touch here and there, a call for new and subtler materials in the grace-notes, so to speak, a more statuesque disposition of the lines, and Monsieur stood back satisfied. Madame was in ecstasies.

"It is incredible! Why did not Monsieur confess he was an artist?"

"Truly, Madame, it is the nature of the model which has inspired me. If one could always so light on the soul ready-made for one's handling! How easy then would be one's task."

Madame answered somewhat at random to that; but the mannequin looked at me kindly, with just a little coquetry of the white shoulders, which said plainly, "Would you not like to have the handling of these!"

I decided finally for that costume, and another to be worn by day, the two to be delivered in the course of the afternoon. And then I withdrew in quest of the hosiery department. My task here was simple, if delicate, and I acquitted myself of it with aplomb, as also of my fancy commissions. And then came the question of the shoes.

Here my directions were explicit. Fifine would have none of your Grands Magasins: A la Merveilleuse in the Avenue de l'Opéra, and only à la Merveilleuse, would satisfy her. And so to that resort of fashion I went. I bought her two pairs; and the price was prodigious; but I had my orders, and there was an end of it.

All this had taken time, and it was past mid-day when I returned, laden with parcels, to the Rue de Fleurus. I entered the flat to find it delivered to silence and emptiness. There was no sign of my visitor in the eating- or the sitting-room—no, nor in the bedroom, the door of which stood ajar. My heart gave a somersault; but instantly righted itself with a laugh. If she was gone, for whatever reason, I had attended strictly to my directions, and could not be held to blame. Moreover it meant to me a problem very simply solved. And yet an odd little qualm of chagrin took me momentarily. I felt I should have liked to know Fifine's opinion on my choice.

And at that instant the sound of a pot crashing in the kitchen made me jump.

So she was there! I bestowed my parcels in the bedroom, and thence hurried to ascertain the cause.

She was standing by the stove, a look between anger and dismay on her face. The fragments of a pipkin lay on the floor.

"I heard you come in," she said, "and it flustered me. I am furious that it should have, but it did. I was trying to bake some eggs, and there they lie. Do you want me to starve, that you leave me like this?"

She was wrathful in her hunger; all the apathy was gone.

"I have brought some lunch with me," I said. "You would have had it sooner if your list had been shorter. Go now to the table, and I will serve it with what despatch I may."

There were oysters—which I knew how to open—little croquettes of chicken, honey-comb in a section, chocolate, and a good bottle of Sauterne. I had them all in a basket, at which Fifine looked wistfully. She went without a word, however; but at the door she hesitated, looking back. "I am sorry I broke the pipkin," she said, and vanished.

When, in a little after, I brought in the meal and, placing it before her, stood aside like a waiter, she glanced at me doubtfully.

"Do you never eat, yourself, Monsieur?"

"Occasionally," I answered, "when my betters are satisfied."

Still she hesitated; but finally set to with an appetite. She had a single glass of wine, which brought a warmth to her cheek and a glow to her eyes. I think it made her generous to me in the matter of leavings, for I made quite a good meal after she had ended and withdrawn, and I finished the bottle of wine. After which I followed her into the sitting-room, where she sat luxuriously smoking one of my cigarettes.

"Now," I said, "*if* it pleases you, and *when*, the bed is inviting for a siesta, the view from the window is benign, and my purchases to your order are all spread out on the counterpane—all, that is to say, save the two costumes, which are to arrive this afternoon."

She opened her eyes. "Why do you want me gone?"

"I have some tidying-up to do," I said. "I must dispose my effects more suitably to the entertaining of so distinguished a visitor."

"I do not want anything touched," she answered. "I like them best as they are."

"But the litter, the disorder, the utter absence of method in the arrangement?"

"If that is all, do not alter them for me."

"It is not all, nevertheless. I have my own bed to prepare."

"Your own!—Ah, true! I forgot. Well, I will go, and ascertain to what horrors you have committed me."

That was gracious; but I remained unruffled in my self-confidence. She did not appear again during the whole afternoon, and I amused myself over what makeshifts I could contrive for my personal comfort. There was a settee in the salle-à-manger, tattered but roomy, which, with plentiful rugs, would serve me sufficiently for a bed; and my washing could be done in the kitchen. The costumes were delivered in the course of the afternoon, and I left them at my guest's door, with a knock, and an intimation that I was going out to buy the dinner. She did not answer, and I concluded that she was asleep.

Asleep, and without a thought of her incredible position, of the hovering danger! I could not believe it humanly possible that any woman, young or old, patrician or plebeian, living in perpetual apprehension of death by secret violence, could conduct herself with such persistent sangfroid. She did not so live in fact; of that I was finally convinced. For some purpose unconfessed Marion had foisted that story upon me, with the sole intention, likely enough, to ensure my closest trust and vigilance. Necessary precautions, no doubt, if one knew the whole truth, but hardly dictated by terror of the worst. By what lesser fear, or policy, it was useless for me to conjecture; nor did the question trouble me. Indeed, from that time, I think, I dismissed the whole puzzle from my mind, being satisfied on the main point, and quite assured that my comrade's soul was darkened by no more mortal trepidations than my own.

For dinner I contrived quite a delectable little repast, and, when it was laid and ready, I announced the fact at the closed door. It opened, after a brief interval, and a shimmering vision appeared before my dazzled and wonder-stricken eyes.

In fact I had chosen very happily, and faultlessly, it seemed, as to fit. The girl's face was quite flushed in the consciousness of the picture she presented. It was a picture, indeed—of tinted youth, sensuous and pure in one, in a silken setting. I was reminded somehow of sun-flushed Pomona in her flowering apple orchards, herself symbolic of the lovely half-visionary blossoms and the rosy fruit they promised. So content was I with this fruit of my own visualising.

"Truly, I am proud of myself," I said.

The smile died on her lips.

"No more than that?" she said. "As if I were a dummy"—and she went past me, while I stood back, ostentatiously withdrawing her skirts. I had never seen a haughtier lady. She appeared so obsessed with her own sacrosanctity, that to look at her uninvited was an offence, to brush her in passing a sacrilege. But a little way on, and she relented, turning to me suddenly with a face between insolence and something strangely like suppressed merriment.

"Really, Cousin, it was very well done of you. Now I can believe what I never should have guessed from your pictures, that you are an artist."

The audacity of it! It caught my breath like a splash of cold water. But it was just as refreshing.

I crowed: "Well, at least I am promoted, and inclined to presume upon that favour. It would never do for your acknowledged cousin to wait upon you like a garçon-de-salle; and so for the future I shall propose sitting down to table with you."

She drew herself up, but relaxed almost at once.

"After all you provide the meals, and have a right to share in them."

"I wonder," I said, "that that did not occur to me before."

She began something, broke off, then suddenly just lifted the hem of her skirt and projected a silvery foot.

"You have a right to see," she said. "I thank you for your choice, Cousin."

"It has come tripping to me through the moonlight," I said, "and is all sparkling with dewy gossamer. A fairy's slipper, and the fairy who wears it to be my guest. Why did you never tell me before that you came of the pretty people?"

"Because I thought you had eyes," said Fifine, and, dropping her skirt, went on to dinner.

I think I had surpassed myself in that meal. Anyhow *I* enjoyed it. Fifine turned to me near the beginning with a question:—

"When you feel hungry you go to market? You just take your gun and hunt for a dinner, n'est ce pas? Do you always so live from hand to mouth?"

"Always, Cousin. It is the rare way to the unexpected, believe me. I have my camp-fire up here, and my cooking-pot, and all the intricacies of the neighbourhood to explore for its replenishing. That is the right way. I have dined with a written menu before me, and dined so without a thrill of the surprise which is the true sauce of gastronomy. We vagabonds are the real epicures—and more than that. The light of our festivity sometimes attracts to us strange comrades—creatures of the outer mysteries, bright or sullen, but always for their strangeness worth entertaining. Here, for instance, comes to me from the shadows a gauzy apparition, most welcome, it is true, yet shining very incongruity in this context of pot-luck and rough-and-ready."

And so indeed it appeared to me; nor otherwise, save by fantasy, could I reconcile this vision of an elaborate evening toilette with its vagrant surroundings. But the fashionable convention, I supposed, when once acquired was ineradicable; and, no doubt, to have dined in undress would have seemed tantamount with Fifine to bathing in public.

But, to my surprise, she took my sarcasm, if sarcasm it was, in good part.

"This apparition is of your own invoking," she said. "And I did not want to deny you that pride in yourself which you had a right to feel. The strange comrade who has come to you out of the shadows is, after all, only your own lay-figure, Cousin; and—and the dress is very pretty."

I glanced at her in some astonishment. Her cheeks were flushed, and she trifled with the food on her plate.

"So spake the young rosebud of its sheath," I said, with a laugh. "Now I am going to fill up your glass."

She let me do it; she was fond, in moderation, of sweet wine, was Fifine; and somehow I liked to see her lips and the "blushful Hippocrene" meet in small kisses—there was a suggestion of pure Paganism in that contact, of nymphs that thought no sin of tasting the good earth's love.

We made a passable meal of it, between smalltalk and persiflage, always in the abstract sense. I accepted things as they had come to me, and, save to ascertain that my guest's privacy had not been interrupted in any way during my absence, asked no leading questions and invited no confidences. That would have been to spoil all the romantic glamour of the situation; and moreover I should not have expected the truth. Since we were reconciled in the matter of social equality, I was prepared, for my comfort, to drift, and suffer or enjoy the charge the gods had put upon me. I came to do both, in fact, but with ever a leaning towards the contented side. And so Fifine and I became comrades.

CHAPTER V

THAT evening after dinner I deliberately tempted the Providence which had offered me Fifine as a mild mental stimulant. There were several of my paintings hanging on the walls of the sitting-room, and, when I followed her in thither, I found her standing meditatively, cigarette in hand, before one of them. I came and stood behind her.

"Ah!" I said, "that is one of the things in which I successfully hid from you what my choice of your dress revealed."

She turned and looked me quite frankly and coolly in the face.

"What is it all about?" she said.

"Call it," I answered, "a psychologic exercise in paint."

"Then it is not a picture?"

"O! yes it is—or at least I hope so."

"But—" she shook her head—"I do not understand. A picture is a picture, and a sum is a sum, and a psychologic exercise is a psychologic exercise."

"You mean they are not assimilable terms. What, then, is your definition of a picture?"

She considered, drawing thoughtfully at her cigarette.

"I think," she said presently, "it is art—just that."

"Well, what is art?"

Again she considered, and answered, "Form."

"Form is an elusive term," I said, "impossible of hard and fast definition. There is no way of proving that any two of us agree about it—no way of ascertaining that our mental and material optics come to the same conclusion with regard to it."

"Then why should you expect people to take your view of it, in—in a thing like this?"

"I don't—in a thing like this. I merely utter my protest in the thing against the accepted conventions of form. It is an impression, conveyed and caught through atmospheric vibration, of what form actually suggested, at that particular moment, in that particular instance, to my individual temperament."

"I think," she said calmly, after a pause, "that that is nonsense."

"What," I demanded, astonished, "is nonsense?"

"All that talk about impressions and individual temperaments. It is only an excuse for idleness—for trying the short cut to laborious ends. It is so much easier to spend an hour over a picture—over a canvas—than a month. A burglar might claim just the same excuse for stealing a year's income in a night, instead of earning it in a year. Besides, if your temperament is individual, what is the good of trying to impose it on people who have individual temperaments of their own. You can't expect them to understand you; so what is the good?"

"None," I said briefly—and grimly. This "mild mental stimulant" was beginning to reveal itself a headier posset than I had ever dreamed it to be.

"Then," she answered, "why do you protest? You know you said you did."

"As a revolutionist, I am bound to," I replied weakly.

"A revolutionist from what?"

"From stereotype and standards. Standards are for yard measures, and bushel measures, and other such commercial or scientific essentials. They are not for art."

"Why not?"

"O, Cousin! See to what they have led us—the lifeless petrifactions of the schools and academies."

"Well, they are art, if they are bad art. And there will always be bad art and bad artists. But *you* want to lead us away from art altogether—into psychologic exercises—impressions that only you can understand. Do you paint for yourself alone, then? In that case why do you complain of your lack of appreciation?"

"I don't."

"O, you do! I know it from Mademoiselle your sister. You are very humorous and philosophical, but you are hurt in your heart that the world will not comprehend you better. I have seen *pictures* by those who think like you—Gauguin, Van Gogh, Matisse—and I suppose, if they did not *feel* like you, that they would hardly exhibit in public galleries impressions which were just peculiar to themselves, and impossible of understanding by others differently constituted."

Why should she *not* have seen them, these mutinous ones? Why, on the other hand, had I admitted this viper to my hearth?

"I, too, have exhibited in public galleries," I said, "and found sympathy and understanding among the elect."

"Well, who elected them?" she said—"themselves? There are always to be found inconsiderable people to applaud what they don't understand. A little man blowing a big trumpet gets some of the credit for the noise, you see."

"But they did understand."

"They couldn't, you know, if we all see with different eyes."

"O, this is puerile!" I cried, with a little shrug and laugh. "You don't like my pictures, or what I call pictures. Very well, then, you don't."

"I think they are stuff and nonsense," she answered, turning away from the wall. "But I *do* like your little mother: she is a real darling."

She was lying in a corner, unfinished—my little clay model of startled yet innocent maternity.

"O! you like that!" I said, a solacing glow about my heart.

"You needn't sneer," she answered. "Why didn't your atmospheric vibrations make a shapeless jelly of her too?"

"That is different. You must allow for the medium."

"I don't. There should be only one rule in Art, I am sure. What applies to this applies to all; and it amounts in the end to form. Everyone with the right eyes knows what beauty of form means. You do yourself, you see; and yet you can go and paint those pictures."

"O, for heaven's sake leave my pictures alone!"

"You shouldn't raise your voice. It squeaks and cracks when you do. I'm sure I'll leave them alone with pleasure." But she couldn't. "I'm glad anyhow," she said, "that *I* don't see things, even for a moment, as if they were all made up of one huge nettlerash."

Poor Pissarro, with his light analyses and colour vibrations! I was bound to feel very small; but I could not help sniggering over the impudent candour of this hussy. She turned, and dropped the butt of her cigarette into a brass pot, and went silently scrutinising the "things" along the walls. Presently she stopped before a little framed piece, an interior with figures, very rich and sombre in tone, but made cloudier than its due by the dirty state of the glass.

"O, I like that!" she said—"I *do* like that. I think you must be an artist after all. Why do you not always paint in that way?"

"Every producer, you know, has his own best for enemy. What do you find in this to like so much?"

"It is a picture—a little bit of truth and beauty brought into the limits of the eye's understanding. It seems to satisfy everything—one's love of colour, one's sense of form, and—yes, just the little place in one's emotions the two appeal to. It doesn't matter a bit about the subject. It is the scheme of colour which *is* the subject, and the figures are only patterns in it." She turned on me. "O, you *are* stupid, to go and paint those other things when you can do like this!"

"Well, I can't," I said. "As a matter of fact it is by a friend of mine. It is very good, as you say; but the critics would have none of it."

"The critics!" she snapped her rosy fingers disdainfully. "They are just the flies on that glass, that have made it all dirty and obscure. But the picture is behind all time to speak for itself; and some day posterity will clean away the dirt with a wet sponge, and the truth will come out. I should like to know the man who painted it."

"Sorry," I said shortly. "He's dead."

Something in my tone seemed to strike her. Her eyes were on me, and suddenly a strange light, like wistfulness or pity, came into them.

"I am sorry if I hurt you," she said. "I did not know—how could I? And I am sure, after seeing that dear little mother, you could paint pictures like this if you would."

"Would you like me to?" I said. I don't know what made me say it. This young callow criticism, refreshing as it might be, was hardly worth the most transitory waiving of my principles. Yet oddly there came into my mind the face, hectic and eager, of the boy Ronsin, whose work, and gift to me, the picture had been—and I was jealous. Yes, absurd as it may sound, because she had said she would like to know him, I was jealous. For my art, or what else? Ah, that I cannot tell. Yet at least I could not deny that, whatever the youthfulness of this criticism, it had seen clearly here: the picture was, of its kind, remarkably good.

"Of course I should," she answered. "You admitted yourself, you know, that it was a fine work."

"It *is* a fine work," I said, "and I am not so dogmatic as to profess that there is only one right theory of art in the world. But every fox looks after his own skin, says the proverb; and dislikes, adds I, the having it flayed from him to adorn a rival."

And so ended our first disputation—which was by no means our last—on the subject. If I was heckled and browbeaten, it was also agreeably clear to me that I had got no fool for my housemate.

Fifine, come out of her shell of apathy, was a surprise indeed.

CHAPTER VI

VERY early I made a strange discovery: Fifine was doing the housework. It did not, perhaps, amount to much, which was likely the reason that the fact was impressed upon me gradually; but, when at length conviction came, I was immensely surprised and interested. The little domestic bienséances, obligatory even in Bohemia, came one by one to be appropriated to meeter hands than mine, so that by and by I was altogether without the occupations which, to speak truth, had served me hitherto as an excuse for much self-malingering in the matter of my professional work.

It began, properly enough, perhaps, with Fifine's quiet intimation that I was to regard her bedroom as her own exclusive property and care; and it ended by her every day making *my* bed, sous ce nom-là, as well as her own. That was sufficiently gratifying; and so was it to find her cleaning up the plates and dishes after meals; but, when it came to her offering to take my place at the electric stove, I was inclined to kick a little.

"It would go against my social conscience," I said, "to accept such a return for the little hospitality I can offer you."

"But I should like it."

"But I should not."

"I know perfectly well what that means," she said, turning on me with a scornful lip: "not in the least that you are shocked at my demeaning myself, but that you are in terror of my cookery."

"That is nonsense," I answered. "How can I fear the unknown?"

"Yet you say you would not like it?"

"Not like your so repaying me, I mean."

"With bad for good, that is to say. Yet you are not the only one in the world who knows how to cook an omelet."

"O, for heaven's sake," I exclaimed, "cook what you like! I am equal to anything, if it comes to that. A man who has dined, day in and day out, on 'arlequins' at two sous the plate in the Marché St. Germain is not likely to be fastidious."

She stared at me incredulously.

"Have you really done that?"

"Often enough," I said, "in my student days."

She tossed her head, turning away: "I do not want to know about those. Please to leave it to me to perform the proper duties of a woman, while you go to your own, which you have been neglecting too long."

The proper duties of a woman! Now could she know anything about them in such a connexion? It was just an absorbing new game to her, I supposed, as her hameau, with its laiterie and moulin and ferme, had been to Marie Antoinette. But a wilful woman must have her way; and so, with a laugh and shrug, I went and left her alone.

And now a surprising thing happened: Fifine, at déjeuner, came up to time with a quite well-cooked little repast. How she had managed it I could not tell, bred as she must have been, if not in luxury, in all that prescriptive ineptitude associated with a class wholly untrained in the principles of self-help. Possibly, it occurred to me, the penurious Marquis held unaccustomed views on household economy; and at that I left it. The young lady, meanwhile, hung, I could see, on my verdict.

"You are a wonder, Fifine," I said.

She started at the term, and drew back.

"Did I not tell you," she said, "I would not be called that?"

"I am sorry. It slipped out unawares."

"Well," she said, relenting in a moment, "it is at least better than the 'arlequins,' is it not?"

"As much better as this time is than that."

She leaned her elbows on the table and her chin on her closed knuckles, and sat regarding me.

"Were you a very bad man in those days?" she said presently.

"Do I give you that impression?" I answered. "How can you look at me and ask?"

Still she conned me with unwinking eyes.

"Used you to go to the cabarets artistiques—*Les Noctambules*, and *de l'Enfer*, and the *Moulin Rouge*, and all those?"

"Not all; but to some, and to some better, in my time. There was the *Chat-Noir* for instance, to whose collection I had the honour of contributing a trifle of statuary."

"And to the *Elysée Montmartre*?"

"O, now and again!"

"To the *Bal des Quat'z Arts* there?"

I fairly gasped.

"How on earth," I said, "did you come to hear of all these places?"

She nodded her head once or twice.

"People have spoken of them before me—and always à coin de l'œil."

"Well, we won't speak of them, with a leer or otherwise. Shall we have a cigarette, Cousin? I am of an inquisitive nature, and I have been to all sorts of places in quest of information. Once, when I was a young man, I was seized with an idea that it would be well for me to harden myself to the sight of physical mutilation, so I got a professional friend to take me to the operating theatre of a hospital. I didn't want to go again; and I am content, also, with my one visit to the students' ball. The impression I brought away from each was something of the same sort—an orgy of crucified human nature."

Still leaning on one hand, and drawing casually at her cigarette, she came out suddenly with a startling question:—

"Who was your particular petite ouvrière when you were a student? Was she very pretty?"

I actually started to my feet.

"You can assume anything you like," I said—"my badness, or my goodness, or my utter ordinariness, which would be the normal mean: only bear in mind that it *is* all assumption."

She gave the tiniest insolent laugh, wafting a puff of smoke away with her hand.

"I will tell you what I think of you," she said; "and why, according to your own statement, your present is happier than your past. It is because with your restless, volatile nature you are incapable of developing a lasting attachment, and your age now saves you from any fear of being importuned for your own sake."

I burst out laughing. "True," I said; "at my years a man should have come to easy terms with himself as to his own superannuation; and perhaps also he should have learned to look a little deeper than the beauty peu profond for his soul's satisfaction."

"O, that is rubbish!" Fifine exclaimed.

"What is?"

"Skin-deep beauty. How can you talk such nonsense and pretend to be an artist? There is no such thing. Just as if the skin could be anything but what the bones and the muscles underneath make it!"

That was not, perhaps, very original; yet a wonder perpetually grew in me over the extraordinary precocity of this young woman of nineteen. Her dictatorialness I could understand: it was just unaffected class assurance. What I could not understand was the positiveness of her views, where her views came in question. As I stood, with nothing to say, she looked up at me.

"What made you come to be an artist at all?" she asked.

"O!" I answered: "I suppose the usual creative itch—the desire to produce beautiful things."

"Comme ça!" She gave a little shrug implying helplessness. "I should have thought the scalpel was more in your line than the pencil."

"Why?"

"O, just because you are so inquisitive. Were you obliged to do *something* for a living?"

"More or less," I said. "But I haven't been very successful."

"Were you born of the people, Monsieur?"

I laughed. "My father was an English *avocat*, Cousin; my mother one of the noblesse; I myself lay no claim to any sort of distinction but what myself may procure me."

She stooped over her plate, slowly extinguishing her cigarette. There was a strange little frown between her eyes, an odd look in her face of some emotion I could have likened to disappointment or chagrin. Perhaps she was regretting now her own calm assumption of superiority. Then, without looking up, she said:—

"But you do not hate the people?"

"I don't know what you mean by the people," I said, "or where they begin and where they end. If you are out for intelligence, I know no one more interesting than a skilled mechanic of his hands; and if you are out for folly, a lord can provide you as well as a sweep. Knowledge, my cousin, and knowledge alone passes all distinctions—at least it is the one master-key in my opinion."

She sat silent a little while; and then she sighed deeply, as if eased of some mental oppression, and rose to her feet, with a smile, verily like ingratiation, on her lips.

"Would it please you," she said, "if, instead of slighting what I don't understand, I were to ask you to explain the difficult thing to me?"

It was quite touching—so pretty, indeed, that I was surprised into humility.

"Why, I told you I was no positivist," I said. "I take it that the sincere among us are all seeking Truth, and what do the thousand different ways, long or short, matter, provided they have that purpose in common? Art and religion should be one there; and for my part I have no more quarrel with an Academician than I have with a 'Futurist,' with a Bishop than I have with a Parsee. Only please don't again talk of short cuts that save trouble. There is more than that, I assure you, in my philosophy."

"Then you are not really idle?" she said, very sweetly, with her eyebrows raised.

"No, really," I answered—"if an active brain counts for anything. I am thinking all the time."

"Yes?" she said—and that was all.

"Well," I retorted, "we think differently, you see; but at least *my* thoughts are consistent."

"Aren't mine?"

"How can you ask it?—at one moment rubbing into me the futility of my producing work that only I can understand; at another implying that I am idle because I don't endlessly produce futility. Well, I tell you, if I put all my thoughts into the shape I should like, I should want a garde-meuble to store them in. But I spare myself and a suffering world that vain burden."

There was still a little amused questioning in her eyes, so that I could have thought I read into them the rejoinder 'The world does not suffer from *some* furniture being stored, but rather the reverse!' She forbore all repartee, however, and answered me only, very simply and feelingly:—

"I am quite sure that is a natural attitude under the circumstances. Still you paint, do you not, if only for yourself?"

"Within reason," I answered; "but my métier is the plastic business. I have plenty of sketches to show you, if you wish to see them."

"O, yes!" she said—"please. That is what I want. And then you can tell me not why you painted them so, but——"

"But why I didn't paint them not so? Very well. Marchez!"

We adjourned to the sitting-room, or studio, and I seated her in a good position and, getting out my portfolios, played judicious showman to my own goods—a fragmentary variety, impressions of men, things and places, forming the artistic excerpta of a vagabond and wanderer. She took them from me, one by one, a little mechanically, and I made no comment whatever, simply briefly stating the subjects and localities. Presently, pausing in her task, she looked up.

"Cousin," she said, "will you give me a plain exposition, in as few and clear words as possible, of your theory of art?"

"The portrayal of all things, animate and inanimate, as we really see them."

"In passing?"

"Yes, in passing: the momentary impression conveyed to us."

"Then, to appreciate these sketches properly, one should look at them only for a moment."

"If you like."

"No, but it is not as I like but as I must. The impression is gone if I pause—the trick, the mere accident of vision which produced them. I know that if I want to understand the true purple of a shadow, the true blue of water, the true gloom of trees, I must look direct at none of these things, but only somewhere near them, so that while not actually seeing them I never lose the sense that they are there and revealing their inner truth to me."

"Aha! You are getting near it."

"Yes, but then I oughtn't to look at your pictures either in order to understand them; and I think you should say that."

"Say what?"

"Why, when you exhibit, that your pictures are not meant to be looked at."

I laughed, though not quite at ease.

"But they are intended to represent what you *do* see without knowing it," I said.

"But you *don't* see it," she persisted, "if you look straight at the things."

I tried another tack:—

"*I do*," I said; "and so will you, if you take the trouble to understand. The truth is that we have learned to look at all objects with sophisticated eyes. The schools have wrought that tangle about us, and the tangles within the tangle, until to our bewildered vision nothing appears as it is, but only as hidebound theory presents it. It is the purpose of us primitives to sweep away at one stroke all that accumulated litter of the schools, and to regard things once again with frank unbiassed eyes."

"But you are not a primitive," said Fifine; "so what is the good of pretending? You belong to the twentieth century, not the first, and have grown up from being one of the world's schoolchildren. You might as well say that in education we all ought to go back to our ABCs. Art must grow, I suppose, with knowledge. For my part I am not interested to know what the men thought who scratched figures on bones and things, but what my own men think, the men of my own time, who try to speak to me in the language I understand. You call it confused and sophisticated: all I can say is that it isn't to me."

"Then you are satisfied with Art as you find it?"

"I am satisfied with its purpose and with its direction, as steadily pursued from age to age. Fancy thinking Botticelli all wrong, and Velasquez, and da Vinci, and wanting to sweep them away to get back to your bone-scratchers. I couldn't live with a bone, however cleverly engraved; but I could live with that little picture on the wall there, because I should never tire of the food for thought it gave me. I think that an artist living day by day over his picture penetrates to the soul of things more deeply than any primitive capturing a passing impression. Not that some of yours are not beautiful bits of colour. But I suppose that was accident."

So she chastised and patronised me. On that subject it was always the same. Call her a frank Philistine, if you like: she had clear views, at least, and she never compromised about them. She was very scornful of my insistence on the free rights of temperament. Art, she said, was the negation of all licence, which had never yet produced any enduring beauty in the world. Look at its decay contemporaneous with the corruption of the ancient monasteries. She had a plenty of information about many things. She called my school (which, by the by, I did not call it) the go-as-you-please school, likening it to a modern fashion of extravaganza in which every performer was at liberty to "gag" as he chose—a mere farrago of unconnected impromptus. She was sarcastic, too, about that deeper beauty I was unlucky enough to say my matured soul had come to crave; she supposed it must mean the bones I was after, to scratch my primitive impressions on.

In fact, I am fain to confess, whether from humour or chagrin, I came to feel out of sorts with my theories, and disinclined for the present to elaborate them. Instead I returned to my clay and made figures.

She was with me there, watchful, mostly silent, yet not without ideas. I owed many a good touch to her sharp intelligence.

And so the days went on—went on as if our compact were for life, and no disturbance to that odd partnership were ever to be apprehended. We kept strictly to the letter of our undertaking with Marion, practising all precautions and inviting no risks. I always locked Fifine in when I went abroad, and I spoke no word to any one as to the change in my ménage. Indeed more and more I came to avoid acquaintances, more and more to limit my issues and returns to the dark hours. A queer attraction was beginning to attach itself to my quarters; I was never long away from them but I wished myself back. There was some lure there in the way of mental stimulant that I found it pleasant not to resist.

As for Fifine herself, confinement and lack of air and exercise seemed in no wise to disturb her. Physically she was of a serene constitution; and her small occupations were enough for what variety she seemed to need. Moreover, on whatever absurd perversion founded, she was sufficiently alive to the supposed danger of her position to endure gladly the inaction and close concealment it entailed upon her. I was aware that her fears, while I believed them wholly unjustified, were entirely genuine, though I had made it my rule to ask no leading questions of her whatever. But her face had become a book to me, in which I found some matter for curious reading.

Our plan of privacy was easily enough maintained, Madame Crussol abetting. I don't know what the worthy lady thought of it all—but not the best, il va sans dire. However, her sarcasms were for my ears alone; I was a favourite with her, when all is said; and it did not disturb me to hear myself called a vieux garçon, still uncertain of his steps at an age when most men had learned to walk steadily. For the rest, whether through prescriptive sympathy, or on the strength of some unconfessed understanding with my step-sister, the concierge managed to hold all undesired visitors aloof. I was so much a rolling-stone that the task was no more than simple: she had merely to shrug her shoulders and say, "He has locked his door on the outside and taken away the key. God knows when he will return."

Indeed I wanted no visitors just then: I was fully amused, and fully contented to be left to the world's oblivion. It was all quite superbly correct—the heart serenely conscious of its own probity, and so forth; what did it matter what gross old door-keepers concluded or suspected? Fifine and I became quite matter-of-fact friends; our rallies were purely intellectual, and not seldom acrimonious; we lived together on a footing of the most dispassionate comradeship. She was seldom haughty to me after a little—save in fits and starts, as if when suddenly remembering a duty, which she would desperately recover, but without conviction on either side. Early she discarded her smart evening dress in favour of others more simple, which she would concoct out of materials I bought for her. She had plenty of money, as she had said, and insisted upon paying her share of the household expenses. She was wonderfully deft with her needle, at which I rather marvelled, until I remembered that I had made a compact with myself to be surprised at nothing. But still on some festive occasions she would play the bedizened sylphid, enrapturing my eyes, and just awakening in me some faintly disturbing tremors. She liked me to design her frocks for her; and in truth I was nothing loth. It was a little thrilling to have a mannequin all of my own, and a very shapely one, on whom to hang my idle fancies. And she repaid my trouble, both by word and effect, though we were always very particular and formal in our relations of costumier and dummy. Never suppose that I forgot my responsibility to my charge, or my tremendous respect for the rank that condescended to me, or that Fifine herself made any motion of unbending in the matter of that mutual understanding. She trusted in me without question, and I never gave her cause to question.

Not that I will pretend the situation found me entirely without qualms of a sort. Nature, it must be admitted, abhors a Platonism, and I was not superior to Nature. Moreover, I could never quite forget Marion's curiously ambiguous language in delivering my trust to me. It had seemed to take so small account of reputation provided the main issue were not involved. Still, no doubt, that apparent confusion had been due to the stress of the moment. Marion could never be anything but deeply moral and religious.

In any case I was—I had Marion's word for it—a gentleman, and determined stoutly to justify that election. I had no choice about it, in fact, since I am speaking of emotions, trifling at best, which I felt were entirely unreciprocated. But I want the credit of my conscientiousness.

And so a fortnight passed; and deliverance came not. My sister did not appear, nor did she vouchsafe word or sign. Was the safe moment yet to strike? I did not seem to care at last; and that was a puzzling symptom.

CHAPTER VII

ONE sopping noon, as I was leaving the yard below on some rather arbitrary commission of Fifine's, I met an old gentleman just entering it. I observed him, but superficially; and was going on my way without further notice, when an odd thought flashing into my mind brought me to a standstill. It was only this, that the stranger, seeing me, had come to a quick stop, as if suddenly petrified, and had thereafter fallen, rather than backed, against the wall to allow me passage while he stared at me. Just that; and what then? Why, nothing—nothing but a recollection of the absurd fable which would have charged me with the circumvention of a monster diabolically bent on the destruction of an innocent victim to his suspicion or jealousy. I did not believe that story; I have intimated as much; yet I felt in duty bound to act as if I did. Who, in short, was this old fellow, and what was he doing here?

He was no denizen of the block: I knew my neighbours generally by sight, and he was not one of them. But why not a visitor? Again, why not a spy or an assassin? With a laugh for my own idiotcy, I yet *did* turn in my tracks and just peep into the yard. He had disappeared. Madame Crussol had him in charge, and she was to be trusted. En avant!

Trying to recall this intruder's appearance, as I continued my way, I could only gather a general impression of bony insignificance, a little white, a little spoiled, a little pathetic, of a damp crow-like figure squatting under a minute umbrella, of two large eyes, like a fledgling's, peering from that sheltering covert—not an heroic figure, by any means, nor one to be associated with secret agencies and stabs in the dark. A piano-tuner, probably: there had been something indescribably hopeless in his aspect, as of one who had spent all his ineffective life in desperately screwing-up things to a pitch destined not to last. I had forgotten him by the time I reached the Rue de Seine, for which I was bound.

But, as chance would have it, his exit and my return again synchronised. As I wheeled under the archway, there was he stepping from the vestibule, and putting up his umbrella in the act. It was a feminine umbrella, very small and very leaky, and somehow it seemed forlornly appropriate to the spare little nervous figure it only half sheltered. He stopped, seeing me, before spreading his tattered wings to fly; then snapped up the spring in sudden resolution and came on. An odd thing again; and this time I took determined stock of him as he approached. He did not evade my scrutiny, but on the contrary seemed lost in one of his own. Something impelled me, quite unwarrantably, to stop and address him as he came up.

"We have encountered once before, Monsieur. You were not by any chance seeking me?"

A sad, plaintive, timorous old face; a deprecating smile; a little contracted gesture of apology, of repudiation.

"No, no, Monsieur; no, indeed. I have accomplished my little mission, entirely to my satisfaction—O, yes, certainly so!"

He was gazing into my face, hungrily, but with a sort of propitiation. His feet, in their little worn ladies' boots, shuffled uneasily on the flags; he was dressed in damaged black broadcloth, the waistcoat cut low over a frayed shirt, whose single stud had been reversed to hide the gaping of the buttonhole; and on his white head was a silk hat, mangy and much dinted, but set at a perceptible angle. His limbs were small, his bones protuberant; and the only points of vital colour about him lay in his vivacious brown eyes and the fresh yellow chrysanthemum bud in his coat-lapel. I apologised for my officiousness, and passed on.

Fifine was sitting in the studio when I entered it. She barely glanced up at me and down again. There was a self-conscious look on her face; a bowl of yellow chrysanthemums, which I had bought her the day before, stood on a table hard by.

"The piano is certainly sadly out of tune," I said; "or was, when I last tried it."

I was certain that her lip twitched—the ghost of an understanding smile.

"Try it again," she answered. "I like to hear you play."

I sat down, and shaped out a chord or two. "No," I said, "it is still as impossible as ever; and that is the mystery."

She did not comment on the mystery of my calling it one; and I asked no question—I was resolute in my philosophy of silence. But here was certainly an unlooked-for development of a situation already sufficiently cryptic. Did she know that I guessed? I think so, or she would not have passed my innuendo unchallenged. But in that case she must have known that I knew how she had betrayed her own retreat. And to whom—an emissary of Marion, of the Marquis himself, perhaps?

Hardly the first, since, if so, there was nothing to prevent her including me in her confidence. If the second, then I was being made catspaw to some mystery to which the other was only a blind. And that I could not believe: there had never been a suggestion of affectation in her part of fugitive, under whatever moral stimulus she had been brought to play it. She might know nothing as to the true cause of her titular father's implacable malignity towards her—as I asked no questions I was in no position to judge—or she might know everything. That she genuinely hugged her concealment and dreaded discovery was proof sufficient that she could be in no secret collusion with the supposed terrific power which had made that concealment necessary. No, here was some collateral enigma, about which it really did not concern me to bother myself. If my guest chose to entertain, unknown to me, mysterious visitors, who for some reason regarded me curiously in passing, she had calculated, no doubt, the profits and risks of the game. I was playing my own promised part squarely and loyally; she must do as she liked with hers. I took a book, and sat reading in silence.

I thought Fifine glanced at me once or twice, as if in indecision or compunction; but nothing came of it, and presently she said:—

"You have not heard yet from Mademoiselle Herold?"

"My step-sister? No," I answered, a little surprised, for this was the first time that any direct reference had been made by either of us to the all-important matter.

She gave a little sigh.

"Do you want me to hear?" I said, putting down my book. "Are you so tired of it all—the confinement, the sense of peril, your company?"

"I do not want to be beholden to my company for anything but itself and its interest."

"Well, you know you are not. You are a locataire—a paying guest."

"Yes, that is just it," she said. "But——"

She hesitated, with a flushed cheek: and I understood. She was running short of cash. Could that be the explanation of the strange visitant? But, then, how could she have applied to him without my knowledge? And who was he? A moneylender? One did not adorn moneylender's buttonholes with chrysanthemum buds. Or perhaps a money-borrower?

That thought was quite suddenly illuminating. I wondered that it had not occurred to me before. The man, possibly, had been appealing to her bounty—and with success. It was a solution; and yet not a solution. There still remained for elucidation the fact of his claim on her, and the means by which he had found access to her presence. However, as he had traced her somehow, and, presumably, to the effect desired, the moral appeared to lie in the direction of some understanding between them, to which the chrysanthemum bud figured, as it were, for the mystic accent. It was a riddle; but I easily gave it up.

"*But*," I echoed, "you are wanting fresh supplies—is not that what you mean?"

"Yes, it is," she answered, shortly and frankly.

"Cousin," I said as frankly, "I am really grateful to you for your candour. It clears the air. Now let me propose, what has often been in my mind, that we keep a common purse between us."

"A common purse!" she said, "into which I put nothing, and from which I take everything!"

"Not in the least: you will put in the account I keep against you for your share, and which you will liquidate at your convenience."

"Convenience is a very doubtful debtor. Are you really satisfied with that?"

"O, yes! Completely."

"You do not want to get rid of me, now you know the burden you are undertaking?"

"That is nonsense. We have come to be true comrades, I hope. And so let that close the matter."

She sat looking down, and purposelessly twining her fingers together. Then suddenly she raised her eyelids, and I thought I detected a moisture on them.

"I think," she said—"you may—that is to say—will you call me Fifine, Cousin?"

Truly there is no help like pecuniary for expanding the human emotions. No wonder that an unscrupulous man with a purse can make his opportunities.

"On condition that you call me Felix," I said; and so it was decided.

But though the compact as to those credit notes was made, and scrupulously insisted on by Fifine, I could see, to do her justice, that she was never easy under the compromise. Her pride of family, I opined, rebelled against that indebtedness to a stranger. So one day I said to her point-blank: "Tell me the truth: you are unhappy at not hearing from my sister. Would you like me to go and see her, and tell her of your difficulties?"

She stared at me with open eyes, into which a positive terror grew.

"What do you mean?" she said. "No, not for worlds! Do you in the least realise the risk you would be running—for yourself; for us both?

Sometimes I think you hardly take what you were told about me seriously. Either that, or you are really bent on shaking me off by whatever desperate means."

"I told you I was not."

"You never said so directly."

"Well, I implied it clearly enough—just as clearly as you imply, perhaps without meaning it, the real reason for your worrying about Marion."

"What is that?"

"Why, that the receiving this contemptible accommodation from me is wounding to your patrician pride."

"Do I seem to imply that?" she said, in a low voice of wonder. Her cheek flushed; a shadowy smile twitched her lips. "It is quite to mistake me—— On the contrary——"

"Well, what?" I asked, as she paused abruptly.

"Nothing," she said; and I thought she looked at me wistfully. After a moment she went on: "And anyhow it would be absurd, because you too belong to the Noblesse, though you *do* pretend to think nothing of such connexions. You do, do you not?"

"I wouldn't affirm such a thing," I answered. "Pride of family is the most excusable of all prides, because it is impersonal—a leaning upon the support of a genealogical tree for one's identity. To claim recognition solely through the achievements of one's ancestry is really a very pretty form of modesty, if looked at rightly. Besides, we owe something to those to whom we owe our own distinguished position, do we not? I admire you for doing that credit to your ancient lineage, I can assure you I do; and should think less of you if you were capable of accepting favours easily, like a commoner soul. Really, Cousin Fifine, you know, your rank is a very attractive part of you to me. Didn't you ever guess it?"

She was looking down again, frowning and knitting her fingers together. She murmured something inaudible—it might have been protest or assent.

"But for that very reason," I went on, "there should be no foolish embarrassment between us in such a matter. Your suggesting such seems like a reflection on my own inferior standing. If you want me to feel on the same social plane as yourself, you must regard this question of funds as totally immaterial. *I* should, believe me, if our positions were reversed; and so, I think, would anybody not a tradesman."

Still she did not answer; but presently, and quite suddenly, she rose, and, going hastily into her bedroom, shut the door between us.

I was surprised—perhaps; or perhaps I was not. Anyhow, let that pass—and some subsequent days, during which nothing more was said on the subject. In the meantime life went on as before, and I, for my part, found it agreeable. We shared our differences impartially, as we did our amenities; and the money question was shelved.

Early in our acquaintanceship Fifine had cleaned the glass of the little picture by Auguste Ronsin that she so much admired. I don't know why, but it always piqued me to hear her extravagant eulogies of this piece, which was after all nothing so wonderful, though it was out of the common. One day, when she was in her bedroom, I took the thing off the wall and hid it. She was not long in noticing its disappearance.

"Why have you removed it?" she asked me immediately.

"I want you, for a change, to praise something of mine."

"Well, I do. Your plats are the most perfect things—models of tasteful cookery."

"Je veux le croire, Mademoiselle. But I refer to the business of the palette, not of the palate. There comes a limit to welcoming praise of other people at one's own expense."

"If I praised a picture of yours it would be in spite of my not understanding it; and what value would my praise have then?"

"O, to perdition with this question of understanding! There are none so blind as those who will not see."

"No, Felix—no, indeed: I want to have my eyes opened, if you will only believe me. Show me your sketches again."

I was nothing loth; there can be no question of vanity in proselytism; and I got out a portfolio of colour notes made in Provence. As before, Fifine considered them without emotion, while I confined myself to the simple enumeration of their titles. Presently we came to one before which she paused in a stupefaction so desperate that I was tickled for once into a brief exposition:—

"Imagine yourself waking in bed on a brilliant June morning, and facing a window outside which the plumy tops of a row of plane trees trellised the blue. What would be the impression to your eyes, winking and blinking between dreams and reality? That was painted at Orange."

Fifine looked up quickly.

"Orange!" she said. "That was where I was born."

I felt a little surprise; but only for a moment. What was against her being born where she liked? And then she went on, with just a little suggestion of flurry: "How much you must have travelled, judging by all the places you have sketched. And I have never travelled at all."

"Have you not? Save from Orange to Paris, of course. Do you want to?"

"It would be amusing to see my birthplace again."

"Well, why not? Let us go together."

She glanced up, with a quick startled look.

"And run straight," she said, "into the arms of my enemies."

"If that is your only objection," I answered, "I don't think it need prevent you."

"Ah!" she said. "You do not believe—I know that."

"Whether or not, my cousin, makes no difference. To slip out cautiously, and leave the impression, if any such exists, that you were still here, would be to my mind an excellent policy. Think of their watching the empty cage while we were ranging the free earth, unsuspected and without fear."

She was conning me with eyes in which some astonishment was visible.

"Do you really mean it?"

"Mean what?"

"That about our running away and travelling together?"

"I suggested it quizzically; but really on reflection I don't know why we shouldn't. From one particular aspect—that of appearances——"

"You needn't go on," she said, interrupting me. "It couldn't be, of course, and, if I appeared to listen, it was only in jest. Besides, I couldn't afford it."

I did not answer to that, because I knew what was in her mind. But the idea which had come into my own remained there to germinate. This hole and corner existence was already figuring as irksome in the light of that wider prospect, and the nomadic instinct in me began immediately to stir and stretch its limbs, like an unswaddled infant laid to kick on its nurse's lap.

"Very well," I said: "we will drop the subject for the time being. Are these things making my methods and principles any clearer to you?"

She shook her head forlornly.

"I am very sorry," she said.

"You want your Ronsin back?"

"Or something in its place. I know you can if you will, Felix. It is only perversity that prevents you. Do, to please me, paint something I *can* understand."

"But that I cannot? Well, shall I paint you, Fifine?"

"Like these?"

"No, like that?"

"There!" she cried triumphantly, and in a delighted voice—"I knew it was only theory, and not incapacity at all. O, do, do, Felix!"

"I hope you will appreciate it at its full value—the abnegation of all my most cherished principles. But I declared I was no dogmatist, and this shall go to prove it. Only you must not build too much on the result. You know, after all, I have not young Ronsin's genius."

"But you have your own," she said; "and, try as you will, you have not been able to hide it under that flimsy stuff."

That portrait of the young woman gave me infinite trouble, but I will admit also infinite satisfaction. As I proceeded, I grew positively enthusiastic over it.

"This shall be something of a revelation," I said—"perhaps even to yourself. I should recommend any artist, wishing to get at the soul of his subject, to live with it on terms of intimacy for some weeks beforehand. You cannot record a face properly on first acquaintance; and, as to hasty transcripts, one might as well pretend to render the depth and mystery of the moon in a blob of white lead."

Fifine, who was a very good sitter—perhaps because she was of a sleepy indolent disposition—laughed at that.

"Why?" I demanded.

"O!" she said, "what a jelly you are!"

"A jelly, Madam!"

"Yes; just as dancingly elastic; and such a beautiful coherent shape until something at a touch divides you completely against yourself."

"You amaze me. Then you do not regard me as consistent?"

"Only in not being so."

"What a very unamiable characteristic."

"Well, I don't think so—or I shouldn't have said it."

I glanced up at her in surprise; then continued my work in silence.

CHAPTER VIII

THE population of our globe, at any given moment, approximates two thousand millions; the section of Immensity visible from it includes some hundred million worlds, most of which, probably, all, possibly, are proportionately inhabited. How much conceit, per cubic inch of his moral and mental capacity, is deducible from a solitary human unit bent on glorifying his own transitory crumb of existence by way of an autobiographical memoir?

It sounds absurd, in whatever terms of dynamics one explains that unit. There may be a force imprisoned in a grain enough to wreck a continent; but, even then, what is a continent to infinity? The unit is as nothing, though he be as packed with condensed power as a cordite shell: he is one speck of cosmic dust, myriad-accompanied, travelling swiftly across a sunbeam from darkness to extinction: he is vivified into his brief moment of meaningless excitement about nothing, and he ends as meaninglessly. Relatively he is of no more account, points no more original moral, than any other of his microscopic relations. Gladness, hope, disillusionment—so runs the scale with them and him, so it has run, so it will always run. There may be notes beyond the mortal gamut, colours outside the rainbow; for living knowledge, for living guidance they neither exist nor have existed. He just runs up the keys, from bass to treble, runs out at the end—ceases.

And yet he will always be talking about himself—and why? Because, I think, in his conscious indestructibility, he is himself in epitome the whole wonder, tragedy and mystery of Creation. He feels these all in his own soul as an individual possession, and feels that they would be his, though his soul lived in utter solitude apart from its fellows—nay, apart from its body. They are the things to be discussed and recorded, and, because they are him, he must have the conceit of his immortality. He never views them in his heart as ephemeral; they do not cease with his material being. Wherefore it is that we are eternally compelled to regard ourselves, our little passions and our brief histories, as stories not ended but begun; and wherefore it is that, in spite of all our cosmic diminutiveness, Fifine and I shall feel as entitled as any others to talk about ourselves.

And what will it all matter in a few years' time? I am more reasonable than most rationalists, and I say I don't know. Nothing may matter; or so much, that any philosophical callousness to which I resolved to discipline my soul now might be found to have worked its own retribution in our eternal severance. I will not risk that, whatever my scepticisms or beliefs; nor could I if I would. Something has suffered in me a "sea-change," which makes such a mood for ever more unattainable; and, if I appear resigned or indifferent, it is for pride and the world's sake. There are some feelings we would not share even with a divinely sympathetic archangel.

It is not to be supposed, however, that all this time my intelligent interests were summed up in Fifine and her affairs. Somebody once said of me—wittily as he supposed and as I did not—that I had got too many irons in my fire ever to let it burn properly. He meant, of course, that I was not one of those monomaniacs who cannot pursue one ideal unless they neglect all others. Well, I am not, and, if I lose anything by the fact, it is not interest. Were we made omnivorous, I should like to know, to feed on boiled rice or beans? The man who could "pinch" his own soul of buds, like a prize chrysanthemum, in order to develop one monstrous head, was always a fool to me. *I* prefer, improving upon Ancient Pistol, to make the world not only mine oyster, but my pepper, my Chablis, my feast of a hundred dishes from hors-d'œuvre to savoury; and so, if you like, the last decanter being drained, to sleep under the table. Most properly, Death is the only drunkard who never wakes with a headache.

Well, Fifine interested me; but Fifine was not my universe. I can recall quite a number of subjects in which I was more or less immersed during those early days of our comradeship: correspondences with Galt, of the English Meteorological Society, on the question of climatological changes in the upper air strata, with some suggestions for an improved recording instrument; with Hénault, of the geological department of the Jardin des Plantes, on the formations of the Rhone delta, especially as regarded the aluminium beds of les Baux, and with others on the same or kindred subjects. Then I was engaged with Gondran, a practical mechanic, in elaborating a design for a bicycle to be part driven by a dynamo-electric screw, the details of which it gave me infinite pleasure to work out; and I was writing a paper for an Art Magazine on Pigments and their Mediums, with a discursus on the genesis and growth of Art, its psychological necessity and devolution.

That last was a subject inviting some minor collaboration; and my treatment of it owed in certain small details to my companion. We used to worry the thing together, and extract a good deal of amusement out of it. Why, given reality, human nature should have come to desire its artificial presentment: the necessity of gathering generalities to a focus for their better understanding and appreciation: emotion epitomised, as spirit is produced by condensation of diffuser liquids: the inexplicable charm of reflected images, originating very possibly the idea of framed pictures: the permanent recording of heroic deeds, leading by a natural process to the appropriation of design to ignobler and less masculine uses—such points, and fifty others, were suggested and discussed between us, until they began to assume an orderly progression in my mind. And presently the article was written, which I am free to confess it would likely have been less promptly without Fifine's intervention.

Still, for the most part, my interests were continued independently of her; though I will not say they borrowed no additional relish from her neighbourhood. Pursuing them, it was like—to use a base simile—working with a dram at one's elbow. To "sip" her in the intervals of reflection was to find one's hand surer, one's brain brighter. Then one day it occurred to me that I was getting rather to depend on this moral stimulant, and that I might feel somewhat lost when, in the nature of things, it should be withdrawn. That consideration surprised me into an effort to do without it, by affecting more exclusiveness in my labours; but the effort was not a success.

I don't know why it was (or do I or did I?); but a favourite topic with Fifine was class distinctions. She frequently recurred to it, and always, it seemed, with a desire to enlist my sympathies on the side of the proletariat—with the kindly intention, perhaps, to put me on good terms with my own less distinguished origin. I took, however, rather a mischievous pleasure in bewildering her—and sometimes myself—as to my sentiments on the subject, though mostly I let her suppose my predilections to be for the "classes"—as thus:—

"The people are the people and will remain the people, not because they are wronged and oppressed, but because they are deficient in certain qualities of the superpeople. Not all the efforts of democrats earnest or democrats self-interested will ever close up and obliterate the line of cleavage; no social reform whatever will make the two one except in name. It is a state of mind, not of condition, which separates them; and that, not class tyranny, was the origin of the division. I think the question of education has nothing to do with it; we have all the same opportunities in that respect. But I think the question of happiness has a great deal to do with it. The people, for all the material misery which infects their masses, are nearer Nature, and therefore further from self-consciousness, than the superpeople, and on that account happier. Finally, the people do not aim at being anything higher than themselves: they aim—and that only when worked upon by demagogues—at reducing the superpeople to their own level."

"Then anyhow you think the people happier than the superpeople?" says Fifine.

"It seems so."

Her bosom swelled to a little sigh (she was sitting to me at the moment), and the meditative brown eyes seemed to search me for some reassuring sign.

"Then," said she, "if I were you, I should know, without any question of qualities, where to seek for happiness."

"Among the people? And you can say that, remembering the happiness I told you I derived from your high-born condescension?"

She sat back, with a little impatient gesture.

"I wish, for once, you would treat me as an intelligent being," she said, "and not always with that sort of bantering flippancy. It is not in the least funny, and does not in the least take me in. I don't condescend, and you know I don't; and, if I did, the only malicious pleasure you would derive from it would be in laughing in your sleeve at my silly vanity. Sometimes, from my lower place, I wonder if you are really as clever as you would like to appear. Are you?"

I could only glance up with a modest expression.

"There was once a great Englishman, Fifine, whose name was Bacon, and he had a pet proverb, 'The vale best discovereth the hills.' Am I, you ask? I leave it to you."

"Then I think you are not."

"Ah! Then now I grant your intelligence, and I will never banter you again. Sit quiet a little. Do you know I am nearly at the end of my task?"

She did not answer, and I worked on. She had never from the start been permitted to see the portrait: it was to be a surprise to her—and, possibly, a revelation. Absorbed in some final technical detail, I did not look at her again; until presently, putting down my palette and brushes with a grunt of satisfied relinquishment, I leaned back and our eyes met.

"My dear child!" I said: "Fifine, my dear child!"

She rose, as I rose; but I hurried to stop her before she could escape.

"What is it, m'amie? You were not really hurt by my tone? Why I never thought your interest in the question was any but a mildly controversial one. I would not have laughed at you for one moment, Fifine, if I had believed you serious."

"Yes," she said, trying resolutely to blink back the drops that would yet collect and fall; "and I wasn't serious, of course. I don't know; but perhaps—perhaps this confinement *is* beginning to tell on me a little; and the long sitting was trying."

"It is the last," I answered. "Come and look, Fifine, and speak your mind about it."

She needed no coaxing; she was the remotest from your weeping woman, obstinate and self-pitying. I took her hand, and she came at once, and stood with me before the picture.

She did not speak for a long time; but at length she turned to me, and I was content in the guerdon of her look.

"Felix," she said softly, "women are really of coarser fibre than men. You see us not as we are, but as your transcendent imaginations paint us. And we know that well enough; and that is why we will always submit to the judgment of men, rather than to that of our own sex, who know the truth."

"You are pleased, Fifine?"

"That you can see this in me? I should not be a woman otherwise."

"But, with the style—the technique?"

"It is all beautiful; only—only you have not yet painted what I can understand."

"Not?"

"No—how I can look like this—to you, to any one."

I knew her very well. There was no coquetry, no fishing for a compliment in what she said. Suddenly she turned, and approached her face one instant towards mine—God knows on what emotional impulse. It was checked as soon as felt; a vivid flush overspread her cheek.

"I am very tired," she murmured. "I think I will go and lie down for a little. Vive le maître!"

"Fifine!" I exclaimed; but she was already at the door of her room.

CHAPTER IX

I HAD started with the word, but I made no attempt to follow: the momentary impulse to do so was reflex and independent of my will. Resolutely I turned to the clearing away of my paraphernalia, whistling as I moved about—ostentatiously noisy. I was savage over having been betrayed even into that one exclamation, significant solely through its tone. It had been surprised out of me; but the warning it conveyed should be unconditional. That glimmer of a Gorgon head had turned me instantly into stone: adamant I would remain thenceforth.

The next day I put a suddenly formed resolve into execution. Telling Fifine through the door that I probably should not be home till late, and that she had better not sit up for me, I went out very early after breakfast, leaving her still half asleep in bed. I had no very definite purpose in my mind but a judicious absenteeism, which I might turn to the profit, or not, of some provisional reconnoitring; and I wished to be abroad betimes in order to avoid chance meetings with acquaintances.

I am ashamed to confess that I did not even know the exact spot of my step-sister's ministrations; but a few enquiries guided me easily to a place so considerable. The Hôtel Beaurepaire stood, more or less about where I should have expected to find it, in the Avenue Henri-Martin. The actual building was pointed out to me by a precocious bebloused infant, shouldering, like a miniature Hercules, a club of bread. The Hôtel presented nothing more remarkable to the street than a huge white face of painted stucco, broken by innumerable tall windows having each its little white balcony and white jalousies, the latter mostly closed. In the middle, great wrought-iron gates, white, also, and as jealously shut, gave upon an inner quadrangle like an inn courtyard. A glimpse of enclosing buildings, of a welling fountain-basin, of oranges and oleanders in tubs, was to be caught through the foliated interstices of the gate. There was no sign of life anywhere visible; and if there had been, my concern with it was purely speculative. Yet I could not forbear lingering a minute or two in a sort of abstract curiosity, to consider the occasion which associated this august residence, unconsciously to itself, with my insignificant eyrie in the Rue de Fleurus. The sense of disproportion evoked by the thought tickled me: it was little Jack against all Blunderboreland—a thimbleful of mushroom self-assurance against the impregnable stronghold of ages. Could we conceivably defy to the end the forces represented in this place, hoodwink its astute councils, succeed in making our own terms before surrender? One thing did strike me as grotesque—my brief startled impulse of the evening before. That might seem possible in the Rue de Fleurus connexion; it was an incredible audacity here. And here was Fifine's natural habitat; from such as this she drew her code, her sentiments, her living colour. It was only a marvel that, by whatever force of fear impelled, she could have adapted herself so easily to those changed conditions. But she had been oppressed and persecuted: I had been told so and must believe it, however monstrous it seemed to me that one so attractive and endearing could have been made the subject of a parent's unnatural tyranny. Perhaps to be allowed to live herself, though in the humblest circumstances, was compensation enough for all the loss implied by what I looked on. Yet she *had* not been crushed; did the fact appear in her conduct, her speech, her imperturbable serenity? And what then?

O! leave all problems to mathematicians. With a laugh I turned away. Why had I come at all? I did not quite know, unless it were, in a sudden access of prudence, to learn something about the place and circumstances of the conspiracy in which I was involved. I had a restless impulse on me to jog the situation somehow, since it was getting congested beyond my management; and this had seemed a first vague step in the direction of movement and change.

What should I do with myself, decided as I was to break, anyhow temporarily, the spell of perilous inaction in which I had become entangled? I strolled aimlessly into the Bois de Boulogne, where the sweepers were at work with their long thin brooms, ruffling the untidy grass which Paris never learns to shave and trim. Loitering slowly on, I heard hurried footsteps behind me, and turned to encounter Marion.

She was mottled in the face—agitation always made her so—and she breathed noisily. Even in that surprised moment I could not help mentally criticising the figure she presented, and uttering a secret thanksgiving that she was my sister only by courtesy. A brother in fact had had reason to feel small pride in the connexion, though in this matter of family credit little allowance is usually made for that unnatural creature's feelings. Yet I thought I could appreciate the hot anguish of gilded youth forced to chaperon, fraternally and shamefully, a figure so aggressively undesirable as this. She had, it is true, conceded to fashion a hat of the feminine swashbuckler type, which blinded one eye and aggravated the inflammatory defiance of the other; but the scornful plainness of her costume and her flat-heeled stride hopelessly discounted any half compromise with custom her head might display. If there is one thing I detest in women it is the long-skirted jacket, and Marion's was so long that it left a quite inconsiderable fringe of dress between its end and her strong ankles.

"Walk on," she said, panting for breath: "don't stop, but walk on."

We turned towards the lake; there were few people about, and the morning was still and misty. Presently she opened upon me in her authoritative way:—

"What are you doing here, Felix Dane?"

I glanced at her, amused, raising my eyebrows.

"You are not asking that seriously, Marion?"

"Yes," she said, compressing her lips, "I am."

"My dear Marion; I am doing nothing, then, but just pleasing myself."

"I happened to be looking from a window," she said, "and I saw you asking a boy to point you out the house."

"My ignorance was inexcusable, I admit."

"Why did you want to know?"

"The scene of your praiseworthy labours? What a question to ask of an admiring brother!"

"I *will* know, Felix." She stopped and stamped her foot, then, warned perhaps by my face, checked herself, and resumed, with a strained attempt at a more conciliatory tone: "You might have consideration for others, if you have no apprehensions for yourself. You don't seem to realise what a difficult tortuous part I am having to play."

"Naturally, when I know nothing about it."

She glanced at me, and away.

"Please come on, Felix. Will you not tell me what brought you?"

"That is better. Call it partly idleness, partly curiosity, partly the absence of any reason why I should not do exactly as I pleased."

"Is there no reason? Can you really say so?"

"None whatever that I know. It was made no condition of an extraordinary situation forced upon me that my absolute liberty of action was to be restricted. I should not have accepted the situation if it had been."

"I am not talking of your rights but of your good feelings."

"Ah? Well, what about those?"

"Are you really so indifferent as to the safeguarding of a trust that you, after all, *did* accept?"

"Be a little more explicit."

"Supposing by any chance Monseigneur himself had happened to be looking from a window just now. Would not his suspicions have been aroused?"

"By the fact of a casual stranger wishing to identify the residence of a family of such importance? What if I had had a Baedeker in my hand?"

"You had not, you know."

"It would only have coloured the moral. I might have had it in my pocket. Anyhow I am sure the great man would have thought nothing unusual about such an everyday occurrence as a sightseer out hero-worshipping."

"You don't know him in the least; you don't comprehend the situation. But of course you are only talking, after your way, for talking's sake."

"*Is* that my way? I should have thought I was a rather silent person as a rule. Do you know, Marion, I could almost imagine from your manner that you were not pleased to see me."

My step-sister jerked up her elbows, uttering a hopeless exclamation. I think she could have thrown me into the pond with the fiercest satisfaction.

"You are quite welcome to imagine it," she said. "Your turning up here is the very last thing I desired."

I laughed.

"Well, it was your own choice, you know, to come and join me. I neither expected nor invited you; and it appears to me that whatever suspicion my movements may have aroused in an august bosom will hardly have been allayed by that rash step on your part."

"I hope to heaven we were both unobserved; but to see you made me desperate. I thought something had happened; that you were bent on some folly which might betray the whole plot. Has anything occurred to disturb you, Felix? I think, seeing my distress, you might be candid with me."

"To be sure I will, Marion, now you ask. Do you realise that three weeks and more have passed since I undertook a certain charge?"

"I know, Felix. I cannot help it."

"And that during all that time I have received no word, no hint from you as to———"

"Yes, I know. I cannot help it, I say." She looked away, as if momentarily disturbed or embarrassed, then faced me resolutely: "Do you want to get rid of her?"

I should have answered, "yes," unequivocally. What motive for delicacy or hesitation could I have? Wisdom and policy alike clamoured for release from a position which, impossibly heroic at its outset, was daily growing more and more compromising in the sentiments it inevitably engendered. My professional interests, my personal honour were both concerned in the response; and how did I vindicate them? I stumbled a moment; and then temporised:—

"I want a term stated, that is all. I have no objection to the young lady, or any fault to find with her. We get on very well together on the whole. But don't you think you are taking rather an unfair advantage of my *good*-nature, not to speak of my—of my not too impeccable *human* one?"

Rather to my surprise the challenge evoked no opprobrious response, nor indeed any response at all for a little. A student of physiognomy might even have fancied he detected in Marion's expression a certain shiftiness, a desire to avoid straight issues.

"I think," she said presently, "that, as to that, you will be guided by your own sense of fitness and propriety. I trusted to it at the first, Felix, and I trust to it now."

"That is all very well, my good sister; but I never understood that the compact was to be an indefinite one."

"It is not to be, of course; only—I tell you this candidly, Felix—the predicament which forced it upon us is not yet safely resolved."

"Does the Marquis know that his daughter has fled from him, and is in hiding somewhere?"

"There is no reason why you should not be told that. Yes, he does."

"And why does he not visit the knowledge upon you, her confidante and abettor?"

"I did not say he did not. But leave me out of the question; I can look after myself. It may be that he respects in me a certain force of character, which is not to be debarred from its duty by threats and bribery; it may be that heaven has granted me a certain power of exorcism over demons; it may be, as I told you before, that he sees in me the only possible clue to the secret of his child's disappearance. That clue will remain safe, so long—so long as you are faithful, Felix."

"H'mph!" I pondered the thing awhile, not satisfied, nor, it must be admitted, wholly discontent. "Then it seems," I said, "that I have no choice in the matter."

"I promise you, as I promised you before," said Marion, "that I will communicate with you the very moment that a present difficulty has resolved itself. Only, for mercy's sake, don't again risk disaster through this sort of collusion. It will be bad for you, for us all, if his suspicions are once aroused. Felix, I will tell you one thing—it is for your companion's sake. He knows—I have ascertained it—that we alighted near the Mont de Piété that night. That is enough to put his agents on the scent; and you must keep her close, if you would not imperil her safety. If she were once traced, and found to be——" She checked herself, gulped, and went on—"you would not like to have her innocent blood on your head, I am sure?"

I stared. It was not her persistent reassertion of that wild fable which surprised me; it was the curiously detached manner of her reference to my "companion." Was it really Fifine's salvation or her father's which formed my sister's leading consideration in this matter? The question was a novel and startling one. Really, if it had not been Marion, I should have suspected here some interest more than exorcismal in the morphiomaniac.

"By no means," I answered—"nor the miscarriage of your plans either. Which means, I suppose, that I must resign myself to the inevitable."

"If you will only have patience, Felix. It will not be for long now, I hope."

"And in the meantime—h'm!" I stood considering. Then suddenly a whimsical thought occurred to me; and I uttered it, more for the humour of the shocked protest it would evoke, than from any least expectation of a favourable response.

"I suppose you wouldn't at all approve of our going a trip together?"

"A trip!" She was obviously and naturally startled; but her tone, I thought, betrayed no particular moral alarm.

"She was born, she tells me, in Provence," I said, "and her journey thence to Paris sums up her travelling experience. It is odd; but I suppose these exotics of the *pur sang* must be kept under cover. Anyhow it struck me that it might not only interest her to visit her birthplace, but that it would be a way for us both out of the killing confinement and monotony of our present existence."

Marion was listening to me; yet I could see that some reflection beyond that engendered by my proposal was exercising her mind.

"She told you that, did she?" she said, staring me suddenly in the eyes.

"What is the matter?" I answered. "Yes, she told it me, but not with any reference to my suggestion, though I made that to her—quite in the elder-brotherly spirit, of course, and with an eye to Plato's moral philosophy for our literary ballast. She might not consent to go, after all; I think that likely enough; only, supposing by any chance the venture appealed to her, would it have your sanction?"

We were strolling leisurely on, and Marion did not at once answer.

"It just occurred to me," I continued, "as a possible resource, no more. It would take us, anyhow for the time being, out of the arena of contention, and if we did it cleverly, vanishing 'like the baseless fabric of a vision,' it might prove more baffling to the chase than our continuing to lie and sulk here under cover. You see, being hidden somewhere in Paris, as they would suppose us still to be——"

Marion interrupted me: "How long would you propose to stay away?"

"How long would you advise?" I said, my eyes beginning to open.

"I don't think it matters."

"Then you have no objection?"

"No; none at all."

She fairly took my breath away. This astonishing acquiescence, where I had expected only obloquy and castigation! Yet I received, in appearance, the thunderbolt nonchalantly.

"Very well, then," I said—"if the question *should* arise."

"You will observe the last secrecy, in that event," she said, "in the manner of your going? I can trust to you for that." And then she went on, putting the case to herself, it seemed, rather than to me: "In the question of scandal, things would rest as they rest now, in neither better nor worse odour. It is for you a matter of conscience, and for her a period of self-obliteration, from which she will emerge, when she does, a restored individuality, having no responsibility to the interval—just, as it were, as if one had crossed from hill to hill by way of a deep sunless ravine."

I did not answer—though that poetical flight from Marion was sufficiently startling—and we walked on for some little distance in silence—a fairly pregnant one on my part. "Certainly," I was saying to myself, "*her* concern is for the morphiomaniac." The idea promised to become an obsession with me. It might be held to explain some things hitherto inexplicable; it certainly, if true, made obscure the probable limits of my guardianship. That was a reflection carrying with it a sense not so much of mortification as of uneasiness. But, in the midst, the thought of that "furlough" so astonishingly conceded rose to encourage and exhilarate me. The free road would dissipate effectively all those drugging fumes generated by confinement. We could be frank comrades, once in the open air, unfettered by convention, responsible to ourselves alone, accountable to no man or woman for a definition of the right which found us wayfaring in company. The prospect pleased me; I foresaw only a single objection to it.

"One thing I must mention," I said, "if there is to be any talk with your young Countess of this expedition. It is, to put it bluntly, funds."

"Funds!" said Marion. She stopped, in some surprise.

"I should never get her to consent," I continued, "unless on terms of sharing expenses. I may as well state the fact. She is out of cash, and already, in some inconsiderable measure, indebted to me. I refer to it only in the connexion of her natural pride—not from any personal motive. She has not confessed the fact to me, nor authorised me in any way to make her position known to you. It was revealed to me quite accidentally."

For one moment I did hesitate as to the advisability of mentioning my suspicions anent the mysterious stranger; but the thought of some possible treachery towards Fifine implied thereby stayed me, and I resolved to keep my own counsel. Marion, after some frowning meditation, spoke plainly:—

"I am a little perplexed," she said, "to understand how, under the circumstances, a fairly ample supply of money can already have exhausted itself. But of course you must not be allowed to suffer by her extravagances. Say nothing about it, and I will write to her in a day or two, enclosing a further remittance. Is that all?"

"That is all."

She seemed to accept my assurance with a sigh of relief: and forthwith, with an air of unconstrained curiosity, put some questions to me about the manner of our life, its domestic incidents, the young lady's demands upon my time and resources, and more especially my opinion of her and my feelings towards her—to all of which inquisition I responded as truth or policy dictated.

"She is a good girl," she said at the end; "a trustworthy girl. Deal finely with her, Felix Dane—and with yourself." She held out her hand. "Good-bye, now, and trust to my promise to release you at the first available moment. Only don't again, for heaven's sake, risk appearances by seeming to force my hand like this."

Begging me to stay where I was, she left me—profoundly cogitative, you may be sure. That obsession had entered my mind to stay. It was gratifying to contemplate the trust of me implied in that leave to travel; and yet, and yet—I could have thought she had no more delusions about me than I had about myself. Really it almost seemed as if Fifine's fate was to her a matter of quite secondary importance; she was willing to confide it to such fortuitous happenings.

I went a long walk into the country that day, tramping by way of Sèvres and Bas Chaville to the little Trianon, with its atmosphere of ghosts and piteous things sighing and whispering among the yellowing leaves. Returning to Paris, late and somewhat exhausted, I dined, cheaply but delectably, at a little Café in the Rue Vivienne, and thence, according to my promise to myself of a late evening, made my way to the Opera-House, where I paid my three francs for a fauteuil de quatrième amphithéâtre (and a very good one) to hear Romeo and Juliet sung.

Now I was scanning the audience from my lofty eyrie, when, my glance roving to the orchestra, whose members were at that moment tuning their instruments, I positively started and sat transfixed. For there, seated behind a violoncello, along whose strings his white fingers hopped and scampered like white mice, was my old plaintive macaroni of the Rue de Fleurus. He had no chrysanthemum bud in his buttonhole now; but I knew him at once; my eyes, sufficiently penetrating at all times, could not be mistaken.

Well, for what he was worth he was identified; and what was he worth? Even were I to take the trouble to ascertain his name, how indeed would it bring me nearer a solution of the mystery of Fifine's indebtedness to him? Besides, it was no affair of mine.

Fifine had gone obediently to bed when I returned home that night.

CHAPTER X

FIFINE received her letter, containing a bulky enclosure, from Marion. I was present when she opened it, and I made no comment, preferring to leave to her the questioning which I foresaw, and which was indeed inevitable. She did not speak for a little, but sat with her velvety eyes fixed on my face, while I dipped, with what show of unconcern I could master, my petit-pain into my cup of coffee. Suddenly she thrust under my very nose a little rouleau of banknotes.

"They are to the value of two thousand francs," she said. "I want you to keep them for me, to draw upon as occasion requires."

"Good," I said. "Behold your conscientious banker. It was unnecessary; but I ask no questions."

"You have no need to," she said; "nor to pretend ignorance of whence they have come and why."

"From my step-sister, I make bold to guess; though how she is able to draw to this extent upon the baronial coffers, without exciting any suspicion as to her motive, puzzles me."

"She has great influence with him," said Fifine; "though I think it likely she has advanced this from her own store, intending to recoup herself from his at a more favourable time."

"Great influence, has she?" said I, looking up.

"Yes, I think so," said Fifine; and she went on rather hastily, as if to avoid the subject: "You will liquidate my debt to you out of it; and then we will go on as before."

"Shall we?" said I. "Then Marion has not mentioned to you——"

"O!" said she. "Then you knew it was from her; and what she was to say besides?"

"I guessed."

"How wonderfully clever of you. Now, Felix, why will you not be frank with me?"

"Let me know first. What *does* she say?"

"Just this: that if we are inclined to take a trip together, she has no obstacle to put in our way. Now, I want to ask you, How did you dare?"

"Hear me out, Fury. I *did* meet Marion: she saw me looking at the Hôtel Beaurepaire, and followed and accosted me; I *did* ask her what would she have to say to our taking a country jaunt together, and when, to my astonishment, she had nothing to express but approval, I *did* assert that you would never agree to such a proposal unless a replenished purse should enable you to take your share in the expenses. But I assured her explicitly that I spoke without your authority, that I did not even know if you would go if permitted, and that, as to the mention of money, it was made entirely on my own responsibility, and from inferences which you had had no intentional part in exciting. You must know, at least, that my only personal motive was to secure your consent to this trip—or, if you don't, you should. I would much rather not be recouped for my little power of hospitality to one who repays me a thousandfold for it through the mere fact of her company."

I got up as I spoke, and went and stood the other side of the table, so as to face her. She did not answer for awhile, nor look at me; but presently she raised her lids with a little smile, and, as it were, a flush of "rosy pudency."

"I never thought you were really serious about this going away together," she said. "It—it seems such a strange thing to do."

There and then I destroyed my boats. I could not look at her longer, in her morning freshness, and play the sagacious self-critic. The burning feminine in her, the ready intelligence, the mental and the æsthetic qualifications, all proclaiming her a comrade of comrades for romantic venturings, ended my scruples in a sort of brain intoxication. Besides, where was the projected harm? Exercise and the liberal air would blow all that accumulated stuff of durance to the winds.

"Why?" I said. "Is gossip rifer under the open sky than in a closed room? We shall be safer from tongues, safer from possible hurt to reputation, to body, than we are here. We will be brother and sister, m'amie; you shall take my name—if you will condescend—and my conscience, and we will journey merrily in company, as witless of criticism as of guile. We will go South, even into the desolations of the Camargue, where no one would think of hunting for us, and, when you will, return leisurely by way of Orange and Fifine's nest to Paris. Say it is settled."

But, womanlike, she would not yield at once. She was full of tremors and scruples—fears of our being discovered and followed, alarm for the unconventionality of the proceeding. I was even exasperated on one occasion into twitting her with her "piano-tuner." "There is no danger," I said, "comparable with that invited by you yourself when you chose to entertain, unknown to me, and in spite of your solemn undertaking, a venerable stranger with a chrysanthemum bud in his buttonhole."

She turned a little pale, I thought, at that, and, looking away, murmured indistinctly: "Madame Crussol allowed him to come up."

"You mean it was not your doing. But he was admitted by you, was he not?"

Then she turned upon me, and broke out impulsively:—

"I would rather not say. Don't ask me, Felix. If it was wrong, it shall not happen again."

"How can I say if it was wrong? But if you have secrets from me, I will have none from you. I saw your mysterieux at the Opera-House the other night, Fifine. He was in the orchestra, and playing a violoncello."

She looked positively scared for a moment; then her face changed, and she laughed, but tremulously.

"It is not my secret," she said, "or I would tell you; I would indeed. Don't be angry with me, Felix."

"Angry, my dear child!" I protested. "I only wanted to impress upon you the comparative unreasonableness of your present scruples. Believe me, if you will, the risk entailed in our leaving Paris is nothing to that courted by you in remaining on and remaining subject to chance intrusions like that."

"Yes," she said, very submissively; "I daresay you are right." But nevertheless it took days to coax and persuade her—until I gave it up in despair. And then she suddenly surrendered.

"So it is finally decided you will not come with me?" I said to her one morning.

"Yes, finally," she answered.

"Then that will do, and I have no more to say."

"O!" says Fifine, "I don't want to prevent you talking about it, if it amuses you."

"It doesn't in the least. I am so sick of the subject that it has no longer the smallest interest for me."

"Yet it is rather an attractive subject."

"You don't seem to find it so."

"I should miss it, perhaps, being gone."

"Fifine, will you come?"

"You remember what I said?"

"No, I don't."

"Not really? Are you sure?"

"On my—h'm!"

"It was 'yes, finally,' wasn't it?"

"To what question?"

"Somehow I can't remember further back than your last."

"That was 'will you come?' Yes, finally, to that, then." I rose instantly. "You will want a travelling dress of some sort. Give me a hint."

"I never consented, Felix. You can't dare to say I did. Something simple but chic—dark blue or stone-colour, would be the best, I think; but I can trust you with the choice."

The choice put me to some pleasant pains, nevertheless; but I need not have disturbed myself. There are angles and angels; there are also women who adorn everything they put on, and those whom nothing adorns. With the memory of Marion fresh upon me, I could only bask in serene contemplation of Fifine's management of material no better and no more effective than that so injuriously misused by my step-sister. It was just a question of self-valuing versus self-spiting femininity. One would be a woman in accordance with, the other, in defiance of, the masculine ideal. Marion scorned sartorial recommendations; Fifine did not. Which is the vainer, do you think, the woman who believes she needs style and embellishment to make her attractive, or the woman who believes in her own perfect sufficiency without either? Even with the hat, it was less a question of what was worn than how. I would have backed my Provençale to make quite an endearing feature of the amorphous basin with which Marion had elected to bonnet herself.

However, if Marion was an angle, Fifine was certainly no angel. She was just a Parisian jeune personne—however she may have been born in Orange—with a natural faculty for making the best of an agreeable face and figure. And she was not *difficile* in the matter of "changes." She was going forth to acquit herself sensibly as the road-mate of a vagabond, and she was merciful as regarded that beast of burden. For I proposed for my reasonable shoulders nothing less and nothing more than a single rücksack, such as I had commonly used in my trampings, which strapped under my armpits and was of proportions elastic enough to accommodate sufficient, and an ounce or two over, for our needs.

And how in the end did we plan our escape? Why, by planning nothing at all, and simply walking out one quiet evening and making our way on foot to the Gare de Lyon. We locked the door of the flat behind us, locking in some pleasant and odd memories, and leaving the key with Madame Crussol, the sagacious and diplomatic, sallied into the street temerarious and tripped upon our way. I neither looked for nor encountered the least interference with our movements, and we reached the station in safety, where I took us second-class tickets for Nîmes. Then, having each of us gulped down a mazagran, hot and black, I bought a bottle of Sauterne and some long sandwiches, and we took our places in the train, only then, perhaps, a little nervous in inaction, and anxious for the whine of the horn that should dismiss us on our adventurous journey. It sounded at last, and we drew away into the night.

CHAPTER XI

WHAT is happiness? Psychologically, I suppose, it is a state of mind, contingent on some pleasing expectation and unhampered by physical disabilities. One cannot be happy *with* the toothache, or *without* the ache of hope in pleasurable forthcomings. Fond anticipation, clear or nebulous, is of its very essence; the fruitful idea is a condition of its being. It must build to exist, like the reef-constructing serpulæ of the Pacific; and when it can build no longer, it ceases with its own productive capacity. It dies upon content, as the chosen companion of the queen-bee's love-flight dies. Yet happiness is not content, though it may achieve it, as labour achieves sleep and life death. It is a thing of subtler texture, of more ardent constitution. One may feel content after a good meal eaten, thirst assuaged, a handsome deed accomplished, anxiety or physical pain relieved, or on rest following fatigue. But that is not happiness: happiness is to be experienced only through the creative and constructive processes of the mind. Following an idea, it may foresee its goal as a bright lodestar; but its essence lies in the pursuit rather than in the attainment of that end.

The happiest souls alive are little children at play. Watch them— oblivious to all material calls; recognising thirst and hunger only when reminded of them—intent upon the pursuit of an idea, which is not travestied by them in their adaptation of incongruous means to certain visualised ends, but is simply imaginatively rendered through the medium of such arbitrary "properties" as are at their service. Cannot one *think* a locomotive out of those little circling cranks of arms, stamping feet, steam-spouting lips? If one cannot, then the unhappier dullard he; a thing not superior to childhood, but its spiritual outcast. There, before those sparkling engine-lamps of eyes, run the gleaming lines, on and on to Waterloo or Euston: the imp's imagination is moving all things to his will, as sure as ever Orpheus drew with his golden lyre the Argo to the sea. He is happy conceiving, and developing his conception to its ultimate fruition. And, lo, then! his purpose fulfilled and the zest consummated, into chairs and tables resolve themselves once more the ships and castles and rolling-stock of that creative dreamland, and he is a little human boy again, sated with play, and with cravings in his tummy that call for just material content.

Yes, children know happiness; and so may the man know it, only in less irresponsible degree. He cannot feel the mortal and play the Robin Goodfellow; but he can read mysteries into Robin's fen-candle enough to lure him on to ecstasy. In this alone is he the child's spiritual inferior—that his imagination is less the master than the slave of his bodily condition.

Only physically well people can feel happy, because it is impossible to associate sickness with the idea of achievement. On the other hand happiness is for the dying, because they are about to achieve death; and always for the loving, because they look to achieve life.

For my part—an impregnable constitution aiding—I have had my plenteous share of happiness in my time; but I have never yet recognised its title to itself save in the sense of happy productiveness. In pleasant idleness, in genial sterility, in drowsy blinkings at the sun, I have spent long periods of ease and satisfaction; but they were negative conditions, not to be quoted in the context of happiness. Happiness is an emotion and essentially procreative.

If, during these weeks I am now opening upon, happiness, supremer than any I had yet experienced, fell to my lot, it was in spite of any early consciousness on my part of a definite lodestar to my imagination. I do not say the star was not there: its light had not penetrated to me, that was all. It shone upon me, when it did, unforeseen and unexpected; and if at the last I had no strength to reject the gift it proffered, I must still plead that the use I came to make of it was wholly unpremeditated. Whatever of its nature at the outset I sought and pursued, lay in the prospect of introducing a fresh and appreciative mind to scenes and influences with which I myself was familiar, and of the new savour to be extracted from them through that rejuvenating medium. I wish to justify myself so far, and with only the one—perhaps eccentric—purpose already hinted at. For, after all, is it not absurd to credit the manumitted, the hyperphysical intelligence with no better than our own cramped and morbid understanding?

Do most people know, I wonder, that less-considered route from Paris, which takes one, by way of Nevers and Clermont-Ferrand, alongside the great hills of Auvergne and the Cevennes straight into the heart of the South? There are two reasons for preferring it before the more popular track on the left bank of the Rhone—the trains are far less crowded, and the view from their windows is generally superb. There is also a reason against; but that is conditional. You may find yourself hung up, at midnight, say, or worse, at some wayside station, with hours, maybe, to elapse before you can effect another stage of your journey. For a brief month or two of the year, however, a through train to Nîmes—supposing you cryptographist enough to discover it in the *Guide Officiel des Voyageurs*—stands at your service in the Gare de Lyon, timed to start at twenty or thereabouts of the clock. It was this train in which Fifine and I took our places, and by a signal stroke of good-fortune—for, as it happened, it was the very last night of the year on which it was to run.

We actually had two compartments of a corridor carriage to ourselves. Think of that, ye crowded cattle of the Lyon-Marseille route! The obliging Chef de train, tenderly and properly susceptible to the claims of beauty, put them, if rather superfluously, at our disposal, and without—I will believe it—an ulterior motive. Thereafter we travelled, as it were, in a two-roomed cottage.

At the beginning Fifine was a little shy of me. She sat aloof and monosyllabic in her corner, as we threaded the shining maze of lines through the City and its environs, and the great sheds and bridges leapt past, and we ran up the scattered outposts of lights until, gradually attenuating, they ceased in gulfs of windy darkness. But as the train increased its speed, whirling behind from its iron tyres the last dust of the town, a corresponding exhilaration seemed to wake in her, and, putting away all fearfulness and constraint, she sat up and clasped her hands.

"It is real, then," she said; "and I have actually done it. How wicked I feel; and how happy!"

"Do you, Fifine?" I said. "That is a fine vindication of my insistence, and a good augury for the fruits of it. And I feel happy too. Supposing we feast our felicity—pile Pelion on Olympus, as it were, and so make transport of our bodily content?"

I produced the provender. As I was uncorking the bottle, I noticed that Fifine's eyes were fixed upon me, with an odd look in them that made mine dilate. I stopped half-way in my task. "What is it?" I said.

She bent forward, and just rested her fingers a moment on my knee.

"Felix," she said, "you—you are going to be my good elder brother, are you not?"

There was a shadow of emotion in her voice—almost like entreaty.

"Why do you ask?" I said. "Is some devil suddenly revealed in me, with this" (I lifted the bottle) "for his insidious *procureur*? I will throw it out of the window, if you like, here and now."

"No," she said, with a smile a little wistful—"don't. Only—" she sat back, with a sigh—"I think—perhaps—I will not drink any wine."

I rose very soberly, put the bottle in the rack overhead, and sat down again.

"There it is," I said. "The Comtesse de Beaurepaire was quite right in suggesting that reflection to me. There is something demoralising to common natures in the mere thought of alcohol."

"Don't—please!" said Fifine distressfully. She leaned forward once more, with a little appealing motion of her hands.

"Don't what?" said I.

"Call me that—attribute such motives to me. I—I did not mean you; but——"

"If you did not mean me, that is enough, then. There are only we two together here, Fifine, and I have no intention, I can assure you, of hunting through the corridor for a pot-companion."

"No," she said. "Please get down the wine again."

"But——"

"I am tired and thirsty! I don't think I can eat my supper without. *Please*, brother Felix!"

We made, after all, a merry meal of it, as the train, crashing past the sentry lights of the last suburban stations, sped shrieking into the black and unknown vasts beyond.

"It is like being put, with one's billet," said Fifine, "into one of those rolling balls you see in shops; and at Nîmes we shall stop, and the cashier will take us out."

"Our ball will have a window in it before then," I answered; "and we shall see things as we roll."

She came and sat by me presently—for convenience' sake, she said. It was easier so to make a common cause of our feasting. By and by, her speech began to drowse a little, and she caught herself back, more and more, from declining upon my shoulder. At last I said, resolutely: "This is good-night, m'amie. You will lie down here, now, and I will go and smoke in the next compartment. When daylight comes I will call to you."

She let me make her comfortable, with the rücksack under her head, and our one rug over her for warmth. Then, like a rosy sleepy child, she smiled up at me.

"Good-night, dear brother."

"Good-night, little sister."

She made an indistinct movement with her lips, sighed, turned her head on one side, and closed her eyes.

I do not know how long I sat at my window in the empty neighbouring compartment, smoking, and looking with vacant gaze on the rush of impalpable things without. Gradually, as I stared, the gliding telegraph wires, sleekly gleaming past in modulations of high and low, resolved themselves in my brain into an endless stave of music, with posts for bars and insulators for notes, the gathered consonance of which, entering into the rhythmic clack of the wheels, seemed to leap into a wild chorus at each recurrent bar-line, and thence to subside and rise again to vault the next. Weariful to madness grew that rocking chaunt, with its flapping regular punctuations, and the stunning prospect of my being doomed to an eternity of it was already beginning to settle hideously on my soul, when of a sudden the strain tailed off into a hollow drum of thunder, which I recognised curiously for the wash and fall of far-away breakers. Walking towards those, and always to hear them receding, I tripped, stumbled, and sank at once into oblivion. And thereafter consciousness was mine but at long intervals, when the grinding of brakes, jarring into the booming rhythm of things, spoke of stoppages at provincial stations, and one's lids were lifted to a heavy knowledge of shooting lights, and shadowy forms drifting, and a pallid fog of steam condensing in the cold air, and one's ears resentfully awakened to a sound of voices, hooting sometimes, or singing, and potential of disgusting intrusions on one's privacy. Yet nobody disturbed us; and in the end I slept so soundly that I came, after all, to be the laggard.

It was Fifine's soft voice calling to me that roused me at length from my stupor. It was clear daylight, and she was standing, glad and fresh, in the outer corridor, looking on the gracious panorama of hills and streams which unwound itself before her. Her hat was off; the rug was wrapped about her shoulders; a strand of hair hung over her slumberous eyes. She made a very picture of dear disorder.

"Isn't it lovely?" she said, in a low satisfied voice. "O, I'm glad we came!"

We had awakened, no doubt, to the cream of it all—those long passages of the mountains after the monotonous flats were spent. The sun had no power as yet to dissipate the ponds of mist which lay in the hollows and choked the deep ravines; but that was only to have our strange land half lapped in enchantment, and to try to penetrate with delight the mysteries of its gleaming floors. They were shy and sly, those mysteries—here, an up-reaching shadow just seen and snatched away; there, white things that moved and vanished; everywhere sparkles of frosty green, and over all, billowing remotely, or frowning imminent, the slopes and scarps of mighty hills. High up in the air we ran, through thundering gorges and over wideflung valleys, and always to perpetual change and perpetual beauty. The railway took the line of least resistance, following the conformations of the range; and yet with such obstacles had Nature striven to thwart its builders, we were hardly ever out of one tunnel before we were into another. All the way, for scores of miles, they pierced the vast and rocky buttresses, and once, when within a given time we tried to strike an average, we gave up impatiently, having counted into the third dozen, and dismissed the silly effort. The line of the hundred tunnels we called it; and indeed I believe that number is but a fraction short of the truth.

Now, as the sun gained strength, the scene, fired by it, grew out to us like a writing on white paper in invisible ink. Soft iridescences were resolved and identified for flowering pastures or fruiting trees; hanging woods detached themselves from clouds; tiny farms, and steadings, and little foreshortened churches were confessed, each in its green place, for what they were; and the cattle, black, or white, or dappled like half-ripe chestnuts, walked on visible hoofs. Sometimes turbulent floods were seen crashing far beneath us; sometimes placid pools mirrored the blue; but most beautiful were the shallow bends of streams, where, tumbling garrulously over white stones and silt, the little broken waters took on the most heavenly hues of lazulite and aquamarine, streaked with transparent green.

Fifine was enraptured with it all. She had first risen, it appeared, about the time of Prades St. Julien, and had feasted her eyes on that old picturesque monastery-crowned scarp, with its calvary and flower-pot tiled buildings, with the delighted relish of an unspoiled appetite. And thence had followed a very procession of enchantments—mediæval strongholds set high on lonely crags, and appearing above the ground-fog like islands in a quiet sea; quaint church-towers, surmounted by bells in wrought-iron cages; turret-gated farms; mystic townlets, seen through the gaps of hills, hanging pearly and opalescent in an amber haze; and everywhere, for foreground, rock and forest and river and mountain, always changing, always unfolding new beauties, spied from a giddy altitude. Twenty times had she been moved to wake me to share in her innocent delight, and twenty times refrained, from timidity or pity for my weariness.

Well, I felt rewarded now. Her enthusiasm was so whole, so fresh, so lovely infectious, it justified, I thought, my happiest predictions. It seemed a golden interval that stretched between now and our return.

At Langogne we got out to drink coffee at the extempore buffet—and thereby hangs a tale. It had chanced that, pacing the corridor of our carriage once or twice during the earlier hours of my waking, I had spied an uncouth figure rolled up on the seat of an adjacent compartment. There was nothing remarkable in that, nor in the fact that this stranger, by evidence of a knapsack resting in the rack above his head, was a foot-wayfarer like myself. The peculiarity—for there was one—lay, as presently revealed to us, in the creature's appearance alone. For, as we approached

Langogne, we heard him bestirring and uncoiling himself, with a sound of vast stretchings and yawnings; and suddenly he was in the doorway. I had a glimpse of him, wild-haired and red-eyed; and then, as we alighted for our twelve-minutes' respite, he followed us out. We encountered again at the buffet, and he drank his coffee quite close to us, his lips protruded abstractedly, his eyes staring inflammatory over the rim of his glass at Fifine. Observing which, I took note of him.

He was rather a short man, with a suspicion of a rounded paunch; and he was dressed in a grey waistcoat, going very high under the throat, loose grey trousers, inclining to the pegtop, and a baggy alpaca coat with brass buttons. A weeping bow of black silk, knotted into what we should call an Oxford collar, not over-clean, dropped five inches down his chest, and his head for the moment was hatless, displaying a huge crop of ginger-brown hair, rather wild than long. An untidy chin-beard, or Napoleon, and a free moustache, raked up à l'Henri Quatre, both of the same hue, somewhat over-clothed a small face a little poodle-like in suggestion; but the utter self-complacency of the creature's bearing was a thing to marvel over and worship. He strutted, he straddled—though displaying thereby some weakness of knee; he preened his coffee-damped moustache: "Look at me," he seemed to be saying; "make the most of this accident, which gives you henceforth the claim to boast to your friends of having once in your life rubbed shoulders with the renowned, the incomparable Carabas Cabarus!"

For that, as we came to learn presently, was his name—*the* Cabarus, the latter-day Provençal songbird, the poet of "native woodnotes wild," the gallant, the amorous, the very last of the troubadours. His eyes—large, watery, prominent, of a pale blue, and really expressive of some mystic melancholy—had already, over the brink of his glass, marked down, and made a provisional capture of, Fifine. Henceforth he walked, pegtops and all, "in aureate dawns of ecstasy, his rhythmic heart one lyric."

Fifine happily so far was unconscious of her conquest, unconscious even of her privilege. Lapped in scenic wonders, I think she had no eyes for human. Back in our carriage, with hardly a glance vouchsafed to the stranger, she withdrew to reorder her ruffled plumes, while I returned to my post of observation in the corridor. But never suppose for one instant that, emotion once wakened in him, Carabas was the sort of man to suffer its incontinent stifling. Obstacles were but as zests to this ardent soul, so confident in his equipments, both physical and mental. Without a moment's hesitation he took his place beside me at the window.

"A satisfying prospect, Monsieur," he said, with a comprehensive wave of his hand, as though he himself were responsible for the scenery.

"Entirely so," I answered.

"Monsieur's first visit, perhaps, to this part of the country?"

"By no means."

"But to Madame, Monsieur's nouvelle mariée, it is new?"

"I have no wife."

"Ah? To Monsieur's sister, perhaps?"

"To my sister, as you say. Yes, it is new to her."

"Bon! I give myself credit for my penetration."

But not for your amazing impudence, I thought. Yet the wonder amused me. Turning to peer unblushingly into our compartment, he caught sight of the rücksack.

"Voilà!" he said. "The snail's pack, containing all his equipment."

"Equipment for two," said I, inwardly tickled.

"So?" he commented; and gave the Gallic shrug. "It is to double the burden and halve the loneliness. I, too, Monsieur, carry my all upon my back like the snail; but, hélas! with me it is the one burden and the undivided loneliness. Monsieur is a happy man."

He did not look unhappy, himself; I think he was pleased with his own representation of his solitariness; but he thought well to sigh, and immediately thereon to check that ebullition of secret grief, as if to hide it from me.

"You travel together?" he said. "By what itinerary?"

"To Nîmes," I said shortly; "thence possibly to Arles."

"By a wonder," he answered, "that is my own destined route. Without doubt this is a providence to bring us better acquainted."

It had not been his route, I could have sworn, until that moment; and at that moment Fifine joined us, unseen by the stranger, whose eyes were suddenly riveted upon a man issuing from a woodside with a gun on his arm.

"Sacré chien!" he growled, in a vibrant undertone: "behold the assassin, bent on his cursed mission to still God's music!"

"Monsieur is no sportsman?" asked Fifine's soft voice behind us. A child of the fraternal Republic, she had no thought of that reserve with strangers which marks our insular prejudices; yet, I confess, regarding her social traditions, this unaffected bonhomie of hers surprised me a little. Monsieur whipped round with a start and his eyes alight. He bowed, posed, stuck one arm akimbo and flourished the other.

"As Apollo was a sportsman, Mademoiselle," he said, "so am I—to capture music as it flies, not, like that murdering caitiff, to destroy it for the indulgence of a base material appetite. Alas, the pretty, pretty becs-fins! See them marshalled on a dish, each corpse a rapturous song, to be lost in the stifling entrails of some pampered glutton. Think next, Monsieur, when you eat a lark, what melody has perished in you."

"It sings in me, Monsieur; I know that," I said. "I will take what comfort I can of the thought."

He turned his shoulder to me, with a disdainful "pouf." "Mademoiselle," he said, "will comprehend."

"Is Monsieur a bird-catcher?" said Fifine.

I thought he would have exploded. He rose on his toes, smacked his chest once, turned, walked away, and came back again.

"I," he said, stabbing his diaphragm with his forefinger, "am Carabas Cabarus!"

A rather painful silence ensued, during which he scanned our embarrassed faces for rapture; even for intelligence. Then, failing the expected response, he condescended, with an audible sigh, to a patient repudiation of the slander.

"No, Mademoiselle, I am *not* a bird-catcher. You will hear of me— perhaps—where you are going; you will hear of me—possibly. The ideal I follow has no material form—at least so it has seemed to me until this moment." (Fifine might here accept the obvious inference which his eyes expressed.) "It descends to me from voices in the clouds; it rises in the scent of flowers; I see far away, against a sky of milky agate, a low moon hung under a branch, pale and yellow as a citron fruit, and, as I advance to seize it, it eludes me, rising like a golden bubble. Sometimes it is the song of birds; sometimes the fall of water; sometimes I see it browsing on inaccessible shelves of rock, the shining goat, the chèvre d'or of our old, old haunted land. But, whence or wherever, it is not for me—that illusive ideal, that spirit of abstract beauty, which, pursuing for ever, I shall find at last only in the grave."

His voice broke a little. Adding—"Unless I am for once mistaken, how divinely, as to the human inaccessibility of my goal!" he put an artistic period to his rhapsody, and, bowing to Fifine, turned away and vanished into his compartment, from which he did not again issue.

Fifine and I looked at one another; her lips quivered and her eyelids; she put a hand to my mouth, and hurried me out of sight, where she caught at the breast of my coat, and buried her face and her laughter in it.

"Is he mad?" she whispered. "I thought at first he might be a spy, who had followed us all the way."

She could not be defrauded of her view, however; and soon we were at the corridor window again. I think it was near Chamborigaud that we passed, perhaps, the most impressive stage of our journey, looking down from a stupendous viaduct that swept the confines of a mighty valley. Thence we quickly ran out of the mountains, and at Alais—that town of commerce and briquettes, the dirty tabloids with which they feed and befoul the French locomotives—we were fairly in the plains. The run thence to Nîmes, which we reached at some half hour after midday, was scenically tame by comparison, though it initiated Fifine in some characteristic aspects of the South. For here, extending for leagues without the city, are low vineyards in profusion, and countless olive gardens, and cypresses, and wastes of tamarisk and juniper all dotted with little red-roofed villas—a country more Roman than Rome.

Well, we walked with our knapsack to the Hôtel de l'Europe—an old building huddled away in a corner of the town, into whose angle is fitted a small public garden which contains a statue of Daudet and some plane-trees, the upper branches of which, dry and mosquito-infested, almost brushed the windows of our bedrooms. And so was accomplished the first chapter of our adventure.

CHAPTER XII

THROUGHOUT Provence and Languedoc there are accredited songsters, severally honoured in the districts which gave them birth. They may be tillers of the soil or owners of it; propriétaires or ploughboys—it is no matter: they are expected and accepted quite simply and seriously, much as our own village folk-lorists are accepted as the legitimate inheritors of an age-long tradition. They continue a succession never broken since the days of de Borneil, Daniel, Riquier, and those other glorious primitives who, in the twelfth and thirteenth centuries, exalted the dialect of Romance to a metrical art. Yet, though they wear the shoes of their lyrical forefathers, these latter-day minstrels are to be likened for the most part rather to the jongleurs, or hired singing-men, who were used to voice their masters' productions, than to the producers themselves, the genuine troubadours who originated the songs. They play, or at best do little more than ring new changes on, antique themes. Still, now and again, a solitary figure, on whom the Paraclete of ancient inspiration would appear in some light measure to have laid hands, will stand out from the rest, and to that extent that his fame will presently enlarge from the purely local to the departmental; and, proportionately, perhaps, his vanity. They are "throw-backs," in the true poetic sense.

Such, I take it, had been the case with this Carabas Cabarus. He was quite a natural bard, individual in his way, and with a real gift for extempore. To do him that justice is right, for all, I think, the admission redounds to my credit; for the man came to be an entire nuisance to me. His skin was as thick as his vanity was sensitive. He seemed to have a congenital incapacity for diffidence, as regarded both himself and his wares. It never occurred to him that he could possibly be *de trop* anywhere.

Well, Fifine and I, having viewed our bedrooms and hurried through a necessary toilette, descended hunger-sharp to the midday meal. Joyful in the novelty of all things, Fifine was prepared to find ambrosia in the thin broth with a sop of toast in it, and the divine savour of the chèvre d'or himself in tough and smoky cutlets. But even she could not idealise the "vin compris." Throughout Provence that way lies disenchantment, and the traveller who would keep glowing in his breast the comfortable lamp of romance should by no means drink the wine, the red in particular, which is invariably provided free of charge. It has a peculiar rankness in it which penetrates through all the acidity, and a single glassful is enough to quench the hottest visionary ardour. I laughed, seeing the face my comrade pulled, and called for the carte-des-vins. One has to pay in these matters nothing or a good deal; but the extravagance is a necessary one, and I had come prepared against it.

After déjeuner we sallied forth at ease to see the amphitheatre and the Maison Carrée. It was opening October—perhaps, saving June, the ideal Provençal month—and one could bask in the sunshine without a thought of enervation.

"Where are you going to take me to first?" said Fifine.

"To the chemist's," I answered, "for a box of pastilles-moustiques. You must burn one by your bedside, Fifine, if you do not want to come down to-morrow with a face like a plum-pudding. And you must shut your window before turning up the light. I marked those trees close outside, and I tell you what I know."

It was a necessary precaution; and we had just effected it, and were issuing from the shop, when we saw an open fly coming down the street towards us. I don't know what moved me to the irrelevant reflection, but I said suddenly: "I wonder what has become of Carabas Cabarus. Thank the powers at least we have given *him* the slip."

The carriage came on, drawn by a horse with a most curious action. He advanced down the incline towards us, flinging his legs inwards with a sort of jolly buccaneering roll which was quite captivating—a free nonchalant big-boned hack, who took the world swaggeringly, though conscious of bowling at his tail no better than a mouldy voiture-de-place. And as the thing approached us, there was Carabas seated inside it.

He was the same, and yet not the same—he had a hat on. Now, taking him all in all, his raiment and his pose, I should have expected here the right Mistral finish, the typical head-gear of the Provençal peasant, limp black felt, and very slightly raked. Instead, to my exhilaration was exhibited a mottled straw hat with an absurdly narrow brim, and a little tail of black ribbon waggling aft of it in the breeze. It was flattened down upon the abundant mane, and I will not swear was not kept in place by an elastic under the chin.

He recognised us, and waved his hand—even with a suggestion of a kiss blown to Fifine. It needed a Frenchman at once to wear that hat and blow that kiss. If you ask why, you have missed one side of the Frenchman—his innocence. I laughed out as I turned away.

"What are you laughing at?" said Fifine.

"The hat," said I.

"What was the matter with it?" she asked.

I laughed again.

"Nothing was the matter with it, of course. It was a charming hat. You might have worn it yourself."

She looked puzzled.

"Well," she said. "But it was funny, wasn't it, his appearing just at that moment. 'Talk of the wolf, and you'll see the tip of his tail.'"

"I did," said I, "and it wagged. But, Fifine, bear what I say in mind. We have not seen the last of Carabas. He has been hunting us through all the Hôtels and restaurants of Nîmes, and he is about to run us to earth."

"Well, it is something to be so sought after for our young attractions," was all she answered, and we continued our way to the amphitheatre.

In the grip of that vast relic a spirit of glowing abstraction seemed to settle upon my comrade. As we sat high up among the shattered tiers, her eyes were the only utterers of the dreams that moved her. I watched them for some time in silence.

"What are you thinking of, Fifine?" I said at last.

She sighed and turned to me.

"What did he mean by that golden goat?" she asked irrelevantly.

"He? Who?" I exclaimed. "That Cabarus? It seems you have made a conquest of him to some purpose. Why, child, he meant nothing more than an old Provençal superstition, which you will fine related in Daudet's *Lettres de mon Moulin*, in the *Legendes* of Charles-Roux, and elsewhere. The goat is merely the symbol of that unquenchable something in us which refuses to be satisfied with the material and the finite. However high or far we may reach, there is always something vague and elusive to be sought higher or further. We find that mysterious object typified in the marsh candle which Jacques Bonhomme follows through the mire; in the jewelled cup buried at the foot of the rainbow; in the sangreal, and in a host of other fanciful forms. We all follow it, one way or the other."

"Yes," said Fifine. Her chin was propped upon her hand; her eyes looked across the gleaming spaces of sunlight; she rested content with that monosyllable.

"If appearances are to be trusted," said I, "you may flatter yourself that, for the moment at least, *you* are M. Cabarus's golden goat."

She shrugged her shoulders, with a little impatient "allons donc!" then turned suddenly and looked at me.

"And what is yours, Felix?"

"My what? My present ideal?"

"Yes."

"Bouille-abaisse," I answered promptly.

"What is that?" she demanded.

"It is a Provençal dish. I came here to eat it."

"Will you not be serious, please?"

"It is perfectly true, Fifine. I shall not be happy till you have tasted it."

"O! So your ideal is to gratify me. That is something, then."

"It is everything, I think. And now it is your turn to confess your ideal."

She looked at me very steadily. "It is to see you realise yours."

"Bouille-abaisse?"

"Something," she said, ignoring my comment—"some dream which you and that man, however much you may laugh at and despise him, may share in common. I cannot say what it is, but I can trace your pursuit of it through all of your works that I have seen. You are shy and proud, mon ami; you affect to laugh at the heroic in yourself; you meet the rebuffs of the world with a pretence of their being justified towards incompetence. But all the time you know the world is wrong, though the great in you will not condescend to parly with it as to your merits. Better, you think, to give up the struggle, to cease your pursuit of the inaccessible, and, falling into line with your detractors, hunt for bouille-abaisse, as the sort of perfection we can all understand and attain. I would sooner be a dog and sniff for truffles."

I sat silent for awhile, a little surprised, a little amused; then answered quietly:—

"The inaccessible is the inaccessible, Fifine. Perhaps it takes a grown man to find that out."

"You might as well say," she replied, "that the stars are not to be searched because they are beyond our reach."

"Well, what has astronomy done for us?"

"It has made astronomers."

"A musty lot."

"I think they are the finest people in the world—spirits almost more than men. Think of their uplifted vigils, night after night, while we are sleeping earthbound."

"Shall I be an astronomer, then, to please you?"

"You will please me by being yourself, by following your own particular star. You know, Felix—yes, you do, that the real ecstasy is in the pursuit, into whatever pains and difficulties it may lead you. I want to see you great, and greatness is all in endeavour, because there can never be achievement."

"M'amie," I said very gravely, "what have I done to bring upon myself this lecture?"

"You have done nothing."

"Ah! I see—that is it. You think me idle."

"Yes, I do."

"Well, perhaps I am. And so you take this accident of Carabas Cabarus, with his goats and golden bubbles, to belabour me for my sins."

"He set me thinking, Felix; I admit it. And there is something in this place, too, that makes me think."

"A ruin is a poor illustration of the value of endeavour."

"I think it is the very best. It shows how greatness would not be debarred itself although it wrought with perishable things in a perishable world."

I sat silent again; then turned suddenly upon her.

"So that is *your* ideal," I said—"to see me passionate in the pursuit of what you think is *mine*—or should be. Have you none, then, for yourself?"

She looked down and away, tracing a pattern with her fingers in the crumbled stone.

"I do not quite say that," she said, in a low voice.

"But you are willing to sacrifice it for the other? That is very unselfish of you."

"Yes," she said, "it is very unselfish of me."

There was something so strange in her tone that I looked at her in surprise. What was her meaning? What was that mysterious aspiration of hers which she would so gladly forego, provided my self-realisation were contingent on its sacrifice? And then, still looking away, she said a stranger thing.

"Do you think men of genius ought to marry?"

"How can I speak for them?" I answered.

"I say you can and shall."

"Very well, then," I replied. "I think, if you ask me, that they should not. A man's imagination is his mistress. He cannot keep his mistress in the same house with his wife. They would be sure to quarrel, and naturally the mistress, having no orthodox title to remain, would be the one to go."

"But—but, supposing it no question of a wife?"

"Then, it is no question at all. Love makes no contracts and is bound by none. It is worldly policy that does all that part. Do you think I would debar my man of genius that best stimulus to his imagination—an unfettered passion? It is all the difference between the golden goat and the poor Billy tethered to a stake in the backyard."

She sat quiet for a long time after that, her face still averted, her fingers playing with the stones. Then suddenly she stirred, and, with a sigh, rose to her feet.

"Are we not wasting our time?" she said. "I feel that there is so much to see. And yet it is so beautiful here."

We were quite alone in the vast amphitheatre. As she stood up, the picture she made—her face, half in glow half in shadow, the vivid life of her contrasting with the golden ruins of the walls—wrought with such ardour upon my imagination, that I felt that, if I failed in that moment to take advantage of the creative impulse its beauty awoke in me, I deserved to be writ down for ever more the emasculate cypher of her strictures. So very quietly I got out the block, pencils, and a handful of coloured crayons which I made it my constant practice to carry about with me.

"Fifine," I said, "don't move: stand just as you are. I am going to immortalise you."

She gave a little start; just glanced at me; then, neither stirring nor posing, obeyed. I was in happy pin: mood, model and place were all in one luminous harmony, and the thing came out as I had conceived it, automatically, almost without effort. It took me but a few minutes.

"There," I exclaimed. "Nemausea of the golden amphitheatre! What do you think of yourself?"

Her face flushed up as she looked.

"You have made a pagan of me," she said—"or the stones have. Perhaps they shall hold you excused for the little freedoms you have taken. But how clever you are, mon ami; and—and how forgiving to me!"

There was a queer little sound in her voice, and she turned away rather hurriedly. I said nothing; but when, having disposed and repocketed my effects, I got up and joined her, the signs of some emotion were still visible on her face.

"Are all the ruins about here of this lovely colour?" she asked, though with an effort, I could see.

"Throughout Provence," I answered. "The sunset of dead Rome lingers upon them all. They stand up in its afterglow, very old and very quiet, the last great witnesses to the glory of its past."

"The glory!" she murmured, rather awfully. "But think of the things that were done here! O, how could they! To build it—*this*, for just a human shambles, and make it beautiful—one huge great torture chamber, and open to the sky—and God!"

"No, that it was not," I said. "There are the sockets for its awning-poles still existing. Come, and I will show them to you."

"I should not like to stand here in the moonlight," she said, not noticing me. "It makes me think of the Towers of Silence. Felix, have you ever seen, or read about them?"

"No. What are they?"

"I once came across a description of them. They are the charnel houses of the Parsees, the sun-worshippers—great lonely buildings, on the tops of which they lay their dead to be eaten by vultures. So in this Tower of Silence here the human vultures once sat and gloated, feasting on the carnage. And they, too, worshipped the sun."

"Very far from being a tower of silence sometimes," I answered. "You should see it in high festival, Fifine, when they have bull-fights—the real thing, you know—à la mort. No need, then, to reconstruct the past, as you are doing; it stands in sanguinary evidence before you. But these are morbid dreams, young lady. Rome was not all circuses, nor is Nîmes all *Courses de Taureaux*. I shall have to confine you to the boulevards Gambetta and Victor Hugo and their like if you take to this sort of thing."

Fifine laughed, and we made our way again into the streets, on exploration bent. Most that was to be seen we saw, and near dusk rested in the beautiful gardens of the Fountain, and drank iced grenadine through straws under the broken shadows of the Temple of Diana. Then we returned to the hôtel in time for the seven o'clock dinner.

As usual in these coffee-rooms, there was the one long table and the many smaller supernumerary. We secured a minor affair in a corner, from which we could command a view of the company. That was fairly numerous—commercial gents mostly—and I confess that the obvious admiration it betrayed for my companion was a source of some secret gratification to me. True, my own interest in her was not a vested one, so to speak; but it is always agreeable to command, even in the abstract, the control of a covetable thing. It had perhaps never occurred to me to regard her so much in that light as now when I recognised myself for the subject of general masculine envy. Fifine, as an admired personal possession, went up fifty per cent. in my estimation—that was only human nature.

We had reached to the chicken and salad course, when Carabas came in. We both saw him at once, and I turned to my comrade, with a snigger.

"Quand je vous le disais, Mam'selle?"

"Hush!" she said: "Don't attract his attention."

But he could not very well have imposed himself on our narrow quarters. In point of fact he did not see us directly, but established himself, with something of an air, at the opposite end of the long table. Then, as, tucking with protruded jaw his napkin under his chin, his eyes wandered abroad, he suddenly spied us, and instantly posed for his part. He invited Fifine quite obviously to observe the deference with which the waiters hurried to attend him, and the hauteur with which he accepted or waved aside their ministrations. "Witness," he said in effect, "the honour in which I am held, and realise, in shame and humiliation, the outrage you perpetrated on a famed child of genius in likening him to a bird-catcher!"

Thenceforth, if he did not eat nicely, he ate consciously, not so much with an eye to Fifine as with a two-fold stare. He appeared oblivious of my presence; he actually, in mute pantomime, drank to her in a glass of that execrable vin de table; though I regarded him with cool amused eyes, he ignored me as entirely as though I were a mere indifferent intruder on the private understanding established between them. And, when we got up to go, he lifted his glass again, and ogled her hideously over the rim of it.

In the hall outside, as I waited to light my pipe, I questioned the landlord, who made his sociable appearance, as to M. Carabas Cabarus, mentioning how we had encountered him in the train.

"Ah! truly?" he answered. "He is on his way from Paris, whither he has been to negotiate the publication of his poems. A native of Montpelier,

Monsieur, where his father was a coachbuilder. Hence his name, given him, perhaps, in irony, for he was a stupid child. But the race is not always to the swift, nor bread to the wise. He who was slow is the first at the goal, and, being there, is poor."

"First at the goal? You regard him highly, then?"

"Surely, Monsieur. There is none better of his kind in Provence. He is of the great succession—a minstrel worthy to be compared with Raymond Ferraud, both for his verse and his excessive gallantry."

Fifine and I went out for a final stroll before bedtime, which in the vagabond's life comes early.

"That landlord," I said, "is a well-informed man. I have read of that Raymond—a distinguished rascal, who actually persuaded a lady president of the puissant Court of Love at les Baux to share his melodious wanderings with him. They called one another in these connexions *commère*—or gossip, as we might say. It is a good thought, Fifine: supposing we adopt it? But, as to this Carabas, the fellow promises to be a nuisance, and I propose that we rid ourselves of him with all possible despatch. I do not intend staying here long: Nîmes is only the antechamber to fruitfuller delights. So to-morrow we will finish with it, and the morning after, very quietly and unostentatiously, slip over to the station with our rücksack, and take train south for Aigues-Mortes and the wilderness. What do you say, gossip?"

"That I am entirely in your hands, gossip," answered Fifine.

CHAPTER XIII

WE carried out our programme to the letter, "finishing" Nîmes the following day, and, as good fortune would have it, without once encountering the objectionable troubadour within doors or abroad. I hoped he had gone on to Montpelier, and that we had seen the last of him—but I had overlooked the knapsack. We *did* the churches, and the Porte d'Auguste, and we visited again the fountain of the Nymphs with its fair climbing garden, up which we mounted to the old ruined Mausoleum called the Tour de Magne, where Fifine was much more interested in the flying grasshoppers, with their marbled jackets and underwings of crimson or azure, than in the supposititious history of the building itself, to which I tried vainly to get her to attend. But she was in a wilful mood, aggravated, perhaps, by the two or three mosquito bites, which, for all our precautions, she had not escaped. With one exception they were on her fingers; and the exception was quite pretty in effect, forming a sort of beauty mark near her left ear. I told her they looked like little swelling buds on a fair stem, but without reconciling her to the disfigurement or the intolerable itching. Poising an insect on her finger-tip, she would not even look at the tower.

"I *will* not be interested in it," she said. "I don't care a fig whether it was a lighthouse, or a treasury, or a tomb; or whether it is built of ashlar or cream-cheese; or whether it is an octagon or an octopus. If you will paint it for me I will love it; if you won't, I shall catch grasshoppers."

"Mayn't I just sometimes," I said, "enjoy myself, without making a business transaction of my enjoyment?"

"That's it," she answered, watching the thing take flight. "You are exactly like a schoolboy. A book, which you might delight in reading voluntarily, becomes a *task* if imposed upon you as a duty. I want you to paint this, so you don't want to paint it. Your attention wanders, just as the schoolboy's would, to all sorts of extraneous interests that don't matter. Your art should be your enthusiasm and your obsession, and the difficult thing should be to get you away from a subject, not to attract you to it. I daresay, clever as you are, you might take a lesson in perseverance from many smaller men."

"Perseverance, Fifine, is a dreadfully plebeian virtue," said I.

"Well, then," she retorted, "I like plebeian virtues. I can imagine even your despised M. Cabarus coming up here and refusing to leave until he had turned its poetic inspiration to some account."

"To the account of scratching his egregious name on the walls, I expect."

"Yes, you may joke. But anyhow *his* mastering purpose is to excel in the gift which Nature has bestowed on him."

I fairly whistled out my astonishment.

"My good gossip, you are talking entirely without book. You know absolutely nothing about his mastering purpose. Why, you have only spoken to him once, like myself; and we have heard what the landlord said. I have just as much right from that to pronounce him a peddling coxcomb, idling away his time between rhyming and philandering. I should define him, if you asked me, as probably an erotic sentimentalist."

"I don't ask you. Besides, I like sentimentality—in reason."

"Well, I don't; and it is never in reason. I abhor it. It is always a manufactured emotion—like spread chords. The people who use spread chords, in playing, or singing, or talking, are hypocrites and impostors. I should liken them, morally, to procurers. They do not feel, they calculate, emotional effects. I have heard Shelley's 'Indian Serenade' sung by that sort in a way to make one sick. 'I ara-aise from dreams of thee in the first sweet er-ser-leep of night.' Bah!"

"Felix!" said Fifine, amazed; "are you off your head?"

"Are you," I said, "when you chastise me—*me* with that meretricious little skipjack?"

"But, how do you know he is meretricious? You have seen no more of him than I have."

"Exactly. My opinion of him has precisely the value of yours; and they are both worth nothing."

She came and put her hand upon my arm, and looked up in my face.

"I did not mean to hurt you, Felix."

"With that?" I answered. "My mail is proof against better than pea-shooters, Fifine."

"You are not offended?"

"God bless you, no, child. I was as much in jest as you were."

"Yes," she said, and turned away.

But, as we walked down the hill together, after a long silence she suddenly broke upon me again:—

"How dared I presume to read lessons to you—and after your yesterday's proof! I think you are the sweetest-tempered man I have ever known, Felix."

I laughed.

"O, no flattery, gossip!" I said. "The last thing I want is to be exalted to a height I should have the deuce's own trouble to maintain. And, as to presumption, I am not so confident of myself as to resent criticism of my methods."

"No," she said: "I wish—sometimes—for both our sakes—you were." And leaving me that cryptic pronouncement to digest, she fell silent again.

Well, we got off early, as arranged, the next morning, and without any hint given as to our destination, though the waiter, who brought our coffee and our *note* to command, was officious in his attentions and enquiries.

"That was because you tipped him too much," said Fifine, as we walked to the station. "You men are always foolish in that respect. It is stupid, because they have no legal right to demand anything at all."

"Tipping is a detestable custom," I answered; "but, when you talk of legality, a waiter has as much right to expect a douceur as any other tradesman. I have heard it said that the real and only definite line of social demarcation lies between the tippable and the untippable; but that is nonsense. We are all open to receive gratuities, in the sense of supercharges on services rendered or goods retailed. The lawyer who attunes his bill to the financial position of his client; the doctor whose fee is this for the poor man and that for the rich; the soldier or the sailor who, through interest, obtains preferment over men, worthier, perhaps, but less fortunate than himself; the politician who uses office as an invitation to bribery; the adulterating shopkeeper; the preacher who rates his eloquence at a pound more or less in the plate; not to speak of the sportsman who accepts his vail in plain terms, and makes no bones about it—what are they all but receivers of tips? It is the bit, little or much, over and above the recognised scale of charges, which constitutes the tip; and the waiter is as much entitled to expect his bonus as any other wage-earner."

"I didn't say he wasn't," said Fifine. "I said you tipped him too much. But I didn't mean to start you going. That is the worst of you: you seem to hold contradictory opinions on every subject one may mention."

"M'amie, my gossip: controversy is the very essence of education."

"O, don't! we shall miss our train. It is past seven now."

We caught it, however, easily, and again had a compartment to ourselves; a boon which, in our then frame of mind, we were not backward in appreciating. For we were full of happiness and gaiety, a jocund irresponsible couple, who had now finally shaken off the shackles of constraint, and were bound for the wilderness where no proprieties were to question nor dangers to apprehend. Even the absurd little shadow of Carabas was to me, in its dissipating, a matter for some small self-congratulation, and I felt our flight into the seaboard solitudes the breezier for its absence. As the long wastes came about us, I flapped my wings, literally, like an imprisoned gull that smells the ocean salt borne inland on a gale, and I croaked out my jubilance. Fifine laughed, protestingly but indulgently.

"What a child you are!" she said.

"And just now I was a pedant," I answered. "Truly some gossips are hard to please."

But suppressed excitement glowed in her all the same. It was her habit to take it sedately; yet I could read the underlying emotion in every pulse of colour that came and went in her cheek. Her eyes might dream slumberous; but in their depths was an exulting spark that confessed their vivid wakefulness. And she cried out once with rapture when there passed close by the windows of the running train a characteristic little procession—a shepherd boy, driving a flock of twenty or so sheep, each individual member of which wore a favour of crimson ribbon knotted into the wool above his withers.

"O, how pretty!" cried Fifine. "We are in Arcady, Felix—and—and I will never eat mutton again."

"Arcady it may be," said I: "but, if so, Arcady has its wolves. Do you see that great dim cliff of a hill over there?" (we were then nearing Vauvert). "That is in the Cevennes, Fifine, and its name is Le Loup."

"It shall stand for the symbol of all the wolves that ever were," said Fifine; "stricken into stone for their cruelties. I say this is Arcady; and it shall be."

"Very well," I answered. "I am agreeable. Arcady it shall be—the land of lovingkindness, where to be fond is not to be suspected. We can be better friends than ever in Arcady, Fifine."

"Can we?" she said, turning to look again from her window. "O, yes! I suppose so."

"Why!" I said. "Don't you want us to be?"

She did not answer, and I left her to her momentary mood, whatever that might betoken. The needle of a woman's mind is an unsafe compass to steer by. It may point warm west, and lead you, if you follow it, crash on an arctic iceberg.

Deeper and deeper into that land of loneliness we ran on, until the vine-strewn levels, rosy and flaming, which at first had accompanied our flight, were all faded, as a sunset fades, into league-wide wastes of melancholy grey. Harsh bents of grass and lifeless sand came all about us, with pools of motionless water, from whose reeds great birds flapped slowly upwards, sailing away to meet a low horizon. And then at last, at near two hours from our starting, we saw, at the lean land's end, the pictured shadow of our goal; and there was the grim old fortress town, its feet in the stagnant lagoons, its long ramparts extending as massive and unbroken as when, at Philip the Bold's bidding, they first rose from the marshes.

Impregnable; unapproachable: but who would want to approach it? That was the thought which occurred to Fifine, when first contemplating that desolate outpost of the ages.

"I suppose nobody could get in, and I suppose nobody could get out," she said. "I hope that satisfied them. I should have thought the best thing their enemies could have done would be to leave them stuck there, and go round another way."

"You have an excellent reasoning power in you, gossip," said I. "But you are no philosopher, or you would know that man is the one organism congenitally incapable of leaving well alone. To let him escape a wild beast by the skin of his teeth is merely to have him provoked to borrow the first inadequate weapon, and go back to try conclusions with his enemy. If you were to throw an empty biscuit tin into the middle of the great Bog of Allen, and loudly proclaim that any man who attempted to redeem it would do so at peril of your deadly wrath, a hundred fools would be ready at once to risk their lives in the reclaiming of that piece of lumber. And, after all, I shouldn't be prepared to blame the fools. I don't know why; except that there is something very inflaming to one's obstinacy in overbearance."

"If you have finished," said Fifine, "we may as well go on."

We went on, and, traversing the stretch of ground which curves between the station and the walls, discovered, a little to our consternation, that it was fair-day in Aigues-Mortes. Booths and caravans lined the approach to the great entrance gate, called la Gardette, and all about them, and thronging the entrance, were swarms of holiday folk, motley and garish in their Sunday best.

Well, there was no help for it, and our only resource was to accept the thing mediævally. The barbaric colour even assisted to that frame of mind; for indeed the workaday trappings of modern France are much of a dingy sameness everywhere, and it is only sparely, as in the case of the cattle-drovers of the Camargue, that one encounters a local survival of the ancient costumes. Dressed almost without exception as our own men, even to the ugly cloth cap, are the labouring and mechanic classes; in places, too, as remote as Aigues-Mortes; while the women have been as ready on the whole to exchange for drab and fustian the livelier raiment of past times. Wherefore this festive frippery, though florid and vulgar in itself, had here its seeming place in the context of stone walls and frowning battlements.

At any rate we tried to think so, as we passed under the archway into that intricacy of narrow streets, and made our way with some difficulty over the filthy pavements.

They were filthy, those pavements. When I had visited the town earlier, it had been in spring, before the grapes were thought of, or the wine-presses disinterred from their winter quarters. Now everywhere the place was littered with the discarded refuse of the harvest, great heaps of decomposing filth, thrown out to await the scavengers, but whether human or elemental who might say. Only their stench was a certain thing—horrible, indescribable, the Genie in expansion of that rank acidity which in its condensed form inhabited the bottled article. It rose from the gutters; from the mounds of fœtid grape-skins piled about the inner walls; from a belated wine-press still in use in the open streets, and revealing itself crusted with the black scum its champings had rejected. Only here and there, in the wider thoroughfares, or in the open *Place*, could one escape the pursuing poison. Still we religiously *did* our Aigues-Mortes, though, I confess, with some failing confidence on my part. And at last I stopped.

"The battlements, gossip!" I gasped. "The battlements—before all illusion spends itself, and we fall stifled!"

Ah! that was another pair of shoes. We took our official pass at the gateway—for the walls are a *"Monument Historique"*—and, mounting by way of the Tour de Constance at the north angle, were quickly in that atmosphere we had come to seek. Here from the summit we could first descry the whole compact quadrilateral of the town, with its many gates and towers, sitting, like some huge mediæval ark, on the shores of the desolate land on which it had grounded and settled. On all sides else were waste and water—marsh, and the long ribs of sand, and weedy dreariness stretching to the horizon.

Well, this tower itself had its particular history; but that is for the guidebooks. For us, in excelsis, were the long battlements, whence one may gather one's glorified impression of the place. High up we wandered, and saw the whole tight little town packed, like a box of bricks, within its walls. The odours reached not to us, but the sun was gay so high, and it was sweet to loiter, and look down on the cradled roofs and the almost empty streets—for the life of them had gravitated fairwards. Once in a little garden we saw a pomegranate tree in rosy fruit—a lovely touch of colour; and once a group of merry girls went by, bareheaded and unadorned, fruit almost as fair. Elsewise, it seemed, we had these deserted ramparts to ourselves, and the view therefrom.

"But grant me still a friend in my retreat," quoth and quoted I, "whom I may whisper—Solitude is sweet."

And at that instant, turning an angle, we saw the whole perspective of battlements ahead fringed with human forms.

Fifine laughed delightfully, hearing my gasp of dismay.

"But they are bending over to look down at something," she said. "We *must* go and see what it is."

I leaned through an embrasure, straining my neck to view.

"O, don't!" she exclaimed, pulling at my coat: "You will fall."

"All right," said I, recovering myself. "It is—why, Fifine, what is the matter with you?" Her face was quite pale.

"You frightened me so," she said. "Don't, please, do that again."

"Well, I will not." I patted her shoulder, surprised and a little touched. "One certainly has no right to take risks in a position like mine—with a little gossip dependent on me."

She lifted her face, with a tiny stamp of her foot.

"I tell you," she said, "that if you were to fall, I should jump after you."

I looked at her a moment without answering; then I said, with a note of huskiness in my voice which I could not quite control, "Allons, donc, Fifine! Then it is certain I must not fall. Come; I am going to show you a Provençal bull-fight. That is what the excitement is all about."

We found an unoccupied embrasure, through which we could command the scene below. Right under the walls, on the strip of land which divided them from the water, they had erected a frail barrier enclosing a goodish space of ground; and within this area was enacting the game which above all others these southerners love. And a game it is, no more, and a manly game, calling for courage and dexterity, and without any suggestion of the brutality which characterises the baser business. They drive in a bull—

commonly one of those, small and black, which are especially raised for these *ferrades*, or fêtes—having a rosette pinned between his horns; and the man who can succeed in snatching this token wins the prize. That is all; but it affords fair enough exercise for pluck and agility. Any one who likes may take part in the sport: you will see some twenty or thirty engaged in it as a rule: and the bull himself is often the most rompish member of the party. Of course he *means* business, but it is very seldom that he gets the chance for a literal *stroke* of it. Still, it is that off-chance which constitutes the excitement; and, if he is a good bull, he affords one a plenitude. The drawback to the thing, as an entertainment, is the lack of colour, owing to the reason aforesaid. These cuadrillas might, so far as their clothes go, be just a body of ordinary young bank holiday-makers, roystering in Battersea-Park. And perhaps it is on that account that, after a bull or two—the bouts as a rule last only a few minutes—the novelty of the thing stales and one has had enough of it.

Fifine was greatly excited at first, and in terror lest the beast in one of his rushes should "get home." "They can never go on misleading him," she said. "He will turn suddenly on a side-skip like that, and have the man on his horns. O, Dieu merci! Did you see?"

"Rest happy, m'amie," said I. "The bull will never do as you fear. And for what reason, do you think. Why, because he charges with his eyes shut."

"His eyes shut?"

"Ah, yes! That is the players' safety. If it were a cow, now, it would be different. She would leave her tale of victims behind her, no question; because she would keep her eyes open. A woman's weapons are not strength but vision. She sees very clearly what she is after, and the best way to get it."

"Does she indeed!" said Fifine, perking her lip at me. "And that is only to flatter her with not being a blundering stupid."

There was a goodish clustering of natives here, come up to view the sport gratis, and so we walked on to regain our cherished solitude. Long time we spent on those ramparts, utterly happy and at peace, until hunger began to remind us of the hour.

"I have not asked you," said Fifine, as we started to retrace our steps, making lunchwards; "I don't even know that I shall; I am not sure that I want to know; I don't know that I care——"

"Good gracious! What is it all about?"

"What your plans are—whether you propose stopping here, or going on to—where?"

"I had meant to stay here, of course—say for a few days. We cannot feel securer than at the world's end."

"O!"

"What do you mean?"

"Nothing. Only O!"

"Now, what is in your mind? But let that pass. Supposing we go and lunch before deciding anything further."

There is only one Hôtel worth its title in Aigues-Mortes—that of the St. Louis, near the little squat Place of its name. It is at best a glorified cabaret, with quite a spacious room to feed in. We entered this room, and the first person our eyes fell on was Carabas.

Now, I ask you, why should not M. Carabas Cabarus be free to visit Aigues-Mortes precisely as and whenever he chose? I put the question to avoid mistakes, and to anticipate any objections you might offer as to his obtruding himself where he was neither wanted nor invited. He was a wayfarer like ourselves, at perfect liberty to wander whither he listed, and accountable in no way to whatever chance prejudices might have been formed against him. Very well; then you will oblige me by accepting him, as we did, with a cordiality which, if it masks any sentiment, shall mask no sentiment of a less lively nature than resignation.

I said "Damnation!" I think; but that was because I had run against the corner of a table. It was an unoccupied table, and incontinently we sat down at it; whereupon Carabas, who had not yet begun his meal, jumped up from his place elsewhere, and came over to join us.

"Bien rencontré, Monsieur et Mademoiselle!" he said, with such an enthusiasm of welcome that really I felt for the moment abashed. "Did I not say there was a providence in our meeting? It is confirmed in this reunion. I asked myself, when I heard you were gone—Whither? I asked also the landlord. The omnibus-man, who was standing near, answered for him. He had happened to be behind you when you took your tickets. 'Ah,' thought I, 'they will welcome a cicerone native to the district, one who can tell them things they will not hear else—a man, moreover, of some reputation; of insight, of a picturesque habit of mind, maybe'—but, bah! it is no matter. To reach my destination by a roundabout way—also, where was the objection? The advantage, rather, since it rejoined me to comrades so amiable—and again, so seductive. Wherefore I followed by the midday train."

"Bon!" said I, quite cheerfully. "Only I fail to see the providence."

"It took the shape of the omnibus-man," said Fifine. "How stupid you are."

Carabas glanced at her approvingly, and at me disdainfully; and at the moment a wan, malaria-whitened young woman, of a type common enough in that infested district, laid on the table the hors-d'œuvre—blackened potatoes baked, or rather unbaked, in their jackets, and a saucer of olives.

But better was to come—to wit, after an indifferent potage, that noblest of Provençal fish-courses, a dish of *petits-rougets* as they call them, small things of the mullet tribe and cooked like whitebait, than which I could desire no sweeter satisfaction for a hungry man. Followed a ragout of mutton, served with a mess of white beans full of the little surprises of vegetable and fatty garnish the French know how to introduce; and the end came in a dish of becs-fins.

Now, appetite being the absorbing consideration, I regarded little else while I satisfied mine, listening only with my elbows, as they say, to the mixed jargon of sentimentality, rhapsody, and unblushing self-glorification with which Carabas, always addressing himself to my companion, filled up the intervals between the courses. Elsewise he was as busily occupied as the best of us—until it came to the birds. And then I watched him with some secret amusement. I saw him glance abstractedly at the dish, and appear as if about to help himself; then, flashing a guilty look at Fifine, he pushed the seduction away, with a magnificently affected air of offence.

"M. Cabarus," I said, "what, sentimentally considered, is the difference between a little bird and a little fish?"

"It is a matter of taste," said he—rather well, I thought.

I laughed and leaned back. He waved his hand, as if he had dismissed a foolish impertinence. He had early, I think, taken what he considered my measure as a trifler and outsider. Yet I could not but wonder over the incredible self-assurance which could thus assert itself against all reason and policy. Surely, if his *objet* were the sister, the sensible thing would be to propitiate the guardian *brother?* But that did not seem to occur to him. I was merely a tiresome obstacle in the way to that perfect rapprochement which nature and circumstance had decreed between him and her. They were souls affinitive, mutually attracted, and, as such and thenceforth, discharged from all conventional obligations. It was ludicrous, if you like; laughable to a degree; yet, if you have observed, you will recognise that attitude of mind, goatish and transcendental in one, as an attitude not uncommon among Latins.

And how about Fifine's acceptance of the implied understanding? Well, a riddle will women always be! First I noticed, to my immense amusement, how, after trifling a little with her birdlet, she left it on her plate untasted. Carabas observed that too, and, you may be sure, drew flattering conclusions from it. Moreover, it was obvious that she was interested in him—and genuinely, for all her pretence of secretly playing upon his foibles for my behoof. His enthusiasm, his sentiment, his play of imagery on the subject of ancient legends, his minute local knowledge, all attracted her; and when, lunch being finished, she drew me aside, I knew what to expect.

"He is really very amusing, mon ami. I think we could do worse, after all, than accept him as a guide."

"Much worse, I am sure," said I. "Tell him to lead on, and we will follow."

Nothing loth, he led on—and in that hat of hats. I just glanced at Fifine, when he appeared in it; but she did not seem to notice. Presently I fell behind, leaving them together, and, slipping away unobserved, sought my own entertainment in my own way.

I re-entered the Porte de la Gardette somewhere near four o'clock, and found the couple awaiting my appearance hard by. Fifine looked disturbed and a little pale. She hurried to me.

"O, where *have* you been?" she said. "We have been hunting for you everywhere."

"Why, to enjoy," said I, pulling out my watch, "what you should not have missed—the view of the town from the outside. But, if you are ready, we must move to catch our train."

She looked at me queerly a moment, her face working in an odd way between question and reproach.

"Must we?" she said. "So you have made up your mind to go?"

"To Arles, yes," I answered. "The prospect of this smell and Carabas combined is more than I can face."

"But he will be certain to accompany us!"

"There is room to breathe in Arles."

"Felix, how absurd you are!"

"Honestly, m'amie," said I gravely, "I could not take the responsibility of recommending you this place for a stay. It was spring when I was here before. I had not guessed its possibilities. If you please, you must come with me—unless——" I looked significantly at M. Carabas Cabarus, where he stood haughtily aside.

"If you dare to say another word," said Fifine, in a low voice, "I will never speak to you again."

CHAPTER XIV

M. CABARUS accompanied us. We had to change trains at Aimargues, and did not reach Arles until long after sunset. He and Fifine had chatted most of the way together, ostentatiously, on her part, to my exclusion. At Arles, I helped M. Cabarus to shoulder his knapsack, a service for which he returned me a rather frigid acknowledgment.

"Our quarters," I said to him, "will be at the Hôtel du Nord Pinus. It will afford us much pleasure if you decide to make yours there too."

He bowed, a little astonished, I thought. But Fifine struck in immediately, in a very cold voice:—

"We have presumed too much already on M. Cabarus's good-nature. Please leave him, Felix, to make his own arrangements."

"They are made, Mademoiselle," said Carabas gallantly, and with a most charming and ingratiatory smile. "Can Mademoiselle doubt it?"

"I am at a loss for your meaning, Monsieur," said Fifine. "I have no claim upon your confidence, nor any desire to share my own with a stranger—" and she turned icily away from him.

I never saw a man more taken aback. He looked as if he had received a tumbler of cold water in his face. And when, Fifine having touched my arm, she and I moved to leave the station, he followed in our wake like a crestfallen poodle, pondering, no doubt, that same riddle of woman which had already exercised my mind.

We traversed the dusty stretch from the station to the town in almost complete silence, until, mounting the slope by the amphitheatre, Fifine pressed against me with a sudden exclamation:—

"O, Felix! How beautiful!"

"We will come and see it at sunset," I said. "That is the great time."

"Yes, *we*," she answered, with a meaning emphasis on the pronoun which gave me an inward chuckle, for Carabas was standing close beside.

She ignored him entirely, even until we had entered the Place du Forum, and stood facing the Hôtel, with our backs to Mistral's statue; and then she turned upon him with the sweetest smile and her hand extended.

"Good-night, Monsieur, and thank you a thousand times for your kindness."

"But I am myself going to stay here," answered the troubadour, with an appealing look at her.

She said "O!" and, turning her back on him, walked straight into the hall.

Rooms for Monsieur Dane and Mademoiselle his sister? Assuredly; there were two of the best vacant at the moment on the first floor. The first floor meant first prices; but was not the lady to be entertained a Countess incognito? "Va, Madame!" said I to the distinguished proprietress; and Fifine and I were shown up. I don't know where M. Cabarus bestowed himself, but in quarters, I expect, less luxurious than ours. We did not see him again that evening; but, once quit of his presence, Fifine's manner to me recovered something of its severity. For some minutes, after we had rejoined company at the table d'hôte, she answered my remarks in only the coldest of monosyllables.

But presently she thawed. It was when a bottle of Veuve Clicquot I had ordered was placed on the table.

"Champagne!" she said. "That is too-great an extravagance, Felix."

"Anything," I responded, "for a summery atmosphere."

She thought it wise to ignore my remark. "What makes champagne so expensive?" she said: "the insignificance of the crop that produces it?"

"It is made from a small grape," I answered, "something like our English sweet-water; but that is not it. One of the chief reasons is the number of bottles broken during fermentation—that, and the complex nature of its preparation—" and I launched out into an elaborate disquisition on stopping and fining and sulphuring, on liqueuring and depositing and disgorging, only to find, when in the full flood of eloquence, that Fifine was not paying the slightest attention to me. I stopped; and she said immediately, in the most shameless manner:—

"Why did you invite him to come here?"

"Invite whom?" I asked.

"You know."

"Well, I thought it would please you."

"It doesn't, then."

"And I thought, after what we owed to him, that as a gentleman I could do no less."

"A gentleman, indeed! Much sense he showed of recognising one when you helped him on with his knapsack."

"Still, you know, Fifine——!"

"No, I don't know. And now you have just got to answer to me."

"For what?"

"Please don't pretend."

"For why I deserted you so basely out there, you mean? I had a wish to vary the entertainment; and I concluded you were quite happy without me."

"Felix, that is to be like a woman."

"Like yourself, m'amie?"

"No; when I went with M. Cabarus, I had no thought of punishing any one."

"Punishing?"

"Do you fancy I enjoyed myself? I was thinking of what had become of you all the time, and I was miserable. I even wondered if you had gone back to Nîmes, and left me to shift for myself."

"O! that is unkind, Fifine. What a brute you must have thought me!"

"No, that I never did. I only thought, all in a moment, that, though I had had no intention to offend you, I wanted to ask your forgiveness."

"Fifine, your glass is empty. Drink to me only—eh? and I—you know, or perhaps you don't know. Look at me, Fifine. I am a fool, and a remorseful fool. Let us be the best of gossips again."

"It is too ridiculous," she said, the tiniest of wet sparkles in her eyes. "That absurd little creature, and his airs and pretensions!"

"You did not find him so entertaining as you had expected, then?"

"Yes, I did. To be honest, I found him, when I could forget my anxiety, very entertaining indeed—on his own ground."

"What is his own ground?"

"Provence, Felix—the Provence of story and poetry. He seems to know everything about it—its history, its legends, its places and people. And he has a really picturesque way of putting things. He told me quite a number of tales—one, very pretty, about a couple called Briande and Bérard."

"What about them?"

"O! It was quite a simple little story. Really all its charm lay in his wording of it; and I could not reproduce that."

"Try."

"I will try to tell the story if you like; but it must be in my own way. It was about a beautiful lady who lived in Aigues-Mortes in the time of the holy King Louis. She was so beautiful that her fame spread far around, bringing innumerable suitors, great lords and warriors among them, to her feet. But she was cold and haughty; and not one of them all was successful in touching her heart. She would never deign to barter that, she said, against rank and power, though it were the Count of Dauphiny himself who should come to woo her; but she would yield it to his meanest henchman did he please her. Briande was her name; and she was called Briande Sans-fleur, for the strange reason that never a flower was to be seen upon her or in her chambers. She hated to have them plucked, and the surest way to her antipathy was for one to woo her with a posy. They thought that sinister and unwomanly; but so great was the force of her loveliness, there was not a gallant among them but would have pledged his soul to her, though she had been proved a witch.

"Well, it happened once that that saying of hers, whether true or false, reached the ears of the Count of Dauphiny, a hard man and a proud; and he laughed, and swore to himself, 'It was designed for a challenge, and that I should hear it. I will woo her, then, but in such disguise that only she shall penetrate its secret. We shall see then, if, knowing what she knows, she will reject the Count of Dauphiny. And after? Ah, low shall lie the head of this Briande Sans-fleur!'

"So he caused it privately to be whispered in the ears of Briande—by one who, in seeming, betrayed a jealous confidence—that the Count of Dauphiny, stung by her professed disdain, designed to visit her in the guise of a wandering minstrel of humble birth, thus to woo and win her by virtue of his sole sweet persuasion, while she, unguessing the truth, should fall a captive to that dear deception.

"And thus it was done; and when one day a troubadour, coming from Dauphiny, was brought into the lady's presence, Briande, guessing the Count underneath those trappings, smiled, and said in her heart, 'He does not win me so.' But she said aloud, 'What is thy name?' And the stranger answered, 'I am called Bérard the bird-fingered.' 'Why so?' she asked—'since birds have no fingers.' Then he held up his hand, the fingers of which were long and white, like the wing pinions of an ibis; and he said, 'As their feathers harp sweetly on the wind, so do these beat music from the air.' 'Sing to me,' she said; and, unlooping his instrument, he both played and sang to her. And, as she listened, something that had never entered there before stole into Briande's heart, and her cheeks flushed and then paled. But when he had finished, she strove with herself enough to ask with scorn,

'What is the station in life of so accomplished a minstrel?' And he answered, 'I am the son of Carel the notary.' And at that she laughed and dismissed him, knowing and contemning the deception.

"Now the next day, meeting him alone in the garden, 'Here is the nightingale,' says she, 'but, it seems, lacking his rose. Prithee pick thyself one, Master Notary, and wear it in thy ear for a grace note.' But he drew back only, shaking his head. 'You will not?' she asked astonished. 'Why will you not?' 'They are the tender offspring of Nature,' he said. 'I would as lief kill a child. And these are pretty children, and children always from their birth till death, never changing or growing older till they close their creamy lids and drop asleep to wake in heaven. No flower is ever plucked by me.' At that, opening wide her eyes, Briande answered him: 'It is no libertine who speaks here.' 'No, by love's grace,' he said, 'but as virgin speaks to virgin.' Then, very softly she said to him, 'I have never yet met another until thee who thinks with me in this. For every blossom pulled on earth our heaven will be one fruit the less. Take up thy song.' Then he sang to her again (words, Felix, that were spoken—I don't know if he improvised them on the spot); and often afterwards again, until by degrees her proud heart melted to him, and then surrendered, and they were lovers."

Fifine paused a moment. "Surely that is not the end?" I said.

"O, no!" said she; "but it all seems so bald as I tell it."

"I don't think so," I answered. "Far from it. Go on."

"Well," she continued, "this Briande, at last so humbled in her self-will, awaited the moment when her disguised suitor, having conquered, should reveal himself to her and acclaim his victory. But he never spoke; and so one day, in proud submissiveness, she bowed her head before him and herself confessed. 'Sweetheart, I have known thee all the time for what thou art—the lord of Dauphiny. I have saved this bird in my bosom until now; but no longer can I stay its singing. Make what thou wilt of thy triumph and of my humiliation.' Then Bérard looked at her like one who hears his death sentence; and suddenly he was weeping and groaning. 'It is not so,' he said; 'but in very truth I am Bérard, son of Carel the notary. It was the lord of Dauphiny who laid this snare for thy pride's undoing, sending me to represent him, and in such wise as that thou shouldst think me him disguised. "And so," says he, "I'll teach her at what henchman's rate I value her regard. Take from her, Bérard; and the more thou canst take, before revealing thyself, the better thou wilt please me." And light of heart I came to do his bidding; and here I stand.' 'Thou hast not done it,' she answered, her lip curling. 'Why dost thou falter in thy villainy?' 'Ah! lady,' he said, weeping for very shame; 'how could I think to pluck the flower of all flowers, who never wronged a blossom in my life?' 'I spare thee for that,' she said. 'But go, and never let me see thy face again.'

"But Bérard being gone left that behind him which he guessed not. And often Briande thought of him, until of her thoughts was born a very passion for the past. 'As was his love for flowers,' she sighed, 'so was his love for me—not to despoil, where perchance the stem was weak.' And, while her coldness to all others grew to a rigid frost, his memory in her heart became a tender spring, amongst whose blossoms she wandered, for ever full of wistful dreamings. And at last she could bear her pain no more. 'I must find him,' she thought; 'or die. I will go alone across the marshes to Les Saintes Maries de la Mer, and beg their intercession that my love may be restored to me.'"

"We, too, will go there, Fifine," I said, as the narrator paused; "and mark the spot of Briande's pilgrimage. A woeful journey for that gentle lady!"

"So she found it," said Fifine; "and often on the long desolate way she gave herself up for lost. But at length she reached the little town, and found the church she sought, in whose shrine———"

"Well?" I said, seeing she stopped again.

"I have forgotten," said Fifine, "whose bones they were."

"Why whose, but the three Marys'—Magdalene, Bethany, and St. James his mother. But go on; what does it matter?"

"I like to be accurate," said Fifine: "and every detail in these stories has its point."

"I don't see one here—unless it is the Magdalene. But never mind that."

"Well, after entering and praying, Briande was leaving the church, when at the very door she met him face to face."

"Bérard?"

"Yes. He was dressed like a priest. Banished by his love, in misery and penitence he had fled thither and, adjuring the world for ever, had given his life to God."

"And is that the end?"

"No; the prettiest bit is to come. They met thus again; but only to know the tragedy of their love and part. Like soiled armour which, being cleaned, looks richer than when new, so, under the rubs of Fate, was Bérard's soul to reveal its intrinsic worth. And Briande took a little house next to the Presbytery, between whose garden and hers was a wall both high and frail, and yet to them a barrier of rock which no speciousness might scale or passion overthrow. And there, on either side, they grew their flowers; and that was the sole bond between them. And, like him, she gave her virgin life to God until she died. Very young she died, Felix, and on the same day died Bérard. And because their end had been saintly and their story was known, amongst their flowers by the wall they buried them, he on his side and she on hers. And, when the spring came, from each grave had shot a rose-tree, from hers a white and from his a red, that climbed the wall with eager fingers until the two met above, and there they mingled; and the flowers when they blossomed were not some white, some red; but each was red and white at once—the Provençal love rose. There!"

She ended, breathless, and I applauded with enthusiasm, making cymbals of my thumbnails.

"You have told it famously, gossip," I said; "and M. Cabarus may congratulate himself on the most faithful and attentive of pupils. You have reproduced his very accents, I will swear, and touched them with Fifine's for music. Yet I think it a finer end than they deserved; for both, after all, were deceivers."

"Why she?" said Fifine.

"She should have declared at once who she suspected him to be, if her pride was all she pretended, and not have risked that temporising with a serpent. Deceit of any sort between man and woman is a dangerous weapon to trifle with; it may at any moment recoil upon the deceiver."

"Yes," said Fifine, in a thoughtful voice, her fingers crumbling her bread; "I suppose it is. You wouldn't like to think I could deceive you, would you, Felix?"

"No," I said. "Candidly I shouldn't like it. But then you couldn't, you know."

"Couldn't I? Why not?"

"Because I am a seer, Fifine, with a gift for second-sight. Now, if you are ready, let us go and take a stroll in the town."

I went out on the steps to light my pipe, while Fifine ran upstairs to fetch her cloak. I was feeling in an odd mood. It was satisfying to know that my comrade and I were on good terms again, yet somehow I found that sense of relief tempered with a certain gravity which was novel enough in its character to set me thinking. Indispensability—the word seemed involuntarily to shape itself in my mind like a spectre only newly realised out of subconsciousness. Yet what possible association could it have with such a transitory connexion as ours? In a brief space of time that would have become for both of us the merest memory, whimsical, a little tender perhaps, perhaps a little pathetic, and there an end. There could be claimed for it nothing of that spirit of inseparability which discovers a mutual unhappiness in even a temporary severance. Yet had I not come to be conscious in myself of a vague feeling of dissatisfaction, of incompleteness, when Fifine was not with me? I must suppose so; or why should I object to her consorting as freely as she chose with chance acquaintances; and, worse, exhibit, as she herself had hinted, the temper of a jealous woman when I fancied myself and my first importance to be ever so little slighted by her? It was not enough for me to tell myself that I simply objected to being called upon to play second fiddle to a *précieux ridicule* like Carabas; I knew that the truth of my small secret resentment that afternoon had lain in the realisation that under any circumstances, and however temporarily, my comrade could dispense with my company. If it was jealousy, it was jealousy not *of* that absurd little *grimacier*, but *for* the integrity of our partnership; and what was the moral of that?

But that was not, perhaps, the most serious side of the matter. The truth was that my own small revolt had served to reveal an almost reciprocal state of mind on the other side—a state of mind which, as now regarded, appeared the inevitable consequence of certain late drifts and tendencies, which, seeming unimportant in themselves, had become a danger in their cumulative result. So that, it seemed, if the word Indispensability was to be ruled out between us, now was the time when the situation should be faced, and readjusted to its most commonsensible effect.

This all came to me as I stood and pondered; and, seeing things thus in a clearer and steadier light, I said to myself that this would hardly do, that there was a threat of my becoming involved in a complication altogether outside my original purpose, and that both reason and good-feeling forbade my disregarding a warning when once it was known and analysed. Not that I would admit to myself even now that I was under bond to any moral compact whatsoever; I had expressly stated that I would not be; only there was Fifine's own happiness to consider. I *had* engaged myself to be her protector, using the word in its purer sense; and if herself proved one, and not the weakest, of her enemies, I was not the less called upon on that account to stand by and defend her.

An heroic resolve—I may claim that for it at least—though destined, like many another of my brightest and best, to an impotent conclusion. In the meanwhile I went so far as to propose to myself an actual tactical encouragement of the ridiculous stranger, with his appeal, whatever it might be, to the romantic in my young comrade's breast. No harm could possibly come of so detached an interest, while I myself should appear to repudiate the least right of sole authority over her wishes and caprices. My one object should be to make her feel that, for all purposes save that of travel, we were independent of one another. Alas! *de sot homme sot songe!*

Fifine rejoined me in a moment, and we went down into the little square, gay with lights and vehicles.

"Mistral!" she said, seeing me turn her southwards. "Am I not to worship first at the great man's shrine?"

"O, the statue!" I answered. "You have only seen its back, of course. For myself I am a little tired of the eternal cult. He is as great a nuisance in his place as the Dairyman's daughter is in hers, or as Kingsley at Westward Ho, where the very engines carry his name about. Mistral did not create Provence, any more than Stevenson created childhood, as some of his fatuous adorers would have us believe. But, come."

"All that is Greek to me," said Fifine, as we sought the front of the statue. "But if it means England——"

"It does."

"Do you ever wish for your own country again, Felix? You have been a great traveller, have you not?"

"Here and there—and I hope to be again."

"But not yet?"

"Why not? Likely this pleasant little episode will give me a renewed taste for it, and I shall be off again as soon as returned."

Thus I seized my opening chance to prepare the way to my resolve. And with what result? Fifine spoke hardly a word during that our preliminary stroll about the lighted town, but early complained of being tired, and went back to bed, after bidding me good-night in a distant voice. And to bed I too retreated shortly afterwards, in a mood between depression and wrath.

CHAPTER XV

THOSE Arlesian days always come back to my memory with a peculiar glow and poignancy all their own. The town itself is one of the very fairest in the Rhone valley, beautiful in its ruins, in its situation, in the stately picturesqueness of its people. I never think of it but I am somehow reminded of Ariel's song:—

> *"Of his bones are coral made;*
>
> *Those are pearls that were his eyes:*
>
> *Nothing of him that doth fade,*
>
> *But doth suffer a sea-change*
>
> *Into something rich and strange."*

For in truth that very sea-change is there, dating from a time when the city stood, like Venice, in the midst of wide lagoons, which extended so far as the great rock of Montmajour three miles northward, and which have since receded to leave bare the vast lonely delta of the Camargue. Ariel and Arles! there seems even a significance in the imperfect anagram; for does not wild music for ever haunt the place, melodiously sounding the dirge of kings long dead, of knights and fair ladies and courtly revels, whose iridescent dust yet clings about the walls, or flutters in golden flakes and scales over the sunburnt roofs.

"Into something rich and strange." So it would appear. Its lumber is the accumulation of rich ages—the loveliness of Greece, the pride of Rome, the polychromatic splendour of the renaissance. All have contributed to produce an impression which I can liken only to that conveyed by opal, or mother-of-pearl, or long-buried glass or pottery. I have felt the same mystery of blended colour in the sweep of infinite downs, in the damasked glooms of Chartres cathedral, or when standing before the great west window at Winchester, with its mad inimitable mosaic of broken fragments, starry, kaleidoscopic, translucent, a waste of wild-set jewels, for which I know not what past genius was responsible, but may his perfect inspiration never fall under the curse of the restorer. And Arles is a spectre of that spectrum—at least so it haunts my inner vision—a town over which the sea of ages has flowed, to leave it finally rich in a myriad tints and corals, the infinite jetsam of time.

Perhaps association colours my view. It may very well be, for it stands emblazoned enough in my memory, where, before walls which a thousand years of sunshine have transmuted into gold, flits ever a rainbow crowd of dreams and thoughts and emotions, not to be separated from the living entities who gave them being and hospitality.

Well, I had struck for solitude, and only once more, it seemed, to be outmanœuvred by circumstance. To Arles we were come, and so with gay hearts to make the very best of a good thing.

To Fifine at least it was all au teint frais. She was enraptured with the antiquities, and more, perhaps, with the modernities—the sparkle of life, the jolly little *Place* in which we were ensconced, the friendly men, the stately women, with their chapelles and cap-ribbons—now, alas, subdued, like Venetia's gondolas, from hues once double-dyed to sombre black— with the spirit of song and dance which still animated this people out of the old melodious years. Very early we went to see the sun set over the amphitheatre—a vision of transcendent beauty. The Rondpoint was almost deserted: we halted high up on the slope, so that our view could command, over and beyond the vast stone cylinder whose base adapted itself to the fall of the hill, the roofs and towers of the buildings beyond. The sun was down below our level; but those house-tops stood up in its glow, making a vividly intense background to the shadowy blue sweep of the arena. Their walls were primrose, their tiles were burning vermilion; here and there a raw advertisement stood translated into terms of jewelled gold and azure. And overhead, in a sky green as deep water, hung a large bright moon, already swelling to its full. There was no breath of wind to vex the quiet of the lovely scene; and only a voice here and there, sounding strange and unreal through the hollow silences, broke like a ripple on the universal peace. I heard Fifine sigh—a song without words, with which I felt in full concord and content.

I take these impressions, as they arise, without order or sequence. Time for a brief space stood still with us, and there are no milestones to mark his way. St. Trophime, into which one enters through a grey façade flush with its neighbour houses—as it might be only number so-and-so in the row— to find beyond deep caverns of antique craftsmanship, and sombre vaulted glooms spangled with gems, and, still further, long fretted cloisters arching away into the inmost recesses of sunlight: the ruined theatre which, sunk in its green oasis among the houses, gave its pagan bones to prop those very cloisters, and yet, shattered and desolate as it stands, speaks more eloquently of the unconquerable pride of the past than any relic I have known elsewhere: the Aliscamps, that old, old place of Roman-Christian sepulture, so sacred—having been consecrated by Christ Himself in a vision—that to be buried there ensured one salvation, for which reason the unhallowed dead, being set afloat on rafts all up the Rhone, would drift down, the *drue de mourtalage* in their stiffened fingers, to find redemption at the hands of careful watchers—all these were subjects for our curious inquisition, and many smaller interests.

Mention of the Aliscamps, or Champs Elysées, recalls a minute incident, which has often recurred to me since, and will again. We were loitering down the lane of tombs—a long alley lined with thin shrubs and trees, and before them on either side set ranks of stone sarcophagi—when, stopping awhile to regard some prospect, as I turned to speak to Fifine I found she was gone. She had utterly vanished; the lane stretched both ways devoid of life; there was no trunk large enough for her to have slipped behind to hide herself. I stood astonished; I hunted up and down, stooping and peering; finally I shouted her name. A little laugh answered me, and she rose from a tomb. In a spirit of mischief she had tiptoed from me, and stretched herself flat in a deep sarcophagus. As I brushed the dust and moss from her clothes, I asked her what on earth had induced her to such an insane prank. "I wanted to play at being dead," she said; "and to wonder how you would feel if I were."

"A pretty thought," I said—"only with a moral a little like that of the frogs stoned by the boys in the fable. Don't play such tricks again, if you love me."

There was just that in my voice which I could not entirely control. She put an impulsive hand on my arm, looked as if about to answer me in kind, but withdrew it without a word.

One whole morning we devoted to a visit to St. Gilles, that town of one considerable church and fifty considerable smells; another to a trip to Montmajour, tramping the three miles to the latter on foot, for the day was pleasant and we were wayfarers after all. There is a little light railway (of whose vagaries more anon), running over the plain, and we had designed to return by that; but after, having left the ruins, we had discovered the *halte*— a task of some difficulty, for it consisted of nothing more than a casual bench in a field by the side of the single line track—and had waited there for our train some three quarters of an hour beyond its scheduled time, we decided that we would rather foot it back than risk the loss of lunch, and so started off—only, of course, to espy the abominable thing approaching when we were just too far away to make a successful return run for it. However, the morning was worth its labour.

It is a ruin to remember among the most striking of its kind, that of the vast shattered Abbey crowning its mighty crag, which rises abruptly from the plain, lonely and austere, like an inland Mont St. Michel. It was surrounded by water once, and could be reached only by boat—a meet and mighty sentinel to command the approaches to that great stone-hewn city of the rocks, les Baux, which can just be descried, some nine miles north-east, fretting the low clouds with its hundred jagged splinters. And yet, whatever strategic advantages it might appear to possess, this Montmajour had to wait, it seems, for a soldier of Christ to realise and turn them to account. For it was hither clomb Trophimus—disciple of Paul and first teacher of Christianity in the Roman Prefecture of Arles, or Arelate—to excavate on the height his little chapel of the rocks with its confessional and cell, and there make converts, who, according to tradition, flocked to him in such numbers as to leave him scarce leisure for grace or meat.

It is a curious little burrow that chapel, and yet, with its single cell—the protoplast from which all the vast superincumbent fabric of the Abbey was to develop itself—by far the most impressive corner of the ruins. There still may be seen, shelving upwards from the back of the tiny follicle, the narrow fissure in the rock through which Trophimus scuttled into hiding like a rabbit, what time the Cæsarean soldiers were on his track. We had not the enterprise to climb and slither the way he went; but no doubt, in the deep dead silence of that retreat, we might have distinguished the throb of a Saint's heart-beats still haunting its dark recesses. The waste pomp and circumstance of the Titanic remains above made no appeal to the imagination like that of the little underground chapel, on whose credit and interest they rested.

So those days return to me, full of the sunshine of both heart and climate. We were lucky in our weather from first to last, never tasting but in fitful spasms the curse of that mistral which dries the kindly marrow in men's bones. They were days to remember; yet not altogether in the unbroken sequence in which I have recorded them. They came and passed; but there were interludes, while still the sun shone, of a moral atmosphere less satisfying. And again Carabas was the cause.

He had soon reappeared, that most persistent and uncrushable of troubadours. He could not believe in the reality of his cold-shouldering; but, like some other people I have met, seemed to think that it was only one's imperfect realisation of his attractions which prevented one's complete enslavement by them. To know him was the one necessity: the rest *must* ensue thereon. So he haunted us—in the streets, in the hotel vestibule, at our table in the salle-à-manger—which, by the way, looked out straight on a little shop in the Rue de Palais, whose windows, full of bric-à-brac, silver tea-strainers, and old embroidered cap ribbons, were a perpetual apéritif to me. He would interrogate us volubly from his place at the long board, enquiring of our sight-seeing, and condescending thereon from the height of his superior knowledge; sometimes he would come over and talk, but always addressing Fifine through me, with shrewd sidelong glances to note the impression his eloquence was making on her. For myself, I met his advances genially enough; I had no quarrel with the man, and his unshakable self-sufficiency was a pure joy to me. But with Fifine it was different. She was as cold and distant to him as the north. I have known a single awkwardness in a man lose him the wife he coveted—turn the balance of her wavering mind from liking to contempt; so, I supposed, that one little solecism of a too smug self-confidence had dished M. Carabas's chances for him.

Good sooth, I pitied the creature: he was so patently perplexed, distressed, at a loss to understand what could have so suddenly turned against him this charming stranger, on the strength of whose tender condescension he had been flattering in himself God knows what dreams of romantic achievement. Certainly Fifine was very ungrateful, seeing the use she had allowed herself to make of his sudden infatuation. I told her so one day, and she wanted to know why.

"One ought not to accept gifts," I said, "and then snub the giver."

"Gifts!" she exclaimed.

"Yes, certainly," I answered. "What are his fables, his imagery, his storied eloquence but the highest gifts a genius can bestow on his fellows? They are as much his exclusive property as diamonds would be, and in accepting them you laid yourself under as great an obligation as if you had accepted a costly necklace from him."

She laughed a little; then looked grave.

"I think, do you know, Felix," she said, "that you are rather stupid."

"Very likely I am," I answered; "but why?"

"Not to see," she began—and stopped. Then suddenly she went on: "I thought anyhow I was considering you in adopting this attitude."

"In that case," I said, "please to consider me a gentleman."

"And the moral of that is," she said, "that my treatment of M. Cabarus proves me to be not a lady."

"I never dreamt of implying such a thing, or of thinking it."

"Well, anyhow I am not a lady in the sense that you are a gentleman. I accept presents from strangers and then snub them. Very well. I cannot return M. Cabarus his magnificent gifts, but I can at least return him what he, I am sure, thinks much more important—his magnificent attentions. You shall see."

"Nonsense," I answered; but she was as good as her word, and thenceforth Carabas, restored to her smiles and graces, was like a soul renewed, strutting in a seventh heaven of confidence and gratified vanity. I had asked Fifine for a breeze, and she had answered womanlike with a gale, with the result that the fellow was blown up to an inordinate figure of pride—of bounce, I might say, in that inflated connection. He assumed a sort of amative proprietorship over my companion, while he tolerated rather than patronised me. And I was the one cold-shouldered now, Fifine seeming to relish that fatuous devotion the more, the more she was besieged by it.

So, I might congratulate myself, were things obligingly accommodating themselves to the exact end I had in view; and, better still, it was now plain to me that my apprehensions as to the state of the young lady's feelings had been wholly without justification. It was all, in fact, as it should be and as I would have it, I told myself; and, though it might appear characteristically feminine to forget sober services such as mine in the intoxication wrought of a flattering pursuit, I was not going to make a sex squabble of the matter. Woman's capacity for absorbing flummery was notoriously beyond man's gauging, and if in that respect quality counted for anything, it was merely the quality which could untiringly repeat itself. And there, I was sure, Carabas was infinitely my superior: his resources in the way of picturesque lip-homage were no doubt inexhaustible. So altogether I resolved to take advantage of the opening the gods had given me to shake free of a possible embarrassment. I would let it appear that I felt not the slightest resentment over the young woman's behaviour, or assumed to myself the least authority over, or personal concern in, her preferences. And then, of course, I was quite satisfied in my mind and happy.

But, before this state of things came wholly to pass—and it was a matter of some days' growth—the poor troubadour had to run his gauntlet, erst-mentioned, of bitter snubs and mortifications. I really commiserated him, as I have said, in his dole, which nevertheless he persisted in courting with the most unblenching stoicism. In these sad hours he even showed towards me a certain spirit of propitiation, though never to the extent of seeming to allow me the least of proprietary interests in the object of his adoration. He regarded me rather as the thorn in the wilderness, which, troublesome in itself, had yet acquired a sort of spurious importance through its connexion with the rose of his desire. Once or twice, when Fifine was not by, we exchanged amenities of a sort; and once I was actually bold enough to question him on a detail of his tenderer confidences.

"That was a pretty legend," I said, "you told Mademoiselle Dane."

"Which legend, Monsieur?" he answered, pricking up his ears at the name.

"That of Bérard and Briande Sans-fleur."

"Ah!" he said, "I can charm a skeleton into life; from a little seed I can produce a fruitful vine. That is to be what I am. Into the alembic of this mind one puts a pinch of dust; and, lo! I return it to him, a golden nugget. Mademoiselle was transported?"

"She liked it anyhow, well enough to tell it me again. Only one point she failed over—Bérard's song."

"She would fail," he said; "but not from want of appreciation. It moved her?"

"I daresay it did."

"Ah! its music sleeps in the whorls and dimples of that little ear, as the voice of old seas haunts the shell; but from the ear to the lips is a journey impossible to most—even to lips so sweetly eloquent as hers. Yet I fain would hear that honeysuckle strive to repeat its lesson of the sun and dew, however brokenly—" he sighed dismally—"but it is not for me."

"The legend," I said, "stands therefore incomplete so far as I am concerned. Will you not do me the favour, Monsieur, to supply the broken link?"

"You wish for the song?"

"Assuredly, if you will be so good."

"It was extempore—but that is nothing." He looked at me—there is no other word for it but balefully. "You wish, no doubt," he said, "to snigger in your sleeve over what you will be pleased to call the meretricious rhapsodies of an improvisatore? It will certainly be more sound than sense, you think, taking refuge from reason under a professed imaginativeness. So are some built, impervious to the spirituality underlying all things, blind to what they cannot see, deaf to what they cannot hear. I tell you, Monsieur, that those who are for ever questioning the truth of literature are incapable of understanding the truth of life."

He seemed almost in a passion. It was positively petrifying.

"I am quite at a loss, Monsieur," I said, "for the reason of this jeremiad, or to understand how it is justified by anything I said. I am certainly no captious critic of either life or literature, and as to Imagination, I try myself to be her humble minister. But leave the song by all means unrepeated. The loss, being mine, need not trouble you."

He was really a little ashamed of himself, I think; though he would not admit it.

"No, Monsieur," he said, gnawing his knuckles—"no. In justice to myself and the completeness of my art I will gratify you. Listen, then: it went somewhat this way."

He chaunted rather than spoke the lines, lyric interspersed with prose, a song of the fashion called in Provençal "*Cansounetto émé parla.*" I do not attempt to reproduce the verse, which was quite picturesque and musical. Its sense was more or less as follows:—

"I followed Beauty as the shadow of a flying bird across the sward. It seemed to wing and settle; and, lo! as I ran to grasp it, it was but a shadow, the shadow of a song that rose into the sky. Quivering it rose, and the shadow quivered to its ecstasy. And as both wing and voice receded up the heights, so did their shadow pale and die from out the grass. Only the shadow of a shadow remained to vex my heart.

"Like the flowers of the *saladelle* were my love's eyes. It was in the chill of winter they gave their blue heaven to my soul. Returning from the long harvest, in summer I resought them, and behold! they were red to me. There is no truth in mortal beauty.

"I followed Beauty in a lonely place; and one, staying me, asked whither. 'I follow a maid,' I said. 'Quick,' he answered, 'or you will never find her.'

"O, elusive is that golden quarry! Headlong we rush over the brink of death, and are still pursuing it. I met a sage, who laughed and said, 'It is the blind side of the eye you set to externals. Will mortals never understand that? The other side it is that sees the truth. Hunt inwards, fool, where Truth and Beauty hide from you secure and unsuspected.'

"Lady, I have never doubted him till now."

Such was the substance of the song which Bérard, or Carabas, sang to Briande, or Fifine. It was marked by the sort of mystic symbolism characteristic of the old-time cantefable and the rather vague rhapsodies of the early troubadours, and, if really first uttered impromptu, vindicated something of the singer's claim to a genuine inheritance. At the end I said:—

"That was a fine improvisation, Monsieur. I congratulate myself on the favour bestowed on me."

"You have perhaps reason to," answered the poet loftily—and did you ever know the like of that for vanity?

It was to prove the sole favour of its kind, however; for thereafter soon came to pass the creature's re-establishment in Fifine's good graces, and my consequent second cold-shouldering by the two. That was to be, I suppose, though without any question of preordination, in which I don't believe. Chance governs the world, and life is a long chapter of unforeseen accidents. In this case, no doubt, Destiny, bent to a particular purpose, seized on the first instrument at hand to effect it. It is the way of Destiny, whom the vulgar call Haphazard. He hears the hour strike, and straight he catches at any chance weapon—it may be a fly in the milk-jug to choke a Pope withal, an avalanche to crush an infant, a piece of orange-peel cast down to throw a giant. On that supposition, and that supposition alone, could Carabas's unasked and monstrous intrusion into our privacy be accounted for. It is true he was a blunt instrument; but then, as no particular harm was intended, he served to do his work perhaps better than another and a sharper.

One morning I said to Fifine:—

"I propose for myself a day at Les Saintes Maries. Do you wish to come?"

"Why not?" she answered quietly.

"Very well," I said. "Only, from a purely personal point of view, I am bound to make a stipulation—that M. Cabarus does not form one of our party."

"If he chooses to come," said Fifine, "how can I possibly prevent him?"

"I must leave that to you, m'amie."

"But that is unfair, Felix—" She broke off, her face flushed, and she made as if to leave me, but altered her mind and turned again. "I have no right whatever to dictate to him as to his movements. Felix"—she put a hesitating hand on my arm—"you said you would take me there."

There was a look of hurt in her face, and of something more—an emotion I could not fathom; but it helped me back to instant sanity. The perversity of my attitude struck me all at once as being in the last degree ridiculous, and it behoved me to hasten to amend it if I would not lose all faith in myself as a reasonable and consistent being. How could Fifine, a child sixteen years my junior, be expected to hold herself the exclusive property of a companion so sober and mature, or to waive on my behoof her perfectly natural instincts for coquetry and flirtation? The thing was harmless; and moreover agreeable to my plans. I uttered a clearing laugh.

"What a dog in the manger you must think me!" I said. "Never mind what I stipulated. Ask him to come, if you like."

"But I never said I did like," she answered. "Cannot we give him the slip somehow, and get to the station without his knowing?"

And that is what we did; though it meant a pretty panic run in the open, the little Gare de la Camargue lying across the river, with the whole stretch of the iron suspension bridge between. However, we reached it and got off undetected, and were quickly on our way again into the wilderness.

And here, indeed, was the real thing—no case of those half measures we had known on the Aigues-Mortes route, which takes one only along the civilised edge of the Camargue. This hour and a half's run in the dancing and reeling little train, which winds up its iron thread of leagues across the very mid-loneliness of the delta, is a far wilder experience, more melancholy, more desolate, and at the same time infinitely fuller of the mystery which inhabits desolations. It is common to hear strange voices, to catch glimpses of strange faces, on hills or in wooded solitudes; but the spirits that peer and flit on lonely wastes are no less in certain evidence because we neither see nor hear them. Only we know that beyond this bent or that, peering through the reeds on the pool's rim, or watching our receding footsteps from behind some bush we have just passed, is something which would not be there if we went to look. Here we learn the story that there is in far horizons: there is no end to its sadness; nor to its sweetness nor hope. And the sky is one vast iridescent dome, like a bubble floating on water, with the flat earth for its floor; and, underneath, what unfathomable secrets!

But I am encroaching on Carabas's preserves, and must decline from rhapsody to commonplace. The prosaic fact is that the light railway from Arles to Les Saintes Maries bisects, roughly, the Camargue, and that the most of one's journey by it is made through a monotonous and unpeopled solitude. It is a very impressive solitude, for those who can appreciate the charm of league-wide isolation from an overcrowded world, and its outstanding features are such as we should expect it to display, the natural offspring of primeval incoherence and desolation—the booming bittern; the mournful curlew; flamingoes (though we were too late to see them), silently trailing their lengths, like whisps of rosy sunset, against a pearly sky, and bill-clapping frog-eating cranes. Reeds are its prominent growth, with, everywhere, unending thickets of tamarisk and juniper; and water, in ponds, in pools, in the little irrigating canals which they call *roubines*, blots the surface eternally. Now and again a clump of silver poplars, or of that most beautiful of its family the umbrella-pine, will rise to trance the austerity with its lovelier mood; but they are rare benedictions. For the most part one seems to travel on the near-barren margin between Life and Death—and so to the symbol and expression of it all, the solitary fortress-church on the edge of the sea.

That is where God and man have closed to try conclusions—power mortal and power immortal locked in one embrace. It is the quaintest, loneliest church in the world—a temple and a stronghold in one. Long, narrow, and crowned with battlements, its crest was lifted to defy what its heart was opened to cherish, the spirit of Christian love and forbearance. There, above, its wardens bristled for the fight, while below slept in eternal peace the bones of those who had inherited direct from the Saviour His lessons of charity and forgiveness. You may see at this day the casket which is said to contain them. It is lowered periodically by machinery, from a chamber above the altar, for the worship of pilgrims. And there is even an odder worship connected with the place—that of Sarah, the Egyptian, who, according to tradition, accompanied the three Marys hither as their servant. She is buried, so it is reported, in the crypt chapel, a deep and darksome cavern excavated underneath the chancel, to which, on a certain day in October, flock from all quarters crowds of gypsies, to pay homage at the shrine of their ancestress.

The whole church is a picture of isolation without and gloom within. It is barely lighted by its few narrow windows; its little lamps are mere glow-worms in a vast concavity; there it stands by the salt sea, solemn and forgotten, like the scapegoat of all religion. It has a village about it, a little village, by now the smallest debris of its past estate. Still it has its great days—and I was thankful we had not alighted on one of them. It was hugely more impressive as it stood.

Fifine was disappointed in it. She could by no means bring herself to associate this forlorn relic with Briande's tender pilgrimage. And the presbytery, when we found it, did not fit in with the poet's description at all. It was an illusion laid, I fear, though I did what I could to claim for romantic licence its prerogatives. But the bitterest moment came with the discovery in the good curé himself of the shrewdest of caterers in the matter of picture-postcards, crosses, medals, and other such local baits for the curious or the pious, with which his office was stocked. An original charter of King Réné, which he produced for our benefit, did little to mend the disenchantment, so interminably and so drily did he drawl over it, while we were suffering to escape. The day, I felt, was a failure.

We were no longer good gossips—that, I think, was the truth of it. There had come something between us, which Fifine was too proud, and I too diplomatic, to own. The fact is a grievance cannot be patched, and there was a grievance here unconfessed. It had to be admitted and pulled to pieces before anything could be affected in the way of an understanding. So, though we were nominally on the usual terms, it was really the false coin of comradeship we were interchanging. We pretended sympathetic goodfellowship, and what was only perfectly obvious was the pretence.

We had brought our lunch with us and eaten it in the train. More than an hour remained to us after we had finished with the curé, and it passed slowly, though it had been killed merrily enough under the old circumstances. There was nothing whatever of interest in the place beyond the church, and we loitered aimlessly in the direction of nowhere. I am sure we both sighed our relief when the time came to return to the station.

In the train, while Fifine pretended to sleep, I sat chewing the cud of injurious reflection. "She is comparing her day," I thought, "with what it might have been had that fulsome yarn-slinging impostor accompanied us. I think, on the whole, and under the circumstances, she might have endured me more benignly. But I suppose it is impossible to woman to yield a point graciously, and without at least some negative nagging in the shape of a self-sacrificial, smiling-martyrdom pose." And that led me to launch out in mental eulogy of the spacious vision which sees at once when all that it is necessary to say has been said—the broad mind which omits to dwell on little grievances, but can show all forbearance and accept all excuses within the royal compass of its catholicity—until it suddenly occurred to me that, while on the subject, I had better perhaps extend the limits of my own vision. And at that I was able to laugh at myself, if a little ruefully, and to re-utter the now rather mechanic formula that everything was working as it should, and as I had the best of reasons in the world for wishing that it should.

We did not reach our hotel until near seven o'clock, and there, of course, was Carabas, seated smoking a disconsolate cigarette on one of the two benches placed on either side the steps. His hat sat on his head like a penwiper; he was lounging at rest, when, seeing us, he heaved himself forward; but the weight of his poetic bow-window carried him back again, and he had to make a second attempt, which brought him to his feet with a stagger and his hat over one eye. Once on his legs, however, his face assumed a mixed expression of relief and plaintive upbraiding.

"Ah, Mademoiselle!" he said, taking possession of my companion; "but this has been a desolate day for some of us."

"Et d'autre part," says Miss, with a naughty smile, "for some of us, a very bright one. You should have come to Les Saintes Maries de la Mer, where the sun shone all day in the sky and in our hearts."

He drooped his head, protruded his lower lip, and regarded her from the top of his eyeballs. It was designed for an expression of despair, and was quite sweetly laughable.

"Les Saintes Maries!" he whispered hoarsely. "There is a stab, Mademoiselle, in your every word. I should have come? Ah, truly! But by what instinct, seeing I was kept uninformed of your intentions? But doubtless that was deliberate, and in order to keep me from interposing my shadow between the sun and your happiness. It is well; then. And yet it is possible my company might have proved not altogether profitless. It is a desert spot, which yet the Magician's wand can make to flower. Truly, Mademoiselle, I think you did perversely in discarding your most attached cicerone."

I laughed, and ran up the steps, leaving Fifine to make her peace as she chose with her injured follower.

CHAPTER XVI

COMING out after dinner to enjoy my smoke in the open, I found Fifine and her preux chevalier already ensconced on one of the two seats placed on the pavement against the house front. It was a still and balmy evening, and the rattling illuminated little *Place* was all one movement and babble of voices. I paused a moment to appreciate the scene, and then, as I descended the steps, somebody addressed me, a little doubtfully, from the second occupied seat:—

"Mr. Dane? It is Mr. Dane—isn't it?"

"*Présent!*" I said, without a thought, and wheeled to look at the speaker. It was a young girl, indubitably English, who leaned forward to scrutinise me.

"Ah!" she said, turning merrily to a pleasant, placid-looking woman, who sat beside her—"he doesn't know me, you see, Mother; I told you he wouldn't." And then she faced me again, a very white row of teeth witnessing to her nationality.

"Wait," I said: "I am not such an insouciant as you think. You are Miss Clarice Brooking."

I recalled her in that moment. She had been a student in Thirion's atelier in Paris, where I had guinea-pigged two or three years earlier during the temporary absence through sickness of its master. Not a very promising pupil, if I remembered; but one, if I must confess it, with an inordinate admiration for the work of the teacher-substitute. But I had liked her, her gaiety, her freshness, her perfectly candid and voluble good-nature; and I was glad—for the moment—to meet her again.

She made a little motion, inviting me to sit beside her, and, as I did so, introduced me to her mother.

"And how about Thirion's?" I said.

"O!" she answered; "that is all over, and you will never be put to the pains again of sparing me the knowledge of the muff I was."

"You have abandoned art?"

"Now please to drop it, Mr. Dane. It would be mere pretence, you know, to say I abandoned what wasn't mine—like jilting a man who had never proposed to you and didn't mean to. But thank goodness the poor creature was saved any further embarrassment on my account by our coming into money. Yes, that is the glorious truth, and Mother and I have been busy for months in visiting all the places we have ever wanted to see and couldn't—making up for lost time."

"Thank you for my part in the benediction."

"O!" She laughed cheerily. "I learned more from you than from any one; but it was all no good; I remained a *rapin* to the very end. To see you paint always made me despair."

"You are not alone in that sentiment. It makes some people even use bad language."

She looked at me questioningly, quizzically.

"I didn't mean in that way. I simply adored your work. Have you not been successful? People say, you know, that success spells mediocrity."

"Those are the people, I expect, who would say anything to vindicate their own want of it. Success is a question of some quality in one which finds its affinity in the greatest number."

"Well, it seems to me, that is the same thing, because the greatest number are perfect idiots in everything but their own business. Are you painting about here?"

"A little."

"All by yourself?"

"No—I have a companion with me."

The moment I had said it a sense of the equivocalness of my position flashed upon me, and I wished that I could have warned Fifine before making that impulsive admission. But it was too late now.

"Does he paint too?" asked Miss Brooking.

"It is not a *he*," I said.

"O!"

Was there a note of alarm, of instinctive recoil, in that single interjection? I wondered. Mamma, who took but a monosyllabic part in the conversation, smiled continually, like one who could be suavely tolerant of most worldly idiosyncrasies; and Clarice herself had been, after all, a student in Paris. Still, I felt I could not leave the matter at that abrupt round full-stop.

"She is a—a sort of connexion," I said, with a slight hesitation, "whom I am accompanying back to Paris at the request of my step-sister."

I spoke somewhat nervously, incapable, on the spur of the moment, of the finessing which was needed at once to betray no secrets and to create no inextricable entanglements. To my surprise the girl responded with alacrity:—

"O, of course! I remember now. Your step-sister is a Miss Herold, is she not?"

I gave a little gasp and murmured an admission, marvelling what was to come.

"You will wonder how I know, perhaps," said Miss Brooking. "It is rather curious, but it is always funnily occurring, that question of associations. She—your step-sister, I mean—governesses Josephine de Beaurepaire, doesn't she?"

I answered, "Yes, in a way," in a voice I strove not to make aghast.

"Well," said the young lady, "I was engaged myself for a short time to give Josephine drawing lessons—cheek of me, wasn't it?—and I heard before I left that Miss Herold was coming to be her companion. I can't remember who it was told me; but somehow I learnt that it was your step-sister who was expected. Is she still there?"

"O, yes!" I sat up with a jerk, in the desperate hope to interpose my body between the speaker and her view of Fifine close by.

"I wonder how she likes it?" questioned the girl.

"Why shouldn't she?" I asked, hardly remembering of whom it was I was speaking.

"O! I don't know," she said. "She may have a different temperament to mine, and of course heaps more wisdom. But I couldn't, myself, have stood another week of it."

"Of what? Of the young lady?"

"Of everything. It was a horrible household. And the Marquis himself was, I really think, half demented."

She was frankly outspoken, you observe. I had turned, facing her, and, watching her eyes, manœuvred to keep their inquisition from escaping beside and beyond me—a quite useless precaution.

"And your young pupil herself?" I asked. "Was she as impossible?"

"*Tel père, telle fille*," answered Miss Brooking—"all affability at one moment and fury the next. I think she was neurotic, poor girl; and she led a fearful life of it with that madman. I couldn't have stood it any longer; it

frightened and offended me; and so I cut the connexion. But I hope——"
she looked at me in sudden hesitation.

"Not in the least," I said. "There is no apology called for on behalf of
my step-sister. She has twice your years, and I should think twenty times
your inflexibility and only a fraction of your sensitiveness. She has done
very well, I understand, and has come to be quite an influence for good in
the household."

"I am so glad," said the girl. "There was room for it, I am sure. And so
you are on your way back to Paris—at once?"

"That depends upon my travelling-companion," I said. "This is all a
novelty to her, and she likes to linger over it."

"Where is she? We should so like to be introduced to her. Will you?"

I rose at once, prompt and desperate to the chance. Under whatever
pretext I must get Fifine away, explaining to her while I covered her retreat.
Once gone, I might devise some excuse for her; but flight was the first
essential.

But when, with a "Certainly, I will," I turned to seek her, I found her
already departed. No doubt she and her cavaliere-servente, seeing me
occupied, had seized the opportunity to slip away together. Breathing again,
I expressed my regrets to the ladies. "She was sitting there, with a friend," I
said, "but a minute ago."

"What," said Miss Brooking—"that very pretty girl? I was admiring her
with all my eyes. Was *she* your relative?"

I stood and heard. On the first shock of those words followed an instant
revulsion of feeling in my mind—from startled relief to incredulity, to
amazement, to understanding; and so to an irresistible impulse to essay a
daring test.

"Did you think her pretty?" I said. "My step-sister always professes to
see in her a certain likeness to your former pupil."

"To Josephine de Beaurepaire?" There was wonder in her tone.

"Yes."

"She must have changed very much then since I knew her."

"You don't see it yourself?"

"O, no! I may have been deceived by the light; but I should never have
thought for a moment of connecting them—not for a moment; unless,
possibly, their figures might be something alike. But Josephine for one

thing was fair—I don't mean a blonde, but with hair of the neutral sort and palish eyelashes. No, really, I can't understand it."

There was no compromise about her. I felt the excitement in my heart as if beating on towards some emotional crisis, but whether fateful for loss or gain I could not foresee.

"O, well!" I said. "It is always a vexed question, that of likenesses. Some people can discover them where for others they simply don't exist. Haven't you ever known an infant that to this person was the image of its mother, to that of its father, while bearing to neither the least suggestion of the other parent? I daresay, if I could see Mademoiselle Beaurepaire, I should be as puzzled as you are to find a resemblance. Are you staying here long?"

"Only over to-morrow. We go on to Nîmes the day after. Mr. Dane—" she cooed honeyly—"I suppose you couldn't—I suppose it wouldn't be possible for you to—to sacrifice a little of your spare time to two poor outcast fellow-countrywomen? It would be so delightful to have you for a cicerone—if you could."

"I don't know," I said. "You will understand me, I am sure, when I say that I am at the mercy of a more exacting will than my own."

I could not, indeed, give any definite answer at the moment—my thoughts were chaos, with still an instinctive dread in them of that introduction the prospect of which had at first dismayed me. On the other hand I recognised in this chance encounter a means to a certain end of unsentimentalising detachment. And more than that—I was really pleased to have run across this young compatriot of mine again; she carried with her a frank deodorising atmosphere which it was pleasant to breathe after the rather close and thunderous experiences of the last few days. I found myself looking at her very kindly: she was not exactly pretty, but as fresh and wholesome as the primroses of her own countryside; and breathing her, as it were, I seemed to feel, wistfully and faintly, a sense of the long exile which, though voluntarily, had severed me from my birthright. England, after all, smells very sweet across the seas.

"Of course," said Mrs. Brooking. "She won't want to be deprived of you for the sake of two strangers."

But Clarice persisted: "Why shouldn't she make one of us?"

"I will ask her," I said. "Don't think me a boor if I leave it at that. And that reminds me: I must go and look after the young lady, and see that she isn't getting into any mischief—" and we parted with a cordial good-night, and I went my gait.

With what intention; and whom to seek? I felt in a very queer state of mind—cynical, puzzled, wrathful, and yet oddly elevated. What should I do—what say? Nothing, I resolved, after I had thought it all well out; but just let things take their course. In masterly inactivity lay the solution of most problems of conduct.

Mademoiselle my sister, the landlady informed me, when presently I returned to the Hôtel, had wished me to be informed that she had retired to bed with a slight headache, and did not desire to be disturbed. So? Then she should not be disturbed by me. I was merely the looker-on in a quaint little game of cross-purposes.

Fifine was before me at the breakfast-table the next morning. As I joined her, the two ladies came in, and took their seats, fortunately at some distance from us. We just exchanged bows, cheerily on their part, nervously on mine, for some dread of the unspeakable still haunted me. But it passed in the next moment and I felt troubled no more. I thought Clarice looked very attractive in her clean frock and dewy morning brightness, which contrasted oddly, I will not say flatteringly, with the more exotic charms of my companion.

"I knew her in Paris"—I volunteered the information to Fifine, who was patently, though with cold looks, canvassing my newly-discovered acquaintance of the night before. "She was a pupil of Thirion's, and under my tuition for some months. She and her mother have come into money, and are travelling. They wanted me to show them the sights for a few hours to-day, and I couldn't very well refuse. You won't mind, will you?"

I did not think it necessary to relate the particulars of our conversation or of my apprehensions. It was obvious that the morning light had done nothing to reform that question of identification.

"They think you a connexion of mine, whom I am escorting to Paris at Marion's request," I went on. "You have nothing to do but uphold that fiction, and steer clear of all compromising details. Just hold your tongue about yourself, that is all. They go to-morrow."

"Why should I do anything?" said Fifine. "They are not my friends."

They were not. I observed her curiously. There was no sign of any recognition in her eyes either.

"But they would like to be," I answered. "They asked particularly if you would not join us."

"Then they may ask. I shall not come."

"Let me introduce you to them at least. I promised to."

"That is your look out. I don't want to make their acquaintance."

"Why not? You put me in a rather awkward position, you know. They will think you very ungracious."

"I don't care what any *maladroite* of an English Miss thinks me. It is hers that is the clumsy bad-taste in interposing herself where she is not wanted. You put yourself in that position, and you may get out of it as you like."

"Very well. You must behave as you please. Only, if I go, what will you do with yourself in the meantime?"

"O! You needn't trouble about me. Fortunately there is one upon whom I can depend more confidently for my entertainment."

"You mean Carabas, of course."

"Yes, of course. He is not like a butterfly to be led away any moment by a new fancy."

"Well, you ought to know—such an old friend, and his attachments tendrils of such slow growth."

I laughed; but Fifine was remote from laughter. She got up in a very few minutes and left the table and the room, her head held high.

I was really placed in an uncomfortable position, and hard put to it, when I joined the ladies, to find excuses for my companion's rudeness. Of course they must have adjudged her in their minds an ill-bred unpleasant young woman; but their tactful kindness sought only to spare my feelings the knowledge of theirs. I said something lamely about her shyness of strangers—for her refusal to be introduced must have been perfectly obvious to them—and I conveyed from her a fictitious message to the effect that she regretted not being able to come, but that she had already engaged herself to a short expedition with a M. Cabarus, an acquaintance of ours. It was not much, but it was more than she deserved, even though my manner, I am afraid, must have given my invention the lie, for I was plainly embarrassed, and as plainly incensed against the cause of my embarrassment. But the two ladies affected, with a much finer tact, a genuine sympathy with the subject of my excuses.

"It is too bad," said Mrs. Brooking, "for us to impose ourselves on you like this. You really mustn't let us, Mr. Dane. Poor girl! I dare say she is wishing us at Jericho; and I can feel with her in her shyness of troublesome interlopers like ourselves. One wants to be free of all social obligations on a holiday. So please don't consider yourself bound to us in any way. We can manage perfectly well by ourselves—can't we, daughter?"

"Yes, of course," said Clarice. "It was only a thoughtless suggestion on my part; and I really hardly expected it to be taken seriously."

"It was taken," I said, "not only seriously, but pridefully. You mustn't deny me that sort of proprietary exaltation which one feels in playing local dragoman to a party of visitors. After exhausting the beauties of Arles, you will leave off with a vague impression that I am somehow to thank for them, simply because my knowledge of them is anterior to yours; and I wouldn't forego that feeling of self-complacent superiority for anything. Moreover, I have no other engagement—I swear it."

They laughed, and expostulated; but in the end we went off together, and made a quite pleasant day of it. Both mother and daughter were of that bright intelligence which gives to the reiteration of ancient commonplaces a perpetual new zest. They were interested in everything; they commented inanely on nothing. I enjoyed myself, I confess it; there was something exhilarating in this contact with the fresh clean North in a fervid land, and Clarice, as a fair young Englishwoman, did her country and me, I felt, the most gratifying credit. We went back to lunch at the Hôtel, to recruit against fresh exertions, and started off again without having seen anything of Fifine. That did not disturb me, but rather otherwise; I had had quite enough of her for the time being, and her presence in the room would have been nothing but an embarrassment. No reference to her was made by the ladies, and for that I was thankful. It had occurred to me only too late that she passed in the Hôtel for my sister, and I was struck aghast over the thought of what strategy would be necessary to accommodate that fiction to the asserted facts of my case. But fortunately our supposed relationship had not reached the ears of the two; nor, so far as I know, were they ever called upon to question my statement. I hope not, at least, for, absurd and illogical as it may sound, I would fain keep my credit unimpaired in the breast of that clean-souled young countrywoman of mine.

I dined alone at the end of the day, my friends preferring to be served in their room after their somewhat exhausting experience; and again Fifine was conspicuous by her absence. But I would make no enquiries about her, or allow myself to be disturbed in any way on her account. She had chosen her own course, and was welcome to bring it to whatever conclusion she pleased. After dinner, I strolled about the town for a time, and at near ten o'clock returned to the Hôtel and mounted to my room. I noticed Fifine's shoes put outside her door as I passed; but I went by without a sign. Nevertheless I was conscious of a slight thrill of relief in the knowledge that she was safely housed.

Our rooms were both of them luxurious—mine little less than the other, a lofty two-bedded apartment, over fine for a vagabond's accommodation, but I will not say unwelcome for its sheeted cosiness. If there was one thing we were both fastidious about it was our linen, which on every first opportunity was despatched to the laundress, and I was moving with satisfaction from my bed a little pile of freshly-washed clothes, when I heard a knock at the door and cried Entrez! Supposing it was the garçon de chambre, I did not turn for a moment, until the silence that followed the sound of the handle striking me, I looked round and saw Fifine. I just observed her face—mutiny still struggled in it with some softer emotion—and then, with my back to her, renewed my sorting.

"What is it?" I said.

She did not answer for a moment, until, it seemed, she could command her voice; and then she spoke:—

"I—I only wanted to ask you, Felix: have you had a pleasant day?"

"Very pleasant."

"I think she is pretty—your friend—in the pale English way."

"I think so too."

I smiled secretively and grimly, as, my head bent down, I busied myself over the linen. A long pause followed—and then:—

"May I shut the door, Felix?"

"No," I answered sharply; then, more reasonably: "Think of the misconception it might give rise to if you were seen leaving—there, I know what the fiction is; but fiction must be safeguarded against truth as much as truth against fiction; and ours has been used before now and found not impregnable. You can talk where you are: there is no danger of any one hearing you on this remote landing."

I thought she would go at once; but to my surprise she did not move.

"What is it you want?" I asked presently, turning to face her, as she did not speak. The look of her, standing so, half disarmed me. She was so patently miserable, with still the proud misery of one who, wishing to atone, struggles against the self-abasement whose first knowledge may be of a place in old affections lost, perhaps irretrievably. Yet I could not keep that harshness from my voice, though I knew she felt it acutely. I had a policy to pursue, no less than a lesson to drive home; and certainly she had given me plentiful provocation for my attitude.

"Nothing," she said—"only to say good-night." She moved as if to go; but still lingered; and suddenly the submission came. "I didn't mean you to be so offended; and—and I suppose it was natural in you to prefer your own countrywoman before a stranger."

"My dear child," I answered coolly, "I must point out to you two errors in that little speech: I did not regard you as a stranger, and I was not offended."

A momentary light of hopefulness came into the eyes turned quickly up to me, but it faded on the instant.

"What were you, then?" she said. "Not anyhow yourself, as I thought I had come to know you."

"Familiarity, young lady, sometimes breeds contempt. Let me hear this fancy portrait described, before I admit or reject it."

"Why, philosophically just and forbearing; always ready to make allowances; humorously tolerant of the weaknesses of smaller natures."

"I acknowledge the soft impeachment with a smirk. And now, how have I falsified your too generous estimate of me? Did I upbraid you for your ill-manners towards my friends, whose only offence lay in wishing to make your undesirable acquaintance? On the contrary, I expressed concern for the situation in which your own obstinacy placed you. Did I not make allowances? Assuredly I did, even to the extent of bearing on your behalf, as some slight amelioration of your discourtesy, an imaginary message from yourself to the ladies. Finally, what humorous tolerance was lacking in my reference to your devoted henchman, whose constancy I acclaim as a thing for admiration, while I cannot, of course, through my baser nature, hope to emulate it? I trust only—to return your kind enquiries—that it proved a source of as great gratification to you to-day as I am bound to confess my *in*constancy did to me."

Though she took unresisting my merciless chastisement, I would not spare her one sting of it. There was something more behind my virulence, you will understand, than mere resentment of a piece of bad-temper, or even of bad taste. But there was yet a stronger incentive: I must be either resolutely brutal, I felt, or irresolutely weak. One concession to the emotional, which fought in me to grant pity and forgiveness to this soft tragic young sinner, and the end for us would come in sure disaster. Yet the tears in her eyes as she gazed at me, with the expression of one who is realising for the first time the truth of a hopelessly alienated affection, were advocates I had a mortal struggle to resist. Let the fact that I *did* resist them stand at least to my credit.

"I dare say you are justified," she said, with a brave effort at self-control, "in speaking to me like that. I don't defend myself, but only my opinion of you, which, being what it was, was the reason perhaps of my venturing to take such spoilt advantage of it. I won't believe now that you are different from what I thought; I have tried you beyond your patience, that is all. But I think, Felix, you might have spared me all that bitter sarcasm. To use sarcasm, I have heard you say yourself, is to try to play the wit with a fool's weapon. It hurts but it does not convince. I would much rather you told me straight out that you had had enough of my tempers and moods, and wanted to be rid of me."

"I could not say that with truth, Fifine."

"O, Felix! how are we to go on like this? Will it change your feelings to me at all to be told that I have been miserable, deservedly I know, all day?"

"What, in spite of your confident dependence on——"

"I have not been with him—I would not go, though he asked me. Most of the day I have spent in my bedroom."

"Starving and punishing yourself? I am sorry for that, Fifine."

"I bought some chocolates. Felix—" she put a light entreating hand on my arm—"take me away from here. O, do, Felix!"

"Where to?"

"I don't know—only away."

"Les Baux is the next on our itinerary. Very well. Only we cannot start until to-morrow afternoon."

"Why not before?"

"Because—" I had a short desperate struggle with myself, and conquered—"I have undertaken to escort my friends to Montmajour, and that will take up the whole morning."

"To Montmajour—where we went together!" There was a note of stricken wonderment in her voice. "Must you go?"

"Yes. I must go."

"You will not expect me to come? But I will come, if you wish it."

"No—if you can manage to amuse yourself somehow in the interval?"

"Yes, Felix."

"I shall be back in good time. They have to start early for Nîmes."

"Very well." She raised her troubled eyes to mine, said "Good-night, Felix," in a desolate little voice, and disappeared, closing the door behind her.

The instant she was gone I went like a lunatic, up and down, up and down, reviling and cursing myself. Once I paused, with my hand on the door, mad to follow her, to shut myself in with her, and, upbraiding my own cruelty, yield everything to a wild reconciliation. But the intolerable moment spent itself, and left me mercifully sane.

CHAPTER XVII

IF passion reveals the God in us, it was a wise policy of the Father God which fettered it with restrictions, lest, in aspiring to achieve angels, we should repeople chaos with abortions. Mercifully the streets and the trains, eating and drinking, business and the social duties, are always with us, to appropriate to themselves ninety-nine hundredths of our nervous energy: what remains for our divinity, the odd fiery fraction, is quite enough for all reasonably creative purposes. The poeticules of our latest movement are all for revolt against this state of things; they glory, openly and personally, in the passion that burns and blisters, which is, after all, I suppose, only their modern euphemism for venery in its vulgarest and most penalising form. That is to exalt unclean gods with a vengeance, and, though I do not go with the orthodox Jehovah in most things, I could follow him gratefully in any relentless campaign he instituted against these little wormy monstrosities of a new Gomorrah. The fact that most of them probably are callow and intellectually embryonic, proves nothing so much as the weak indulgence of an age which allows such undeveloped juvenilities to pipe their pretentious eroticisms unsmacked. When Art claims the right to discover and worship beauty in filthy disease, or in the iridescent scums over human corruption, it is time that Art was put away by its friends in an asylum for the neuroticly impossible. So far as I can make out from the published evidences, that asylum should need at the present moment considerable enlargement.

There is, in fact, no beauty, and there never can be, in incontinence; the point is too self-evident to need labouring. Restraint is the quality most to be studied in aiming at perfection of form, and to achieve it one must be content to concentrate on the hundredth fraction. Spiritually and materially, that man will find the highest happiness who is satisfied to yield the bulk of his being to the workaday and unemotional.

Morning lowered the pride of my own starry exaltation, and found me with a normal pulse and a brain swept clean as a housemaid's step—with a deep thankfulness, moreover, that I was reawaking to a day of untroubled commonplace, and not to one of unquiet, responsible remorse. In action I looked to dissipate the last fumes of an intoxication, whose memory, though it lingered without nausea, was yet no proof against that glad consciousness of moral security. I whistled as I dressed.

Fifine did not come down to breakfast; and I was off with my friends before she had appeared. I knocked at her door, bidding her to expect me back about midday, when I should hope to have finished my task, and she answered "Very well"—coldly, I thought, and in a manner which I was relieved, I told myself, to recognise for one of reassuring indifference.

However, she was punctual to her appointment; and I found her awaiting me in the coffee-room, when I came in—a little late myself—after seeing the ladies off to the station.

"Well, they are gone," I said. "And now for relaxation and refreshment following duty."

She shot a quick glance at me; but relapsed immediately into the rather apathetic attitude with which she had accepted my reappearance. She looked a little pale and dark-eyed; but I was resolute to make no comment thereon, nor to imply in any way an understanding sympathy with her state. I expressed my contrition for my unpunctuality, and that was all.

"It doesn't matter in the least," she said. "I don't think I am very hungry."

"Nonsense," I answered. "You *must* eat, after that—" I checked myself, on the brink of the undesired subject. "Besides," I said, "we have this journey before us, and with only a problematic meal at the end of it. I don't build implicitly on the resources of the place we are going to—unless it has altered considerably since my time."

"Very well," she said impassively: "I will try."

"How have you amused yourself during my absence?" I asked.

"I went to the Muséon Arleten with M. Cabarus," she answered in an indifferent voice: "we stayed there till it was time for him to go."

"To go! What, has he actually taken his departure?"

"Yes—for les Baux. He went in a hired automobile."

I sat back in my chair, and looked her fixedly in the face.

"Did you tell him *we* were going there?"

"Yes, I told him."

I said no more. Presently an uncontrollable fit of laughter began to shake me. It was too ridiculous. Was I for evermore to be haunted by this incubus with the inflated paunch and disordered head? But the moral was no less obvious than the absurdity—I could not shut my eyes to the fact. I had been crushing under in myself a sentiment which had no authority for existing. Perhaps, even, she had known all the time whither he was bound, and had manœuvred so as to induce me to follow in his footsteps. I could not quite believe that; but anyhow I felt myself handsomely made a fool of, and the thought of my own discomfiture appealed irresistibly to my sense of humour. One thing was now certain, that I might quit my conscience of any feeling of regret for my own harshness or irresponsiveness.

Fifine looked a little astonished over my hilarious reception of her thunderbolt; but she said nothing, and we finished our lunch almost in silence.

"Now," said I, when all was done: "what time did you say our train started? You looked it out, didn't you, as I asked you."

"Yes," she said. "It was at three-twenty."

"Then we will pay our bill, collect our traps, and, by your leave, start leisurely for the station."

All of which we did, arriving at the little terminus in ample time. It was somewhat disconcerting, however, to find the platform empty, the office closed, and no sign whatever of train or passengers.

"This is odd," I said; but presently sighting a porter in the distance, I went to enquire of him. The result was illuminating.

"What time did you tell me our train went?" I asked Fifine, as I rejoined her.

"At three-twenty," she repeated. "I copied it down, and can show you."

She showed it me, in fact—a little note in pencil on a scrap of paper.

"Read it, please," I said.

She obeyed—"Thirteen-twenty"—and stopped. "O—o!" she exclaimed—a prolonged interjection of dismay.

"Exactly," I said. "Thirteen-twenty is one-twenty, goose. There is not another train for just two hours."

She stood looking up at me. Her lower lip went down, positively like a dear pitiful baby's in deprecation of the expected and well-merited scolding.

"O, Felix," she said. "I'm *so* sorry!"

I could have shaken her; I could have laughed; I could have snatched her to my heart and kissed her—it was so moving, after all, to see this change in her from that one-time confident assurance to propitiation and entreaty. In these latter days all her precocious dictatorialness seemed to have deserted her; and yet she did not know that I knew what I knew; to all intents and purposes she still figured to herself for a free agent. It was Carabas, the eternal Carabas, who had wrought the sad confusion.

"Never mind," I said. "It will make us rather late, and it will be a little dull waiting; but we must kill the time as we can, and be glad it is no worse."

She thanked me for my forbearance, though with only a pathetic look.

"Wouldn't you like to go back into the town," she said, "while I wait here for you? Please do. I shan't mind, and it will make me feel less guilty."

"Very well," I answered, after a moment's reflection—"if you are sure you won't mind."

"Quite sure," she replied; and so I left her.

I knew why I had acquiesced; it was from policy, policy—I put it firmly to myself. It was from policy, also, no doubt, that I wandered no further than to the main platform—to which the other was related but locally— where I smoked and loitered aimlessly, acutely conscious all the time of my self-exile, obstinate to maintain it, yet never losing jealous mental sight of the forlorn figure awaiting my return a short stone's-throw away. But I prevailed against inclination, even to the end, and did not return to Fifine until the train was actually in the station.

It was well past five when we started, and already there was an ominous drooping about the lids of the sky. Three-quarters of an hour's run, with the stops at an *halte* or two and the little midway station of Fontvieille, would surely carry us into something deeper than twilight at Paradou, which was where we had to alight for our final destination. I had not before approached les Baux from this quarter, and was ignorant as to its distance from Paradou, the character of the way, and the possibility of procuring a vehicle of some sort. However, let come what would; we were in for it.

It was a wild little train, a mere giddy colt of a thing, which rattled us through scenery for ever growing more into communion with its untamed self—great stretches of rock-strewn heather, and clattering gullies, and vast ramparts of hill which continually rose about us more savage and menacing. We could see the white road creeping up the valley, as though stealthily pursuing us, now touching us with a coil and gliding swiftly from the contact, now receding to worm itself through purple thickets, whence it would reappear far ahead, wheeling as if to strike us as we passed. The light sank from the sky, like blood from a dying face; the country grew featureless first, and then slowly indistinguishable; once through the little sparkling oasis of Fontvieille, we found ourselves committed without reserve to uncompromising darkness. Still there was a twenty minutes run before us, and I found myself anxiously peering by and by for some sign of twinkling reassurance amidst the glooms ahead. There had been carriages at

Fontvieille; should we find their like at Paradou-les-Baux? And while I was still peering, the train slowed down, stopped, and we were at the station.

It seemed a mere isolated platform in an otherwise lightless desolation. We were the only passengers who got out. With a rather sinking heart, I took, after the train had started on its way again, the solitary official—who seemed to combine in himself the parts of stationmaster, ticket-collector, signalman and porter—into my confidence.

"The distance to les Baux, Monsieur?"

"By road," he answered brusquely, "three miles."

"An easy road?"

"But far from it. For yourself difficult; for Madame impossible."

That was discomforting; but it was not accurate. The road, as we discovered next day, was a carriage road and easily distinguishable, though decidedly steep.

"A voiture?" I suggested.

The stationmaster shrugged his shoulders, and called to an urchin, who was hanging about by the platform wicket. A brief colloquy ensued between the two as to the probability of Charloun's cart being available. Finally, in order to ascertain, the boy ran down the hill, on which the station was situated, into lower gulfs of blackness. He was absent ten or fifteen minutes, when he re-appeared with the information that there was no possibility of our procuring a trap of any sort whatever.

"A guide, possibly?" I asked.

It was certain, was the answer, that no one could be found at this time of night, and the day's labour over, to put himself to the trouble.

"This is pleasant," I said to Fifine; and turned again to the stationmaster:—

"There is, without question, an inn?"

O, yes, there was an inn, it appeared, one inn, but hardly of a quality to appeal to travellers of our distinction. It was merely, in short, a cabaret. "Still, if Monsieur and Madame——"

Monsieur and Madame held a short counsel of desperation, and agreed—if one may apply the term to Madame's passive acquiescence—that it was a question of the undesirable inn or nothing.

"Conduct us to it," I said to the boy, "and you shall earn the fifty centimes which travellers of distinction are accustomed to bestow upon the deserving."

He led off, and we followed—down the gulf-like hill. There were no stars, and the wind blew upon us coldly.

"I'm afraid," I said, "that there's no help for it, Fifine. You'll have to resign yourself to being parted from your troubadour for a few hours."

She did not answer for a little; and then she looked suddenly up at me.

"How cruel you are," she said. "I never should have thought it of you once."

There was an odd catch in her voice; but she commanded it, and spoke clearly and precisely. Thereafter we walked in silence—a surprised, half-vindictive one on my part. Not that I was wrathful with Fifine, but with Fate. However unexceptionable my motives, it would not allow me, it seemed, the unequivocal expression of them, but must always be impelling me to say the provocative thing when I had meant only the playful. At least, so I told myself; but then one is not always quite honest in one's self-confidences. It is extraordinary how gullible we can be when our own inclinations prompt us to mischief.

At the bottom of the hill we came to a crossroad, turning to the right along which we presently sighted the yellow end wall of a country caravansary, on which was emblazoned the magnificent legend "Grand Café Bellin." It was, in truth, as we discovered on reaching it, a humble enough hostelry, standing in an arid little compound, with a row of plane trees before its windows; but it offered shelter, at least, and possibly some hope of refreshment. We knocked on the door, and a formidable cross-eyed woman opened and demanded our business.

At first it was all *impossible*; the cooking was done with and the fire down; but finally she was prevailed on to admit us grudgingly; and we were shewn through a reeking little kitchen—which opened straight upon the compound, and where, it seemed, the whole staring household was assembled—into a great barn of a room, furnished with bare benches and tables, at which were seated a number of boors, quite *à l'hollandais*, only drinking hot coffee in lieu of beer, and playing dominoes and cards with greasy little packs. There in a corner we sat, watching the curious scene, and awaiting meekly the moment when it should please the high-handed landlady to serve us the wherewithal for a meal. It came, and sooner and ampler than we had dared to hope—thin soup, a mess of mutton bones, the usual tough smoked cutlets, the usual rancid wine; but we were hungry and thankful, and remote from a critical mood. We blessed providence and ate; and afterwards sought to ruminate at ease, watching the coming and going, the rough but mannerly company, the animated expressions and the sober recreations. There was a billiard table at the further end of the long room; and presently I went and challenged to a game on it a young quarryman who was idly knocking the balls about. He was unwashed and heavy-booted; the lines of his common face and coarse clothes were filled thick with the dust of his labour; but he accepted with perfect courtesy—and gave me a complete thrashing into the bargain, his strokes being as deft and resourceful with a cue as they must have been violently destructive with a pick. We had a *petit verre* together afterwards—the only palatable cheap drink in Provence—and parted very good friends. I went back to Fifine, and found her sitting quite patient, but with a strained tired look in her eyes.

"It is bed for you, by your leave," I said. "Shall I call the girl and get her to show you up to your room?"

"I think," she answered, "I—I will not go till you do, Felix."

"Why not, Fifine?"

"I don't know. I would rather not."

"You are nervous, little goose. These rough surroundings frighten you; and you are recalling terrible tales of things done to belated travellers in lonely inns. Are you not?"

She smiled faintly, but did not answer.

"Believe me," I said; "you are safer here than you would be in the Hôtel Ritz, and far less likely to meet with impertinences. But, of course, if you feel so, I will come. You ought, it is very certain, to be in your bed."

"It is a shame to victimise you so. I am very sorry, Felix. I have been trying to fight it down; but I can't—everything is so wild and strange."

"Of course. Poor child!"

I caught up the rücksack, went to the door, summoned the little solemn-eyed Provençale who had waited on us, and bade her conduct us to our rooms. She went before, carrying a lighted candle, up a flight of stairs as steep and narrow as a ladder, and ushered us at the top into a dim windy chamber, sparely littered with furniture, whence opened a couple of doors into two box-like little cubicles, or compartments—our bedrooms. Each contained a bed, a tiny washstand, one chair, and a minute chest of drawers with a scrap of looking-glass on it. They were dingy, the discoloured paper was peeling from the walls, the boards were bare; but, wonder of wonders, each boasted a single switch and electric light. They were more civilized in

Paradou than we had opined, and I hoped that Fifine's nerves would take comfort from that reassurance. I made her choose her room, and deposited in it, as was our custom, the rücksack, having first removed from it my own necessities. Then I bade her good-night, and told her to sleep in peace and security, seeing my own cubicle was contiguous, and the wall between no thicker than match-boxes.

"If you whisper, I shall hear you," I said. "Call to me, if anything frightens you."

She promised, and I went—went perforce, though the look in her face made me feel as though I were abandoning a scared child to its night-terrors. There was a mosquito blind to the window in my room, and, raising it, I saw that it opened upon the row of plane trees, and the little compound faintly illuminated by the light from the common-room below. All else and around was dense obscurity—only that little spectral oasis shone isolated in a desert of night.

I sat there long, smoking and meditating. Now and again the door underneath would swing and bang, and a figure would cross the paddock of light and disappear into the glooms beyond. Gradually all sounds in the house ceased; and presently, after a wink or two, the light itself shrunk and was gone. Only still the faintest luminosity, proceeding from somewhere undetected, lingered in my neighbourhood. It took me a minute to discover that it shone through the close web of Fifine's mosquito blind. So she was awake still; or slept with her light up.

And almost immediately I heard a little stifled call.

"Felix!"

"What is it, m'amie."

"O, do come to me! There is something horrible!"

I laughed, as I got to my feet; then set my teeth, with a groan, as I softly slipped off my shoes.

"All right," I whispered back; "I am coming."

I opened noiselessly one door after the other, stepping like a panic-stricken thief. She was sitting up in bed, her hair coiling about her temples, the sheet clutched to her chin by her two convulsive hands. Her eyes met mine, piteous, deprecating, imploring.

"What is it?" I said.

"There!" She nodded her head frantically, looking beyond me at the wall. I turned; and saw a slowly-travelling centipede—truly a monstrum horrendum. It was about an inch and a half long, its body was encased in overlapping dusky-red scales, and its innumerable legs, unlike the brief pedicles of its more northern brethren, were as long as a house-spider's, but like fine hairs. I seized up one of Fifine's shoes that stood outside the door, flattened out the visitor with it, and he fell defunct.

"O, what was it?" She shivered. "Have you killed it?"

"As dead as Charity," I assured her. "It was just a shield-bearing centipede, Fifine. Nothing worse. You find them about here."

"Will another come?"

"I should think it unlikely."

"Felix—will you—will you sit by me till I go to sleep?"

"I ought not to, you know, m'amie."

"I will shut my eyes; I will not speak to you—not one word. Felix, I am very lonely and miserable."

"Hush, child. Close your eyes, then. I will stay only on condition that you are absolutely true to your promise."

She lay down at once, turning from me to obey. I just pushed to the door without latching it, and went and sat as far from her as possible. It was a strange vigil that followed; and yet I never once felt chill throughout it. The blood was always throbbing through my veins like a living fire; little reels of vertigo seemed to take me from time to time, half blissful, half delirious. When my thoughts grew masterful, my soul grew weak; and in those kind and pitiful moods I had to force myself to keep my place, lest a single movement should precipitate a tragedy. But I could not hide the truth from myself any longer. We must go home, I said to my suffering conscience: we must end it and go home. Did she guess the torture in my mind—had she even invited it? In that case I had a formidable task before me indeed.

I don't know when she slept at last; probably the ferment in her brain, coupled with her consciousness of my presence, kept her long awake. That she could sleep at all, trustful in that consciousness like a child, was sufficiently moving to me. And somewhere in the little hours she *did* sleep: I knew it, when it came, by the soft regularity of her breathing; and thereupon I rose, and padding it like a burglar, went away from her room into my own. Yet I could not pass her bed, I had not that self-command, but I must pause by it for one moment to look in her dear unconscious face. There was the tenderest flush upon the upturned cheek; the lips were the least bit parted; to look on innocent sleep is to know the bud before the flower, the locked secret, the loveliness nearest heaven. God forgive me!

CHAPTER XVIII

I AWOKE, somewhat late, and stretched myself with a sense of luxurious felicity. Then I clasped my hands under my head, and lay luminously dreaming. It was very still. The sun came in at my open window, filtered through a confusion of vivid leaves, and made of my common coverlet a woodland tapestry, intricately woven of gold and grey. Half closing my eyes, the oblong of light became to them crystal and liquescent, as if it were water blotted with innumerable globes of oily green. Those floated and travelled spasmodically, whisking back, as soon as started, on the movement of an eyelash, but always venturing again on voyages of insistent discovery. It was their business to carry little cargoes of sunshine and emerald into my brain; and presently I ceased to resist them, and they swam one by one into port and unloaded.

That betokened a surrender on my part to the delicious inconsequence of the hour. Self was entitled to consider self an imponderable quantity, in that interval of suspension between the attractions of night and day, and I let mine swing to what bias it listed, only blissfully watching, as it were, its direction. There was no question about that; nor did I desire there should be. It took me into glowing reveries which I indulged to the full, so long as that sense of irresponsible neutrality lasted. Yet it did not last long; bias itself was fatal to it, for bias must sooner or later convey a sense of weight, and a sense of weight brings us promptly to earth.

I came to earth presently, with a renunciatory yawn—and than a vast physical yawn there is nothing more dispelling to illusionment. I sat up in bed, and called to Fifine through the frail partition.

"Are you awake?"

She answered, "Yes," and I demanded again, "Is your blind up?"

"Yes," she said; and I put it to her thereupon:—

"Do you remember that waking impression of mine, that puzzled you so, of the plane trees seen outside a window on a bright morning? If you do, wink once and blink once at your window, and then tell me what is the visual effect on you."

There was a pause; and then, "O, I have winked a fly into my eye!" wailed Fifine.

I burst out laughing.

"Shall I come and remove it for you?" I asked.

"No," she answered—"you mustn't. It will be all right in a minute."

"Bon!" I muttered to myself, à propos the momentary impulse which had thrilled my nerves. "She is wise in the daylight, God bless her!"

We joined company below, even with something a sense of an old comradeship recovered, though Fifine's cheek flushed a little when she first saw me. I drew her out for a stroll while our coffee was preparing, and we walked together happily, tacitly eschewing all perilous topics. It was a lovely glowing morning, and the little village, sitting in its slipper of the hills, unfolded its simple charms prettily before us, rebuking our gloomy estimate of its last night's inhospitality. But there was not much to detain us; and, breakfast finished, we were soon on our way for the mountain stronghold, which was the true siderite of our desires.

A siderite, in sooth, it appeared, burning sky-high. We were climbing all the way, and I had to strain like a pack-horse, loaded as I was.

"Is the knapsack heavy?" said Fifine. "But really, do you know, Felix, we are justifying its existence for the first time."

"I shouldn't mind that," I said, "if it didn't take such advantage of the favour shown it. Now I know why the rack in the train creaked."

"Poor man," she said. "Shall I help you?"

"Yes, take the rücksack, Fifine, and I will carry you. M. Cabarus would call that halving the burden to double the joy."

It was a mistake to utter his name—and ironically. I don't know why I did it—from natural perversity, I suppose. It re-created between us a little shadow, which was never wholly dissipated during the remainder of our walk.

At about a mile from Paradou we came, always climbing, to a sign-post, and thence, making to the right, in a moment there opened out before us the veritable wild glen of our pilgrimage, a vision from end to end of tumultuous beauty.

Is any description of les Baux wanted in these days? I suppose during the last dozen years or so it has been more "exploited" than throughout the whole interval of centuries dividing it from its heyday of power and prosperity, when the singing-men came flocking from all quarters of the land to its exotic love-pastures. Once and for long its towering silences existed but in vague report for the ordinary traveller. He heard of them, but as things not easily attainable—hazards a little remote from his purpose of orthodox sight-seeing. But the motor-car has altered all that; it has rendered accessible, to the read-as-it-runs class of tourist, fastnesses hitherto respected for their isolation and inhospitality. He whirls over from St. Remy, stops an hour to lunch, bolts a hasty snack of local gallimaufry, and rushes on again. Sadie and Goldshtein, with their voices nasal and nosey, invade the austere solitudes; and, though they may vex them but fitfully, the aggregate of their gothicisms must have done something to take its keen edge off the strangeness and romance of the place.

However, that desecration is relative, and, after all, quite inconsiderable. One may still spend a week, a month, a year, in les Baux, and never, if one likes, know more of the casual demons than is conveyed through the distant low of a horn, or the vision of gliding heads above a stone wall. And in time, no doubt, the speed-lust will spend itself, and these casemated defences of the mountains return to their primal loneliness—to be once more periodically discovered by earnest schoolmistresses and sentimental poets desiring copy.

Now, right in our front as we clomb, rose a mighty forehead of cliff. It was as the face of a sphinx, veiling the mysteries of the hills beyond. We passed it, and their stupendous contours unfolded themselves before us— rock upon rock, lifting to the sky, in derision of the toiling road, which struggled vainly to put itself on terms with that impossible ascent.

And as it toiled, so did we, atoms perspiring in the dust. The little farms, the patches of vine, the olive and the mulberry gardens in the valley below, sunk ever deeper and deeper as we laboured up and on. There was heavy green on the Titan groups across the glen; they were furred with thick pelt of juniper, and spike-lavender, and bushy rosemary. But on our side all appeared near naked rock, clambering by way of scarp and shelf and overhanging boulder to a giddy altitude, where it broke against the sky in a wave of jagged masonry, hardly to be distinguished from the mountain which gave it birth.

There clung the shattered stronghold, a city in itself, still rooted in the rock from which, manured by blood, it first grew rich and lusty. It bred fierce hawks and gladsome swallows once; it breeds them still. The old life contest between the gentle and the cruel is not ended there, but Berald, in the form of a hen-harrier, will still swoop on the little dove-wife Françoiso to drive his cruel beak into her heart. The hill of colossal ruin, like his wood to the melancholy lover in "Maud," remains "a world of plunder and prey," though its vivid antique spirits, bad and good, be all harlequinaded in these days into their fairy similitudes. Do you seek Guilhem de Beauvoire, who walled up his own mother for her sins, or Raymond de Seillans, who made his wife eat unknowingly of the heart of her lover? Turn this stone or that, and you will likely find them squatting in the shape of little scorpions underneath. There, in the sanctimonious form of a praying mantis, stands a false priest—rapacious, hypocritical. And as for the frailties—Briande, Béregère, Iseult, Bels, Midons, Etiennette, and what not—are not their very names become butterflies, as pretty and as light, on which the spider and the lizard will feed if they get the chance.

The lovely things came down and looped about our heads as we climbed on—commas, like baroque tortoiseshells, pale clouded yellows, Bath whites for every one of which, if netted in England, a collector would have given a small fortune. They danced before us, like giddy laughing girls, taking us, no doubt, with our pack, for some wandering jongleur and his commère— perhaps Raymond Ferraud himself and the beautiful Alète de Mauleon— and beckoning us on to the appreciative Courts of les Baux. And indeed we were only suffering to attain them, magnificent as the prospect about us was.

However, for myself, I was now on familiar ground, and could calculate the remainder way. It ran up to the valley end, where, above a tumbled sea of boulders, rose a sheer wall of rock, against which it appeared to fling itself and cease. But in reality, short of the cliff it turned on a sharp curve like that of a hairpin, and, mounting thence at a steeper gradient, brought us in brief space to the village eyrie and the comfortable hostelry de la Reine Jeanne.

We were glad and content to have reached our goal at last. It looked an unpretentious house from the outside—painted stone grey, and entered up a little double-sided flight of steps put parallel with its front. But, within, everything, though on a modest scale, was bright and clean, and the slim young landlord as inviting as his surroundings. He saluted us with cheery hospitality (Madame his wife was, alas, indisposed—her first!), and answered our request for rooms with the smiling alacrity of a right host. He could speak some English too, having served his term as waiter in a Marseilles hotel—which seemed rather wonderful in that context of wild rocks and praying mantises—and was altogether rather an admirable Boniface to have alighted on in the wilderness. There was only a single difficulty, he said—which after all was doubtless not insuperable—the difficulty of accommodation. The house, as one might understand, was of limited capacities, and circumstances had further curtailed those. There was but one exclusive bedroom, and that was already bespoken. What remained consisted of two rooms in one—that was to say, as it were, a bedroom, and bed-dressing-room, but with a door between. To leave the second, it was necessary to go through the first. Still, if Monsieur, and—

Monsieur filled up the tentative hiatus in the manner which occurred to him as the most tactical and uncompromising: "And his belle-sœur"—and turned to Fifine:—

"What do you say, m'amie?"

I was just apprehensive that she might flush and look down; but I did her intelligence an injustice.

"Il ne choisit pas qui emprunte," she said, turning away, with a little laugh. "It is either that, I suppose, or the troglodyte caves" (a number of which I had pointed out to her by the road). "Let us go and see the rooms anyhow."

She exclaimed with pleasure when she *did* see them—not on account of their really luxurious comfort and cleanliness, but because of the view from their windows. And truly it was magnificent, looking, as we did, from the back of the house over the way we had come, and the whole extended panorama of the valley.

"It must be the little room for me," said Fifine steadily in a moment.

"As you will," I answered.

"Obviously," she said, "as you will arrive later to bed, and leave it earlier than I."

The landlord was all gratification.

"It is, after all, just a matter of sentiment," said he; "and there is no particular virtue in a corridor. Still, if Mademoiselle prefers it, M. Cabarus, who announced your forthcoming, would doubtless exchange with Mademoiselle."

Fifine turned to me.

"Would you like, Felix?"

"No," I answered shortly. "I don't fancy a poet for a neighbour. He would talk in his sleep. It will do very well as it stands."

I left her to her toilette, while I descended with the landlord. There was a small smoking-room off the salle-à-manger, and we sat there and talked together over a bottle of wine. The man was new to me, and, comparatively, to the place; and the one fault I had to find with him was that he was a modern product, and as such anxious to popularise his position. Still, if that ambition spurred him to no worse than he had already effected, it gave one small ground for complaint. Trim comfort and fresh white sheets were by no means regrettable innovations in les Baux.

"This M. Cabarus," I said presently, "is a great man with you, I suppose?"

He laughed a little—actually. He was not born Provençal, you see; and his reverence for its traditions was a matter of policy.

"He brings custom, Monsieur," he said. "Yes, he is a very important man to me."

"Does he often visit here?"

"I should think, Monsieur, there is no one individual more constant. The hills inspire him, it is there he most seeks his beautiful chimeras; he knows every foot of them; he is out on them now. You are familiar with them yourself, perhaps—the Roman Camp, the Val d'Enfer, the Château above us? You should take Mademoiselle up to the Camp opposite. It is there one obtains one's finest view of the ruins."

"Ah, yes! I will take her, maybe; but it is a long climb for her, and I do not know the way very well. These chimeras, then—what are they?"

Again the landlord shrugged out a little smile:—

"What are they? I do not know; you do not know; he does not know. The Almighty He produces everything out of nothing: M. Cabarus he produces nothing out of everything, and spends all his life hunting for what does not exist. It is the way with poets. Someday, perhaps, he will walk over a precipice in the fog, and find what he seeks at the bottom. It is certain he will never reach it else."

But the virtue lay in the chase, I concluded. That was where Fifine would have discovered it. In the meantime, the landlord being called away, I awaited her descent with impatience. We might at least enjoy a last little exploration together, before the chimera-hunter returned to re-sight in her his mystic quarry. And then?—Well, the virtue was in the chase—and the flattery, no doubt, in being chased by the virtue. It must be gratifying to know oneself the provocation to what most became a man—endeavour. And, as for me, I was simply contemptible in my lack of ambition.

I yawned, and dawdled, and fingered some antiquated literature on a side-table. There was a six months old copy of the London *Spectator* among it, left probably by some newly-travelled curate in process of cutting his wisdom teeth. Bulwark of orthodox respectability, it seemed curiously out of place in this context of harping troubadours, and wild love-courts, and Nature in her most recklessly disordered mood. One associates the *Spectator* somehow with nothing so much as the British Sabbath—on which day it is mostly read—and its decent conventions of silk hat, black coat and decorous Church parade. It never sins against the established or the social rubric; it is the incorruptible champion of common sense; in Mr. Sparkler's phrase, it has "No nonsense about it." Sometimes, even, I have a suspicion that the Creator figures to it as Himself wearing the regulation coat and tall hat on Sundays; whereas my god wears nothing in particular, and is not at all prone to pontifical complacencies in the matter of social law-giving. Les Baux to my eyes seemed a little profaned by this practical-minded interloper, as no doubt the interloper considered itself profaned by les Baux. I felt, for myself, that it was censoring me, in a way that no free-born Briton ought to endure; so I took the liberty of tearing it into quarters, which I dropped into the waste-paper basket. Then I felt as if I were free to do what I liked.

Fifine still delayed to come, and I strolled out to the steps overlooking the street. All above me went heaping up into the blue sky a massive confusion of rock and ruin, so commingled that one had to gaze hard to distinguish shattered wall from shattered scarp. To my left descended the steep road we had mounted—and, rising into view along it, appeared the perspiring form of M. Carabas Cabarus.

He detected me at once, and came on at a quickened pace. His waistcoat was opened, revealing a bosom of grey flannel shirt and braces well bowed over it; in one hand he held his straw hat, in the other a bandana handkerchief, with which he mopped his face incessantly. He made a hurried gesture to me, of recognition, of detention, and fairly ran at last. He was so hoarsely breathed when he reached me, that for a minute he could not speak.

"You have arrived, then, Monsieur," he laboured out at length.

"We have arrived," I responded.

"Ah! *We!*" Confident satisfaction expressed itself in his tone. "Voilà qui est excellent!"

He turned away a moment, fanning his face with his handkerchief, then addressed me again: "Mademoiselle is resting from her fatigue?"

"It would seem so."

"Bon! The occasion is opportune." He poked a fat forefinger at me. "Would you favour me, Monsieur, with a few minutes' private conversation."

Surprised on the moment, I foresaw the next what was coming.

"Why not?" I answered. "Let us go up the hill, Monsieur. Among the ruins we shall not be interrupted."

He came, I thought, reluctantly. Perhaps he had had enough of the rocks for one morning. We climbed the irregular street, and, passing by the church, sought the open hill-side above, where, beside a heap of fallen masonry, we rested.

"Now, Monsieur," said I, "for your communication."

"Ah!" he exclaimed, like one having the advantage of me in his knowledge of a flattering secret. He dwelt on its taste a moment before inviting me to share in it.

"I am waiting, Monsieur," I said.

He propped one foot on a stone, and his right arm over his bent knee, and standing thus, his handkerchief drooping from the pendent fingers, apostrophised space rather than me:—

"There comes a time in the life of the spiritual enthusiast, the most ardent pursuer of the sublime and the ideal, when, in the presence of some ravishing beauty, not perfect, yet halting only on the threshold of perfection, he must pause and say to himself, 'The conditions of this life are fatal to my success. Why for ever drop the substance for the shadow?' This passion for the elusive, the unattainable, has perhaps its closest analogy in human love, by way of which, though we may not reach the stars, we may attain to a nearer view of them. There is the heart, as well as the soul, to consider, and perhaps, aspiring together in unison, they may touch altitudes hitherto inaccessible to the one alone. The chimney-corner knows the worn huntsman, the tired mountaineer comes down from his heights to sit beside his hearth, and, in dreams of wife and child, project his vision into the beyond of his unsatisfied longings. So why should not I? I am weary of the unfulfilled solitudes, and the sense of man returns upon me as I descend. If the grail is not for me, because of that human weakness in my blood, my search for it has at least shewn me the means by which I may yet doubly strive to approach the nearer precincts of its mystery. Though I am not Parsifal, Parsifal may come to call me father."

He flourished his handkerchief, blew his nose, and gazed into the infinite.

"M. Cabarus," I said, "you have my sympathy in all this, and as much of my understanding as I dare exercise. But I am a practical person myself, and I must really ask you to be more explicit."

His pale blue eyes slewed themselves slowly round to regard me.

"Precisely," he said. "It was to be expected."

"Am I right in assuming that what you are proposing, and reconciling, to yourself, is a descent from your heights upon matrimony?"

"With your permission, Monsieur," he said.

"What has my permission to do with it?"

He waved his hand airily.

"Much, Monsieur—or nothing, as it may be. I put the proposition to you formally, as to the one who appears to stand in the position of legal custodian to the object of my devotion."

"You allude to——?"

"Precisely, Monsieur. To your sister."

"Why do you say 'appears to stand'?"

He shrugged his shoulders renunciatory.

"Doubtless," he said, "marked discrepancies will appear between children of the same parents."

"What! You challenge me on a question of family honour?"

"Monsieur, Monsieur," he answered hastily: "I do not challenge you at all. The world is too full of problems for one to quarrel on a point of resemblance."

I laughed.

"What if I were to tell you that Mademoiselle is my step-sister?"

"Then the problem would be no more than one of coincidence."

"What coincidence?"

"That she bears your name."

I laughed again, getting out my pipe to fill it.

"Truly, it seems the long arm, Monsieur," I said. "But, assuming that you are right in approaching me in the matter, your proposition amounts to no more than that you are desirous of marrying my—ward."

"With all my heart, Monsieur."

"And is she to have no voice in the matter?"

"I am not so arrogant," he said, with a sovereign uplifting of himself which belied his words. "It would be false modesty in me, on the other hand, to feign an unconsciousness of the gifts, of the reputation, I could offer her as an equivalent for the priceless gift of herself. Still, for the present, I ask no more than unrestricted permission to make my proposals to that sympathetic paragon of womanhood; and if I assert some confidence as to the result, knowing with what favour she already regards me, I beg you not to attribute it to any conceit of my qualities, but to the sure conviction that Destiny has allotted to us, in conscious affinity, the realisation of the unborn Parsifal."

"Well, that is enough, Monsieur," I answered—though with difficulty. "All I can say is, go in and win."

He looked at me, like a café-chantant monarch, bestowing, by accepting, a favour.

"I have your permission to pay my court?"

"Absolutely. I answer nothing, of course, for the result."

He waved that remark away, as inconsiderable and not worthy of note.

"More," I said. "You shall have every opportunity you can desire to do so; and there is no time like the present. Go back to her now; say what you will, and without fear of interruption from me. I want to explore those hills across the valley—particularly the Roman Camp—and I shall probably be absent most of the day. Tell her so; say that I will take food with me, and that she is not to expect me back till I appear. You two can lunch together, walk together, bill and coo together, if it suits you. So au revoir, Monsieur, and bon chance."

He detained me an instant as I was going from him.

"Do you know the hills?"

"A little; not much."

"Do not stop on them too late, then. They are full of dangers and pitfalls for the ignorant. Moreover, if I am not mistaken, there will be mist to-night. Take warning, Monsieur."

"A word to the wise is enough," said I, and turned and left him.

CHAPTER XIX

I TURNED and left him, I say; and he went a swift course, and I a slow one; yet in the end the race was to the tortoise. I had no least intention of making it one at the time; I was quite sincere in my purpose to obliterate myself temporarily, and leave the situation to resolve itself independently of me. For, in truth, for all its comical side, it was becoming intolerable. We could not for ever keep company on these terms; something definite must be decided one way or the other. I did not, I told myself, care what was the upshot of their meeting; I wanted only to know where I stood, and to adjust our plans accordingly. If the absurd thing actually came to pass—and it seemed to me too preposterous for belief—then a rapid return journey with my charge to Paris must be made, to deliver me from any further responsibility as regarded her actions. In the meantime I had no legal authority whatever over those, either to oppose or encourage. My impulsive undertaking had brought us into a position which I was only to realise at too late an hour to command. If she chose to be wilful, I was helpless.

So much for the impersonal side; and how about the personal? Why, the result did not concern me, save from a purely practical point of view. Have I not said it; and is it not a jealous man's first instinctive defence to lie to himself? He is like a savage with a blow-pipe, who, inhaling a great breath to expel a poisoned dart, draws the barb back into his own throat. And that I had done, and, for all my affected nonchalance, it rankled venomously.

And yet I could not have declared even then what I desired. Flattering relief from unflattering dubiety was perhaps nearest it—since, to speak truth, the idea of this Carabas as a rival was positively insupportable to me. And afterwards, supposing that reassurance granted? I could not be blind to a certain anterior tendency in things—at least as it had affected myself— nor to the inevitable consequences, had not that tendency been violently checked. Did I want it resumed, then, simply in order to deny it? Unlikely, at least; and if not——?

I was in fact an irresolute, uncommendable jackass, if with some lingering instincts yet for rectitude and disinterestedness. And, on the strength of those survivals, I sought weakly to justify myself, saying, If I have been full of inconsistencies in my moods, so has Fifine been in her contributions to them, at one moment seeming to imply what at the next she would seem to refute, whereby I was provoked into an attitude of loverliness, which, though fictitious, was demoralising in itself. If she had only stood resolute to our compact, I should never have thought of her but as the good gossip and reasonable comrade.

And straightway I cursed myself for my meanness. That I should seek to shift the blame for my irresolution to those shoulders upon which no burden but love should ever be laid. She inconsistent—Fifine inconsistent? Yes, by the sweet testimony of her womanliness, without which she would have been as little Fifine as the companion of my choice.

The thought brought an instant pang with it. To touch upon her womanly side was to feel the sharp sense of loss of all which that might imply in possession. And yet how could one talk of losing what was never his? A paradox, for lovers to answer through their dreams. I leave the explanation to them; and there is one.

I would not yet, you see, confess myself of their kin; but I held myself as it were detached, prepared to advance or retreat as circumstances suggested. Our days, Fifine's and mine, had been full of perversities and contradictions, but we had reached a point at last when our sentiments must confess their true inner properties, and declare for either attraction or repulsion. Then we should see.

After parting from the Frenchman, I went down the hill at a long slant, striking again the road, by which Fifine and I had come, at some half-mile below the village. I had no very definite plan in my head, save that of a politic absenteeism; at the same time I had no intention to let my emotions get the better of my enjoyment of a perfect day. My correspondence with Hénault suggested to me the idea of a closer examination of the Neocomian limestone of the opposite range, together with an exploration of the ground about what was known as the Roman Camp, where it was possible I might alight on fragments of metal or pottery of an interesting description. That would do as well as anything to give a savour to exercise; the only question was food. I did not relish a return to les Baux, with the possibilities it entailed of a most inexpedient encounter; yet where else was I to procure what I needed? After a moment's reflection, I set off with a determination to walk back to Paradou. It was but three miles, and, quit of the rücksack, I could easily take it into the itinerary I proposed for myself.

It was past midday when I reached the Grand Café Bellin. The household greeted my prompt return with astonishment, attributing it to some fatality, but were reassured and diverted on my putting it down to the accident of a lost letter, which I fancied I might have dropped in my bedroom. Was there such a letter? Was there in fact the least necessity for my inventing any such excuse for my reappearance? No; *but I wanted to go up and sentimentalise over the empty room.* The feeling, the pretext, had seized me in a moment, and irresistibly.

I went—but not into my individual cubicle—and I stood there a minute, humouring, half pathetically, half jestingly, my own folly. Then I bent, and just touched with my lips the place where her head had lain; and looked round and saw the centipede lying where it had fallen; and smiled, and shook my silly noddle, and went downstairs again. No doubt, the good inn folks regarded me as a lunatic for putting myself to all this trouble and exertion on behalf of a trumpery letter: my sanity would have been much more in evidence to them had I confessed the sentimental truth. So are they built; and so are we not. That was the irony of it: they thought me a fool for doing the very thing that I did to avoid being thought a fool.

"No, it is not there," I said; "but no matter. One may waste time less profitably, I find, than in renewing one's acquaintance with Monsieur and Madame Bellin."

They were pleased at that—blarney is a recognised currency in France—and paid me with a generous measure of the bread and figs, which, with a bottle of wine, was all I took from them for my al fresco meal. Then, my pockets comfortably loaded, I bade adieu to the inn for the second time, and started on my roundabout way back.

It was a lovely quiet noon, but with a brooding stillness in the air which brought Carabas's warning into my mind. Still, at the worst, I had before me long hours of unobscured sunshine, enough and to spare for all the use I wanted to make of it. At the sign-post, turning off from the road, I struck straight across the valley, and was soon among the lower intricacies of the opposite hills. And there I sat down among the rocks, and, for a good beginning, got out my provender.

There was nothing in it inimical to a sober and temperate view of things; indeed the wine was rather a febrifuge than a stimulant; wherefore it was, perhaps, that I soon found myself excusing my late ebullition of feeling to myself on the score that it had been conceded to a purely abstract idea—the thought of a pleasant comradeship ended, or about to end—and that I should never have dreamed of so committing myself to that demonstration unless I had been sure that the tender sentiment it embodied was predestined to unfulfilment. Nobody was compromised by it—least of all myself, in whose independent soul it had figured for the mere indulgence of a whimsical fancy.

All of which was quite sensible and satisfactory. And then I bethought myself, with a gleeful chuckle, that I possessed, in the shape of a flask of right cognac in my breast pocket, a jocund corrective to the dismal stuff I had been swilling; and out it came, to change, in a few moments, the whole complexion of my mind.

So do great conclusions hang upon little means. It was a fly that once made the throne of St. Peter vacant, a gnat that, entering the ear of the arrogant King who thought to storm heaven with his flying chariots, hurled all that vast expedition to the ground. A few drops of Prussic acid will suffice to poison the whole stream, with its thousand tributaries, of the living ichor; a thimbleful of liqueur runs the same course in stimulating fire. Now, as I sat, without yielding my title to a spiritual independence I did certainly begin to consider it from the point of view of its losses rather than its gains. Or, rather, my mood lapsed entirely from the critical to the sentimental, and not my sacrifice, but the constitution of what I sacrificed, came to absorb me.

She had a hundred pretty ways—now I studied her thus impersonally, as one might a figure in a book—yet not one but was a sincere expression of her feelings, and without conscious art. I always loved the quality of her voice; it was slander that could call its leisured music apathy. One thought of her as one did of sleep—the "swooning to death" of Keats, and in as sweet a connexion. Because sleep has more and dearer discoveries than waking, a deeper understanding, mysteries of the subconscious spirit too shy to face the light, but confessing themselves dearly out of the darkness. So she seemed to me, a thing of daylight reserves, enough to obscure but not to kill the promise of the lovelier soul that hid within. And, with such potentialities, how rich a possession might she not prove to the man who won her.

What were she and Carabas doing at that moment? I got up suddenly on the thought, and began to move off among the rocks, turning my face instinctively homewards. But as suddenly I swerved to the left, with a little testy laugh, and addressed myself resolutely to my business of exploration.

For some time I went at random, fairly involving myself in the huddle of low hills and slades into which the mountains here ran down, suggesting, as it were, the subsiding waters of a cataract. They were pretty intricately confused, and tessellated everywhere with patches of bush and waste ground, with occasionally a cultivated field of olive or almond set amidst. My purpose being on the whole to kill time, I took little thought as to my bearings, only noting in a general way the trend of the hills, and the position of that particular one which I intended presently to climb. It remained a dead calm, sultry, and with little incitement in it to exertion; but the haze was palpably thickening; and presently I came to realise that, did I wish to attain the Roman Camp, the sooner I set about making for it the better.

I was by then well to the south-west, in a wild hill-tossed country, of the particular height which I understood to be my goal, and since I was virtually lost it seemed that my plain course was to take as much as possible a bee-line for it—which was what any Roman himself would have done. Wherefore I set off—only to find that what meant a bee-line for a bee might mean a scarce passable switchback for a human being. Plunging through thickets; ploughing along clayey bottoms; struggling over boulder-strewn slopes, only to discover that they were isolated mounds I might have skirted; threading my way through thronged groves of olive and mulberry, to lose my direction and be aggravating minutes in refinding it; most often painfully forcing a passage through massed bushes of juniper or tamarisk, and never once crossing a friendly track or lane that would have helped me over a difficulty, slowly I toiled on towards release and reassurance. And when at last, after hours of labour as it seemed, I *did* break into the open, and saw what I conceived to be the hill of the camp towering mistily in its full height before me, I threw myself with a groan down on the rocks, and set to cursing all bee-lines literally up hill and down dale.

So I had not attained my goal yet; I was not in the way to attain goals, it seemed, however fair and desirable. Fate, on the whole, was treating me pretty scurvily. And I had done nothing, absolutely nothing, to merit the curse of Tantalus—or to merit that form of it, since I had not coveted the grapes for myself, which was implied in the sight of another man's enjoyment. Soft, bloomy, delicious things! Damn the fellow, with his globular paunch and thick relishing lips! How women could let their beauty be so profaned! I had often dwelt on her profile seen against a background of silvery light or purple drapery, and loved its infinite childishness—the smooth rounded cheek, the short rather insolent nose, the upper lip projecting but the tiniest fraction of an inch over the lower, an endearing feature. And she could value them all at no better than material for that fulsome traffic!

I jumped up, and began to ascend the hill. The sun, during the half hour I had lain resting and brooding, was already sloping deep into the west, and there was a chill heaviness in the air which portended evil. I was conscious of it, even while the fire in my brain drove me on, reckless of consequences. What did it matter, even though I had to spend the night on the mountains? I had only myself to consider; there was no one else affected by my obstinacy. I had said I would explore the Roman Camp, and I meant to do it. I would show that my will could be resolute, even though to a foolish end. I meant to paint a picture presently that should give all my slanderers the lie; and then there would be a finish to this talk about my idle futility, and the charge that had been brought should be regretted, and bitterly regretted, and in vain.

So the callow calf-lover solaces his injured heart with dreams of stern qualities in himself realised too late by the unappreciative, of silent rebuke, and noble retort in the shape of self-sacrificing heroisms by fire and water, ending possibly in a quiet grave much bedewed by the tears of aching, hopeless self-reproach. I did not perhaps project my imagination to those extremes; but certainly I indulged it to the extent of shaming my sober years, so that in a minute, overtaken by the humour of the thing, I burst into a laugh and was myself again.

"I am going to hunt for broken pottery," I said aloud—"nothing more nor less; and if in the process I get benighted on the mountain, well, it will be my own fault, and there's an end of it."

Up, then, I toiled, and the fog crept about me, drifting sluggishly down from the Camargue. It was thin as yet, and not more than enough to give an air of indefiniteness to the rocks above. Presently I came to a great bramble-grown bluff, twenty feet in height, up which I had the greatest difficulty in finding a way; but I achieved it at last, and, topping the ridge, found myself on the main plateau of the hill, an apparently limitless waste of dense bush.

Here, though I did not realise it, was the actual site of the Roman Camp, whence ordinarily a magnificent view of the valley and of the Château-crowned heights opposite was obtainable. Now I stood isolated in a little world of mist-encompassed green, littered all over with prone boulders, of differing, but mostly huge, dimensions.

Ploughing through the bush, I worked my way slowly on. It was a tedious process, but I could not venture to hurry it, as twilight was momentarily deepening the obscurity like mud disturbed on a river bottom, and any rash step on my part risked a wrench and sprain in one of the innumerable hidden fissures with which the whole surface of the under-rock was sewn. Many times, in spite of my caution, I slipped and half-lost my footing; many times trod suddenly on air, when I had thought firm ground was beneath me. And then, with a shock, I had started back, and was standing gaping. Right before me dropped a precipice, going down into unknown depths, and another step would have carried me clean over it.

It was only then that a sense of my rather impossible position began to penetrate me. But I was not going to give up without a struggle. Evidently I was on the wrong tack, and must bear away in a different direction. Gingerly I proceeded—only to be brought up in a few minutes on a like experience. Then I stood still and reflected. I had hopelessly lost my bearings; I did not know on what part of the hill I stood at that moment, and there was no distinguishing feature to guide me—only a tumbled confusion of rock and juniper heaving itself on all sides into swift obliteration. At the best, I knew, the descent on the north side was a long and a difficult one; under these circumstances, even if I could find and trace its course, it must prove hazardous beyond the worth of risking. I could see nothing for it but to camp beside some rock, and there await, as patiently as I might, the shifting of the mist, with or before the return of daylight.

No great hardship, after all, for a toughened vagabond, and no very new experience. I had slept on a hillside before now; I had run into a ditch, bicycling in the dark, and had slumbered where I had fallen from pure exhaustion. Here, save for the slight chill of the crawling vapour, all was cosy and secure—no wind, plentiful cover, and litter for one's bedding ad infinitum. It was imperative only that I should bestow myself in comfort and safety while yet I could distinguish between air and matter. Very warily, turning from my latest peril, I trod a cautious path to where a massive boulder heaved itself out of the green, and, dropping under its friendly shelter, prepared to abide my destiny.

I had tried a shout or two first; but that, I knew, was a pretty forlorn hope. What other fool but myself would likely be abroad on the hills on such a night as this? Then, very surely as I sat, the gloom came in about me, until to have dared a step in that blinding investment would have been madness.

So there was nothing for it at last but to face the facts, and make the best I could of them. If I was conscious of any qualm on Fifine's account, I quickly dismissed it as, if not unreasonable, immaterial. I was not the less in the hands of Fate because she knew nothing of my predicament; while, at the best or worst, my welfare had ceased to be a leading consideration with her. Carabas, no doubt, would find means to assuage her anxiety, if any such she felt on my behalf.

It was odd sitting there at freedom on the open hill, and yet feeling oneself as securely caged as though fettered to a stone shaft, like Bonivard, in a subterranean dungeon. After a time I got out the handful of figs remaining to me, with the flask, still two-thirds full, of brandy; and, having discussed that simple meal at leisure, lit my pipe, and lay smoking and sipping with an ample serenity. It was perfectly still; even the mist, born of the sun-baked levels, seemed to have a quality of warm steam in it, and flattered rather than discomforted. Gradually, after I know not how long an interval, drowsiness overcame me, and, sinking comfortably into my cosy eyrie, I slept.

* * * * * * *

Something or somebody was calling to me, and by name. My subauditory senses had been conscious of the fact long, it seemed, before any association of it with reality occurred to startle them. But now, and more acutely, the sound penetrated, cutting through the web of sleep; and the next moment I had leapt wide awake, and was sitting up listening.

"Dane, Dane, Dane! Holà, Monsieur! Holà, Monsieur Dane! Do you hear? Answer, then! Dane, Dane, Dane!"

"Here!" I shouted, scrambling to my feet, and facing in the direction of the voice. The mist had thinned somewhat, and was penetrated, moreover, with a white diffused light, in the shine of which all immediate details of the surrounding plateau were faintly visible. I thought at first that day had dawned upon me as I lay, but in a moment recognised the silvery radiance for that of the full moon, which appeared to hang in the heavens right above the banks of vapour. And not fifty yards away from me stood a solitary figure, ghostly and motionless on a rock, and looking like a half-gilded statue in the glow from a lantern it carried in its hand.

For an instant my drugged wits failed to respond to the vision; then, with a laugh, I began to stumble forward—and stopped.

"Hullo!" I shouted. "Shall I come to you? Is it safe?"

Though I repeated the cry, never a syllable answered me. It seemed strange. Surely, the hallooing, whose echoes still rang in my brain, could have come from no direction but this. I dwelt puzzled a moment; then, deciding to take silence for assent, continued to advance. I went stupidly, still fuddled in my mind, lifting and putting down my feet mechanically, and hardly looking where I trod. The figure, never moving or uttering sound, began to take to me near shape and substance. I was already within speaking distance of it, when it appeared to move, and a cry came from its lungs, sudden and furious:—

"Halt!"

I had wit, or instinct enough to stop on the instant—and lucky for me I had. That moment returns me now in a black shock of memory. As I stood, vaguely wondering, the figure came down from its stone; approached me; halted abruptly within six yards of where I stood—and it was Carabas. In the sick shine of the lantern he carried his face looked livid and contorted. He stood a moment; then leaned down the lantern, and swung it to and fro.

"Voilà ce que c'est!" he said, in a thick scornful voice. "Another step, and you would have been in."

I stood like a half-sobered drunkard, staring down. There, in the very heart of the bush, gaped between us a damnable black pit, man-hewn, obviously the shaft or ventilator to some quarry, and sunk to God knew what terrific depths. There was no fence about it; even by day one might have stumbled into it without any great accusation of carelessness.

"Did I not warn you of the perils of the hills?" said the Frenchman, in the same thick, sneering tones. "A word to the wise, grand Dieu!"

At the sound of him my wits returned to me, and in a clap of fury.

"Why, in the devil's name," I bawled across the gulf, "didn't you direct me sooner? You saw I was coming straight for it."

"I thought of course, you knew."

"You thought?—My God!" The truth sprung upon me in an instant. "You *meant* me to go down—on my own initiative, so as to quit your lying conscience; only you turned craven at the last. Own up, you infernal dog!"

His eyes looked across at me, ghastly; but, to my surprise, skirting the edge of the opening, he came round and dared me face to face.

"Ananias!" he said. "What right was mine to cross God's judgment on a liar?"

I regarded him for a little without answering, searching in my mind for some explanation of this extraordinary behaviour, and finding none. I was by now quite cool and self-possessed, and conscious of a full command of the situation.

"If that is to imply," I said, "that you have sacrificed your conscience to your humanity, it is to imply no motive for it that I can understand. Why did you want to kill me?"

"I did not want to kill you."

"But you saw me walking to my death—fortuitously, perhaps—and lifted no finger, until the last moment, to interfere. What would that have been, at the worst, but moral murder?"

"No matter. It did not happen."

"Clearly through the interposition of Providence, working automatically on a coward's fears. But, supposing it to work as automatically on his intended victim's resentment, and that a sacrifice of some sort was demanded? I have twenty times your strength and will, and a thousand times your provocation. What is to prevent me from sending you where you proposed sending me, and leaving it to be inferred, as no doubt you had designed it should be inferred about me, that you had blundered to your doom in the fog?"

Involuntarily he had started back at my words. The lantern clattered in his hand. If he could be, like Falstaff, a lion on compulsion, it was plain also that he could be a coward on instinct.

"I saved your life!" he cried hoarsely. I walked towards him. As I approached, he put out his arms, lantern and all, as if to ward me off. "Monsieur, Monsieur; let us be reasonable; let us talk together. Before God, I came to risk the night perils of these hills in order to find, if possible, and rescue you. I knew you were coming here; and I knew, if you did not, of these quarry openings. Was I not calling you, here, there, everywhere—and did that look like premeditation? And when at last you answered and appeared, it was mere accident which interposed that temptation between us. And I resisted it, Monsieur—I resisted it."

I laughed shortly, halting before him.

"M. Cabarus," I said, "you are not qualified, it is obvious, for the heroic part you set yourself. But rest content: I am not going to kill you. After all, you did, as you assert, save my life in a way; though why you should ever have wanted it ended beats me."

He sat down on a stone, quite overcome, and, putting the lantern beside him, buried his face in his hands.

"But for you she might listen to me," he half sobbed, from that covert.

I heard, astonished.

"She? Who?" I demanded.

"O, Monsieur!" he said, "why equivocate? She who you informed me was your sister, or your step-sister, and who is in fact nothing of the kind."

Answer of any sort for the moment failed me. Then, "She told you that?" I asked quietly.

"She told me."

"What provoked her to it?"

"I—I!" He uplifted both his face and hands despairingly, apostrophising the moonlit heavens; then dropped them in dejection. "I taunted her with you, and she answered in a fury. For myself, I had never but half believed in that story; and, in the bitterness of my rejected vanity, I goaded her to the admission—alas, to what result!"

I stood canvassing the forlorn creature, even with some contemptuous pity in my heart.

"Rejected?" I said. "Then I am to understand you have tried and failed?"

"Failed," he repeated, in a voice of grief.

"Now, listen to me, M. Cabarus," I said. "It is, I acknowledge, no question of a sister or a step-sister; but it *is* a question of an honourable trust, which I may not specify, but which to this moment I have maintained. When I bid you this morning to the test, I bid you, as one totally disinterested for himself, to a venture which would have honoured any man in its achievement. You understand me? It was to achieve an unsullied name. But I never professed the least authority over any one's tastes or predilections. That anyone was free to do as she liked, to accept or reject as she liked. If you chose to presume absurdly, and arrogantly I must say, on a brief acquaintance, that was your business. I should not have stood in her way: I did not stand in yours."

"Ah!" He looked up at me, with a strange woeful expression: "But unconsciously, Monsieur—unconsciously, we will say."

He rose, with a profound sigh, and lifted the lantern.

"Judge you, Monsieur," he said, "if, for all my vanity, my soul is small. This morning she spoke to me—words of bitter scorn and upbraiding, difficult to forget. She was angry to see me appear without you; she received my proposals with amazement, heaping insults on my head. Sweet poisonous flowers they were, dropping from those incomparable lips. Yet, mark; when anxiety rose and grew over your failure to return, it was to me she came to appeal, to my wounded soul she addressed her suit. I was responsible, she said, for your absence, for letting you go to wander among the darkening hills alone. And when they whispered of mist and pitfalls, her fears grew wildly clamorous, and she entreated me, yes me, to imperil my own safety, to issue forth and seek for you among the clouds, careless of what befell me so not a hair of your head should be injured. And I came, Monsieur; unable at the last to witness unconcerned the agony of mind of her who had so abused me, I counselled my own heart to nobility, and came to seek you."

He turned from me. "Follow," he said; "and I will lead you down into safety. So I requite my defamer. Only let me entreat you, Monsieur, to humour in me by the way a silence which indeed my heart is too full to relieve with words."

How could I answer but by acquiescing. It was a strange descent, that from my rocky prison—in the white ghast light, following the bright spark of the swinging lantern, while vast shapes and shadows seemed to bend and look at us as we passed. It needed a sure knowledge to accomplish it without mishap; but at last it was done, and we stood at the head of the valley, where the road branched upwards to La Reine Jeanne. A clock struck eleven as we paused; I turned and held out my hand to my rescuer.

"I am sorry," I said. I felt that it did not become me to utter more.

But he could not bring himself to accept the proffered advance.

"Your way is now clear to you, Monsieur," he answered frigidly, backing a little from me. "You will need my services no longer."

"But what are you going to do with yourself?"

He made a comprehensive gesture, expressive of the saddest renunciation.

"What does it matter? Who cares? It is only another illusion vanished——"

And he turned and left me, drooping through the mist, and bent on what lamentable vigil only the spirit of desolation might know.

Well, I at least could be held in no sense responsible for the event. As I rapidly mounted the slope to the inn, I thought I could perceive two forms standing on the steps overlooking the street. I shouted a word of cheery reassurance, which was as jocundly answered; but, when I reached the place, only the relieved young landlord stood there to greet me. He was, of course, full of concern, enquiry, eager congratulation. As to Carabas, he assuaged my apprehensions with an easy optimism. It was not the first time he would have elected to spend the night abroad. When the inspired fit was on him, there was no holding him within conventional bounds; and doubtless the events of the evening had tended to set alight in him the ever-smouldering spark of genius. I need not disturb myself about him. As to any other possible provocation, if he knew or suspected such, he was discreetly silent on the subject; and I, for my part, felt curiously shy of any reference to Mademoiselle, or to the part her anxiety had played in the questions of my non-appearance and late return. I had a glad recuperative "nightcap" with the good fellow; then, loth to keep him longer from his delayed repose, took my candle in hand, and mounted softly to my bedroom.

Once shut in there, my boots left outside, I tiptoed softly, fearful over the least noise I made, hardly daring to breathe. Not a sound came from the next room; not a word, not a murmur. She was asleep, then; and that was well. And yet she was not asleep, and I knew it. Only a few minutes before she had been out there on the steps, waiting and listening in an agony of mind. But she was reassured now; she could rest. It would be wise to leave all explanation to the morrow. And yet that resolve had hardly been made when I knew that I was powerless to keep it. The thought of the long hours to pass in that dead-locked silence between us was already insupportable. I could not suffer it, and hope for forgetfulness. I must speak, if only a word—to say good-night. And yet, God help us, I must not speak. I fought against the longing while fight was possible to me; I set my teeth and endured and resisted. But the moment came when I could endure no longer.

"Fifine," I said softly.

There was no answer; and I waited a minute, and spoke again.

"Fifine; it is all right; I have come back. I am so sorry, Fifine."

Something answered me then—a little sound, but enough to send a flood of wild emotion surging through my veins. I rose, I went to the door.

"Fifine," I whispered; "shall I come in?"

No response; and I turned the handle noiselessly and stole in. She was lying fully dressed upon her bed, her face turned from me, her whole body shaken with suppressed sobbing.

I stood remorsefully looking down for a moment; then—I could not help it. I went and knelt by her, and slid my arm under her neck, and took the soft troubled body to myself.

"Fifine!" I whispered. "It is no good our trying to resist it, is it? It has to be. It is no good, is it, Fifine?"

And she whispered back, with a long quivering sigh, "No——" and her arms caught and held me convulsively.

CHAPTER XX

IT had all been such dear egregious folly, that contest of tempers and jealousies and wilful self-misrepresentations. We used to laugh about it together in those after days of perfect concord and understanding. It had been the ferment, we supposed, necessary to the rich wine of love we had come to drink so deeply. All restfullest things are born of unrest: the brawling stream ends in the quiet lake; there is no sky-blue like that that flowers out of storm; life itself is wrung from anguish into infant sleep; through strife and tumult we draw to death, the profoundest peace of all. So now, in proportion with the former riot in our souls was the lovely tranquillity that succeeded it. There was no question of conscience to disturb us; for conscience pricks through sense of guilt, and we knew of no evil in ourselves, but rather an excess of charity and lovingkindness towards all men and things. For the first time in our lives, perhaps, we were in near concord with the Christian concept of Grace. A greater force than convention had pronounced upon us; not we upon ourselves, or either on the other. We had but acquiesced in what was decreed, guiltless, both, of soliciting the issue. All that was over; the storm had been and it had passed, breaking into this heaven-born flower of serenity. Was that God's punishment on us or God's commendation? I only know that no thing on all the earth would we have harmed; that our hearts brimmed over with a universal tenderness; that we would have gone to martyrdom for the faith of infinite love that possessed us. It is difficult to think that sin which bears such divine fruit.

But, let that pass, I entreat you. Forget the flaw in our idyll, if such exists for you; take its rhapsodies as authorised—really a minor point—and grant it the full-blown licence accorded to conventionalised bonds. Then I shall be safe to expatiate intimately, if I wish to, on a tenderest subject.

But on the whole, I think, I prefer to treat that subject abstractly. I am not so hardened in gracelessness as to wish to steal their liberties from the sanctioned ministers of Grace; and these matters seem to me, in my sinfulness, rather too holy for discussion. Wherefore, if you please, we will be content with my saying that Fifine made me a sweet friend, stately shy before others, keeping me rosily at a distance in public, but ready with all amends when we walked and talked alone.

Dear God, what a girl—what a woman! And how I loved her—how I loved! I had never known her before, I thought: I had never known myself—of what I was emotionally capable. Then in those days I learnt the unconfessed secrets of my own soul—what it would have meant to me had

I lost her. The knowledge gained, I could hardly bear her out of my sight: it was to part with my better self; to wander guilty and bewildered. Only when she rejoined me came reassurance with the contact. She had accepted no evil: I had meant none. She was good, good—in all that goodness means of essential purity. I cannot too much insist on it. It was the self-sacrifice of utter devotion to a pure ideal. Here is what she once said to me—I will reveal so far—her grave eyes loving into mine:—

"Felix, for my sake now you will strive again—will you not?"

"How strive, Fifinette?"

"To achieve; to be your greatest; to realise the very conscious best that is in you."

"Why not? You have given me new heart."

"It is so dear to hear you say so. It was for that"—she hesitated; then putting her two hands on my arm, looked up earnestly in my face: "it was for that, Felix, I gave myself to you—soul and body, my own love; that you might—perhaps—justify the sacrifice to me."

"Was it a sacrifice, Fifine?"

"You should know. But I should never regret it, never for one instant, if it came to be so dearly requited. I want you"—she laid her face down on her hands, where they rested—"so much—so much I want you to see it in that light. I could not bear to have you think that—that I yielded, to no higher emotion than——"

"You can leave it unsaid, Fifine. I am going to do great things, and you shall have the credit for them all."

She thanked me with an affectionate look. Was she not pure? Could orthodoxy have shewn a better case for love? But let the matter rest there. If stones are to be cast, here am I, blithe to be made their target. I am jealous for her good fame; not a copper farthing for my own.

But, while I insist on that specific truth, I make generally no pretence of drawing the portrait of any Fifine but the one commonly known to me. I would not have her pictured by any means as a self-renunciatory young penitent, or as piously shedding the very qualities and characteristics which made her the desirable thing she was. We contended as much as ever, if now with a novel spirit of delight in the understanding which sweetened direfullest controversy; she showed no sudden increase of diffidence in her attitude towards my work or my opinions, but stated her own views as confidently and dispassionately as she had always done; the bright intelligence, which could seize so readily on the essential in any subject or object, and whose manifestations, owing to our estrangement, had been suffering of late some temporary eclipse, reappeared as active and as fearless as ever. And joyfully I welcomed this rush of sunshine from the withdrawn cloud. It was gay to see her, in the sweet assurance of her power over me, throw off the shackles which had been cramping her, and resume in great gladness the lovable enigma of herself—girlish, ingenuous; yet with that odd suggestion of worldly knowingness and knowledge which was always such a stimulating puzzle to me. If there survived a shadow of a shadow between us, it was this: she had a secret from me; and I had a secret from her—that I knew she had one. Yet mine was in a sense a justification to me of my love; and so the shadow to me was but as a shadow thrown by sunlight. I thought I knew what hers was—the true explanation of that silence, that withholding; and now I know indeed. She was afraid even yet to speak the truth; she dreaded unspeakably the chilling effect it might possibly have on me and my belief in her. Poor child—if she had only understood!

And so, to that extent we lived a lie to one another; yet it was a falsehood of infinite pathos and tenderness. In all else but that we were wholly one and inseparable, in trust, in truth, in perfect confidence.

We had it all out, of course, on the subject of those erst-peevish perversities and misunderstandings. There is no joy like a converted jealousy; quarrels become relishes when they can be discussed impartially. I told Fifine of my savage decision, on the hill that fateful night, to achieve the world-conquering work which was to refute and overwhelm her with a sense of what she had thrown away. She laughed; but, like the dear love she was, immediately stroked me down, in remorse for the pain her apparent insensibility might be giving me.

"Gossip," she said—for we had resumed that pretty address as being singularly appropriate to our state—"you will come to do for love of me, will you not, what you designed to do for my punishment. My heart will sing then for its very shame."

And indeed it sang, and sang me on to inspiration. I did my utmost, in those golden days, to vindicate her sacrifice to her through the persistent endeavour that her soul so prized. I schemed, and designed, and made innumerable colour notes, while she glowed beside, my patient, enthusiastic ministrant. Yes, and my prompter too, for she was no despicable critic either as to ends or means. We would make a compromise of our theories, our principles, with even perhaps a slight leaning of the balance towards the traditional; and in the result—well, those were but plans, elevations, as it were. The whole, into which the infinite parts were compacted, exists for any one to see who likes.[1] It is the only work of mine in which heart and soul and brain made a common cause of it to achieve perfection. It has not achieved it, of course, for Fifine was not perfection. But what approach to it it makes was her doing and hers alone. There is sunshine in it, which they call sunshine. I wonder sometimes if one from the idle multitudes who pass it by ever chances to penetrate the secret of the truth from which it was drawn.

Once we climbed up to the hill-top on which I had been fog-bound, and found the pit into which my stumbling steps had nearly precipitated me. It was a very death-trap, even as regarded by day, sawn clean and square into the bowels of the rock. Ruthless the greed which could thus assert itself, callous of human safety. They had been quarrying everywhere since my former visit, cutting wholesale into the majesty of the hills. But now, though late, the government, we heard, was interfering, with a view to stopping the brutal devastation. Might its powers, we prayed, prove despotic in a free land! We looked over into the black gulf, and could see no bottom. Fifine drew away from it, sick and shuddering; and suddenly she was clinging to me. Yet I had been careful to make light of my escape; and Carabas I had altogether spared in my half-jocose reference to it.

"Sit me down," my girl whispered: "I shall be all right in a minute."

We rested on a great stone, and for a time she could only breathe in silence.

"O, Felix!" she panted presently—"O, Felix!"

"My gossip—this is not to be your reasonable self. Here I am, you see."

"I should have been a murderess."

"Now, Fifine?"

"I should, I should. It was my perversity drove you up there."

"Now that it was not. It was Cabarus if it was anybody. You could not know he wanted me to make that opportunity for him."

It was a tonic reference. She sat up, her bosom still tumultuous, but with a scornful frown lined between her eyebrows.

"Opportunity!" she ejaculated—"that imbecile!"

I laughed—the base comfortable chuckle of the successful suitor.

"For loving you?" I said—"or what?"

"How dared he—the presumption! And when we had known him so short a time!"

"Really, gossip," I said, "I think he had some excuse."

"How?"

"You seemed to like him—I want to tread delicately."

"I liked his imagination—when I could dissociate it from his ridiculous vanity."

"Fifine; tell me honestly. And that was all? You never even considered him in the light of a—of a possible husband?"

"O, don't be horrid!"

"Women will, you know, take these incredible fancies."

"Felix, I could understand myself falling in love with a gorilla——"

"Thank you."

"But not with a poet. That he could picture himself, think of himself, as *your* successful rival! I almost laughed, although I was so angry. To see him return alone—and for that purpose!"

"You did not spare him, I fancy."

"Indeed I did not. Why should I? I was enraged; and after all I had been hoping from our reconciliation."

"Well, I am sorry for him."

"It is generous, and like you. For myself, I think he deserved the worst he got."

"Don't forget he saved my life."

"Nonsense. He did nothing of the sort."

"I mean he rescued me from a very ticklish position, and at considerable sacrifice to himself."

"What sacrifice? He knew the hills; he could have walked them blindfold, he said."

"But to agree to come, after all that had happened—his disappointment, his—his merciless drubbing."

"Well, he owed me some compensation for having insulted me so."

"I must sympathise with him, gossip, nevertheless. Don't I realise what it would mean to lose you."

She cooed to me over that, like the lovingest of doves. What vanity it is to think to chop logic with a woman. She can see no reason in the world, I think, why, if the lusty adored of her heart be hungry, she should not snatch food out of the hands of a starving beggar to feed him.

"Well," I said, "I am glad for his sake he thought fit to take himself off; and certainly I am glad for ours. A serpent in one's Paradise is disturbing; but a wet-blanket is fifty times worse. I would rather chance a burglar than a chill any day—or night."

And indeed poor Carabas had disappeared the morning after our parting on the road, and we had seen no more of him. Whatever conclusions he had formed as to facts, he had assumed from them, I opined, no hope for himself, and had withdrawn timely from the unendurable spectacle of his own discomfiture as reflected in another's triumph.

"What made you tell him we were not related?" I asked.

"Did he say so to you?" demanded Fifine contemptuously. "That only shows how unworthy he was to be entrusted with a woman's confidence. He made me so angry with his innuendoes about our relationship that I simply had to tell him the truth, to vindicate your right to regard me just as you liked; only, I said, your liking happened to be that of an honourable man towards a trust—a thing which he couldn't understand. And, to prove it, he went and told you, the mean toad."

"Never mind. And the less said about my devotion to a trust the better, perhaps."

"Aren't you devoted to me, Felix? That is all I care about."

"You would believe it, Fifinette, if you had seen me drivelling over your pillow at Paradou."

And thereupon—but I am not writing a catalogue of baits for kisses—spoon-baits would be the better term. Every lover is a law unto himself in that respect.

We were three weeks in all at les Baux—a rosary of enchanted days. I should like to linger over that halcyon time, my life's one long unbroken spell of happiness, were it not for what I must regard it through—years like a dingy window looking out on a jewelled morning landscape. The crown of sorrow—you remember Tennyson's words? Yet in a way, I think, that was rather a maudlin complaint of the poet's. Are not the "happier things" always behind us—dropped behind, and following us, perhaps, at their leisure? Maybe when we stop some day, our journey done, they will overtake us. Would not that be beautiful, my Fifine—to turn, and find you, with your dream and your glory? And in the meantime I am not going to mope and snivel because a certain incomparable loveliness in my past cannot be repeated. Perfection never can.

Had she, through all these shining days, a least suspicion that I guessed anything? She must have wondered surely how it was I could inwardly face the prospect of our return to Paris, with the inevitable moral it implied of separation, or of utter catastrophe, and yet could act now as on the apparent assumption that our union was eternal. She had put off conclusions for a time by begging me, by my content in her, to cut the very name of the Capital from our catalogue of references; to live as if it had never existed or was to exist for either of us; not to allow one harsh extraneous thought to enter through the gates of our golden Paradise. Yet she could not have supposed my intelligence hoodwinked by that pretty subterfuge into overlooking a consequence which must have seemed inevitable to me, and which only her own confession was in the way to nullify. But what she guessed or reasoned I never knew; only, poor love, it would have saved her so much self-torment could she have made up her mind to throw herself upon the ordeal, and, in that time of passion, betray the truth.

And in the meanwhile what was my own attitude towards the mystery? Why, emancipated as I was, simply one of love-in-idleness, I think. Fifine was Fifine to me, and that was all sufficient. If I thought lazily beyond that bare fact, tasting even a piquancy in speculation, it was to present myself with the portrait of a young lady of very feminine but independent views, having a knowledge, or at least a cognizance of the Bohemian side of Paris, entertaining seedy violoncellists, and capable of coming to definite conclusions with herself on a variety of subjects, from art and dress to conduct. Comely too, and yet unspoilt, be it said; and, if a worldling, one with the highest capacity for self-sacrifice to an ideal devotion. A fine spirit, but warm and sweet and very human—such was the picture.

Where Marion came in? Ah! that was a puzzle indeed. By no conceivable process of symphysis could I make her and Fifine combine; though the knowledge that the latter was what she was, or rather was not what she professed to be, explained to me some things in my step-sister's attitude towards her and me hitherto inexplicable. It explained nothing else, however; it left me stranded exactly where Miss Clarice Brooking's ingenuous revelation had deposited me outside the Hôtel du Nord Pinus.

That same Clarice, I confess, was another of my killing baits. Fifine had asked my pardon very humbly for her inexcusable behaviour to my friends. It had been due to extreme jealousy, she very frankly admitted—to a wound even now not quite healed, and whose pain had driven her to reprisals. It was horribly silly, no doubt; but then—my own countrywoman, and the attractions of that delicate pink and white. She had envied her her complexion; she had envied her—this with a hot averted look—her earlier knowledge of me. Was I quite, entirely, absolutely sure—

Yes, I was quite sure, my Fifinette; and quite sure of always drawing you on the subject, and of extracting my ample rewards therefrom. Machiavellian is passion in these matters.

So in the lovely valley the lovely idyll spent itself, until of its very perfection came the sense of inevitable rounding off and closure. Nothing disturbing came near us all the time; but we wandered free spirits of that haunted glen, absorbing into our glowing blood the very atmosphere of its enchantment. The little pavilion of the incomparable Queen Jeanne, with its pretty sculptures and oddly jointed ceiling, snugging into the corner of a grassy paddock in the valley, was a favourite resting-place of ours. But in what antiquities of rock and gorge and crumbled human dwelling did we not steep ourselves, from the eyries of the prehistoric cave-dwellers and the worn stone sarcophagi of the early Christians, to the toppling renaissance fronts and doorways that mingled on the hillside with the wild architecture of the first Seigneurs. All immense, all significant, all spectral despite its ponderous actuality; teeming with the infinite dust and debris of bygone story; ruins like rocks and rocks like ruins, one indistinguishable confusion and torrent of stone. Long ago from the floor of the little church they had unearthed the body of some beautiful unknown châtelaine. She had golden hair, like the maid of Pornic, that stretched down on either side to her feet. It was all that survived from the desecration, and it was deposited in Mistral's museum at Arles. Fifine had seen it there; and, of course, Carabas. He had promised her a poem on the subject when they should stand together over the pilfered grave. And now was the grave of his own heart robbed of its golden vision. Poor troubadour. It gave me a moment's melancholy to hear of his intention. Fifine laughed, relating it. Such is the difference between men and women; yet women are infinitely the pitifuller. The elemental riddle of them, of their inconsistencies with themselves, has never seemed to me so well epitomised as in the fable of the Amazonian Queen Thalestris, man-conqueror and man-scorner, travelling alone to give herself to Alexander, that she might become by him the mother of a boy-hero.

One day Fifine, putting a hand on my arm and looking up into my face, spoke to me wistfully of a thought that had come into her mind.

"Felix, we have been very, very happy here, have we not?"

"I answer for myself, m'amie. And how about you?"

"I had never thought there could be such joy anywhere. It has been almost too perfect for believing."

"You mean something. What is it?"

"Only that—don't be vexed with me—I think I should like to go, before the edge of the tiniest little cloud comes to peep at us over the horizon."

"What cloud are you looking for? I see no sign of one."

"No more do I. That is just it. But my heart seems so full: it cannot hold more without brimming over. And I want to keep this memory, just as it is—so full, so complete; a little immaculate Paradise, and all our own."

"It is Paradise, as you say, Fifine. If we leave it we shall have to put on aprons perhaps. It is not time yet to talk of clouds—especially since the serpent departed."

"I don't care what the world says. I am not ashamed. But I might be, if the cloud appeared. Won't you, gossip dear—just to spoil me? And there is another reason. Somebody I know will be getting anxious about me. Shall I tell you who it is?"

Why did I not say yes, and so lay for ever that last lingering shadow between us? She was prepared, I knew, in that emotional moment to throw herself upon my love and confess the truth in a breath. But like a fool I would not let her. I was jealous that she could consider any claims above mine.

"No, I don't want to know," I said. "If we must go we must; but we will carry with us, if you please, as much of our Paradise as is expressed in a complete isolation from all persons and things unconnected with it. You know we haven't visited your birthplace yet—which was really our first pretext for this adventuring. You aren't proposing to go straight home to Paris, anyhow, I hope?"

"O, no!" She gave a little sigh, of part sadness, part relief perhaps, over that baulked impulse. "Only if we might begin journeying that way. And I should love to visit Orange."

"Very well; we will turn our backs on the Cherubim and the flaming sword, and march out into the wilderness. *Adieu paniers! vendanges sont faites!*"

"No!" cried Fifine, in a full voice—"then I will not go!"

"Wilful?" said I. "Then that convinces me you were right; for is not this little, little difference between us the first faint warning of a cloud?"

It was with hearts full of emotion that we left the next morning the long valley of our delight, with its golden sunshine, its quiet hospitality, its unforgettable memories. Shall I ever go there again? Maybe when someday my lonely journey ends, and I sit waiting my overtaking by the "happier things" I have left behind. Then, perhaps, but not before. And, in the meantime, on what butterfly wings hovers my beautiful faithful Psyche among those ruined "Courts of Love"?

CHAPTER XXI

I AM not going to relate in detail the processes of our homeward journeying. One must necessarily in leaving Paradise put on the common vesture of mortality; and, though the deathless glamour of past days remained to us for all eternity, a sense of the finite conditions of life, of its partings and uncertainties, returned to possess us, like a premonition, the moment we stepped beyond the bounds of our love-haunted Eden. Wherefore, having fully depicted that sovereign realm of delight, it would be a work of rather sad supererogation to dwell at length on our sojournings, as we made our way easily northward, in the subkingdoms of happiness. Beautiful it all was, but with a beauty more of evening than of sunrise. We were drawing to the night that has no voice but that of lonely introspection.

From les Baux we walked over the Alpines, six miles or so, to St. Remy, passing by the way those two famous fragments, tomb and triumphal arch, which are all that remains of a once prosperous Roman town. Standing solitary under the hills, they would seem to have been spared, in their chance juxtaposition, as a symbol and epitome to all future generations of the glory and vanity of the human story: Life's victory, Death's victory over Life, and Time, the last and mightiest, the conquerer of both. I might have read into them, had I possessed the seer's vision, the moral of all idylls in the world, including our own.

From St. Remy the balmy we took, having lunched and wandered an hour or two about the place, the prosaic motor-omnibus to the fruity little town of Châteaurenard, whence we bowled by the long white road, dusty and monotonous with its eternal plantations of esparto grass, into Avignon, reaching that city after dark, and in comfortable time for dinner at the Hôtel du Louvre, where we had elected to pitch our camp. Old house of the Templars (one meals, actually, in the very vaulted refectory of that ancient order), we felt, enjoying its pleasant hospitality, so little remote as yet from the spirit of antique romance, that our ex-Paradisian "fall" was hardly enough to disturb or abash us. We had fallen "soft," indeed, and, during the three or four days we stayed there, lived in a somewhat renewed glamour of enchantment. The year was now drawing on and in, closing upon the last days of October; but still the season moved in golden accord with our mood, showering peace and quiet sunshine upon our heads. Fifine had of course as a child lifted her trivial skirts and pointed her pretty toes to the *"L'on y danse tout en rond,"* and nothing now in all the grey old city delighted her so much as the broken bridge, on whose imagined stones the feet of countless generations of infants have danced and pattered. It moved her more than the mighty palace of the Popes, than the Cathedral, than the stupendous ramparts, than the great ruined fort of St. André, looming misty and gigantic on its hill across the river—though there, when we came to visit it, the old baker's dies for stamping the loaves of bread outside the ovens *did* fascinate her almost as much. They impressed her so, she said, with their suggestion of domestic fitness and tidiness.

For Fifine was tidy: have I never remarked upon it? Our difference in that respect was her perpetual lament. She could never be at ease in the presence of casual litter; a piece of paper flung in a grate, a picture hung crooked on a wall, would spoil the whole æsthetic value of a room to her; she folded her clothes at night; her toilette accessories had each its definite place on her dressing table, and any natural disorder was no sooner done with than she must be removing its evidences. Tidying-up was an obsession with her; I used to laugh at her about it, but it was no good.

"What is the use," I would say, "of sweeping up dust only to resettle, of making clear spaces for the fresh deposits that are sure to follow? It is a purely human monomania that of tidiness; nothing in nature sets us the example."

"I daresay," she would answer. "But dogs and cats and birds and trees have no sense of preparing for anything; and I, as a human being, have."

"What are you preparing for?"

"I don't know—the next world perhaps. It is just an instinct, like washing your hands."

"Washing your hands isn't an instinct, you goose. It is an acquired superstition."

"Well, so perhaps is tidiness. But anyhow it is a superstition founded on the Bible."

"How?"

"Isn't there something in it about keeping your house swept and garnished?"

I hooted. "No, that won't do. That was the house that proved so attractive to the unclean spirit and his brethren. You are hoist with your own petard, I am afraid, my Fifinette."

"O!" said Fifine. "Well, anyhow you won't make me believe that tidiness is a sin."

"No, it is only a 'preparation'—for what? fresh untidiness, say I. When you have paid all your bills, and filed the receipts, and checked and balanced your bank book, and swept the hearth clean, and sat down with a satisfied sense of accumulated scores settled, and of being able to start again with a clean slate, what follows? Why, the falling of new ashes into the fender, and the recovering of the slate with the same old fatuous irreconcilabilities between receipt and expenditure."

"Well, you know at least periodically how you stand, and where," said Fifine; "and that is a consolation."

How was it a consolation? How can a coat removed from the floor, say, and hung on a peg make one feel more sure of one's position? I have often tried to understand, and cannot. Or is there really in the instinct some subtle feeling of the temporary sojourner in a strange land, prepared for eventualities, ready, because unencumbered, to move on at a moment's notice? Travellers, explorers, are often the tidiest of men, clearing up behind them, as they advance, having its place for every article of their kit, and scrupulous to maintain it. To me, nevertheless, it is no comfort to know how I stand, if the result is to prove every item in the ledger against me. I am interested in my own solvency or insolvency, moral or material, only as regards their practical effects, and those occur automatically without my troubling my head with anticipations, or with manœuvrings for or against them. At the same time I am quite willing to admit an argument in favour of the *super*-natural instinct of tidiness, since Nature herself is atrociously untidy. Those who possess it may be spirits, finer than the common, who bring unconsciously from some other sphere the desire to mend, in their little piecemeal, the lamentable disorder of things mundane. Then human tidiness *may* be, in fact, the surest evidence of immortality; and indeed I hope it is. For if I laughed at it in Fifine, I loved its staid pretty manifestations enough to desire with all my soul to find now in their memory some comfort and assurance.

One entire day we devoted to a visit to the Pont-du-Gard, a super-impressive experience, since, owing to the lateness of the season, we had the whole stupendous mise-en-scène, lovely valley and striding aqueduct, to ourselves. We lunched gaily, sitting on the flat rocks of the river, and then climbed the hill, and walked through the huge artery of the bridge, which, drawing from the heart of Usèz, once flushed with life all the ramifying veins of Nîmes. The conduit is dry now, drained of its living force with the decay and death of the ancient city it supplied; but one still thinks of it somehow as a thing animate, a thing actually organic and sentient in the days when the throbbing of its mighty pulses shook the league-long hills by which it travelled.

That was our last ex-mural expedition; and the next morning, with a sigh of regret for what we were leaving, and of reluctance in the thought of the further stage it meant for us *away* from Paradise, and *towards* the uneasy problem of Paris, we shouldered our pack (figuratively) and took the train north to Orange.

This was, however, an event of its kind, since—ostensibly, at least—it stood for the mid-maze of our enterprise. We were travelling, if you remember, with the main purpose to visit Fifine's birthplace, and I could not but be, secretly, a little curious to learn how she proposed to herself to deal with a rather nervous question. It was hardly to be assumed but that, as the offspring of one of the richest and most powerful nobles in the land, her advent would have occurred amid environments the most notable the town could boast; whereas—but it is true I knew nothing as to the facts of her origin.

However, she resolved the difficulty quite quietly and naturally, and in the most convincing way possible; though I thought a little flush came to her cheek with the explanation. We got in about eleven o'clock of the morning, and were walking up the long avenue that leads from the station to the town, when I said to her:—

"Well, m'amie; how about the site of Fifine's nest? In what direction are we to seek it?"

"Indeed," she answered, "I know no more than you."

"You do not?"

"I was a baby at the time, you see."

"But not always a baby?"

"Always, as long as I was here. I remember nothing, absolutely nothing—only the oddest, most shadowy little impression, like a dream, of a great thing like a curtain, and a confusion of pots and pans, and dark people moving about among them."

I laughed. "It is queer, isn't it, that survival of first impressions—what decides it. Accident, perhaps; the accident of their alighting on a peculiarly sensitive patch of brain-matter. Hullo!"

We had been walking at haphazard, and had emerged suddenly into a broad open *Place*, which, dominated by the huge blind façade of the Roman Theatre, suggested somehow, with its scintillating crowds, an operatic stage before the rise of the curtain.

"There is your impression," said I—"realised to the life!"

It was actually so. Strewed all about the ground, with little alleys of commerce dividing the groups, was an infinite confusion of pottery—jugs, dishes, cooking utensils, and what not; and, pervading it, a number of picturesque figures, swarthy of face, hot-dyed of dress and neckerchief, the whole constituting a sort of gypsies' fair. Fifine stood as if dumbstricken.

"Perhaps now," I said, "the clue of memory taken up will lead you back to your birthplace?"

She shook her head. "No. But it—O, mon ami, I feel as if I want to cry!"

"You shall cry, Fifine, when we reach our quarters. Come; we will go to the best I know."

It was at the Hôtel de la Poste we put up; and I specify the fact for three particular reasons: it was from the window of my bedroom, in the Pension attached to that hotel, that I had had—as I was able now to point out to Fifine—my earlier impression of the plane-trees; it was in its salle-à-manger that I found my first opportunity to introduce to her the delectable mysteries of bouille-abaisse; it was in that room also that occurred—but let me come to it.

This dining-room was not, perhaps, of the cheeriest. It was ill-lighted, far from spacious, and fairly crowded, when we entered it, with a mixed assemblage of farmers, shop-keepers, and bagmen. A certain commercial importance attaches, I fancy, to Orange; and moreover market-day, had, no doubt, contributed its quota to the complement. Anyhow we had some difficulty in securing places at a table in a dark corner; but, once established, we prepared, after our custom, to enjoy ourselves thoroughly. And, lo! the first item on the menu was bouille-abaisse.

I crowed. "Tiens! The goal of our long romantic quest lies revealed to us at last. We are about to achieve our ideal; the spirit of abstract beauty offers to materialise before us. Eat of this ambrosia, my gossip, and count for its sake the toil well vindicated."

Fifine laughed, rosily, but in her little sedate way.

"Poor M. Cabarus!" she said. "It is a shame so to mock at his ideals. They were not the less fine and sincere because his personality failed to recommend them. It was a great soul, was it not, Felix, in a grotesque setting? But externals ought not to influence us. They mean nothing."

"Of course not," I said. "I have known the most abstemious men libelled in their waistcoats."

She laughed again, with a little protesting "tais-toi"—and the bouille-abaisse was placed before us. I watched her taste that Provençal delicacy, trifle a moment with it, put down her fork and lean back.

"You do not like it?" I asked, grinning.

"I think it is simply horrid," she said, making a face.

So we had come to Provence for nothing after all. However, for myself, I swallowed my disappointment with relish.

It was towards the end of our meal, when the company was somewhat thinning, that the event occurred. I was conscious of a sudden convulsive pressure of Fifine's shoulder against mine; looked up—and there was Carabas entering the room. We sat aghast and spellbound, but he did not observe us in our dusk corner. He sat himself down, as usual, at the long table, pulled off his gloves (brown kid gloves, and extensively worn), placed them, with his straw hat, on the chair beside him, examined the menu, looked up from his scrutiny with a full sigh of gratification, and round on his immediate company, self-conscious, challenging, and summoned the waiter with a gesture. That garçon, prompt, deferential, relaid the accessories, swept away contiguous crumbs, retreated, and reappeared—with a dish of veal.

"Bouille-abaisse!" exclaimed Carabas, in a voice that all might hear.

"Ah, pardon, Monsieur," apologised the waiter. "There is none left."

"It is on the menu."

"It is, in fact, as Monsieur says. But it is not in the kitchen."

"But this is infamous," said the visitor, very loud and indignant. "It is here, but it is not there, you say?"

"The demand, Monsieur will comprehend, has been excessive. There is not so much as a spoonful remaining."

"No demand should discover a good landlord unprepared. It is his business to keep faith with his guests. Tell him to come and explain."

The landlord came, apologised, expressed a thousand regrets. All propitiation was in vain. The disappointed troubadour fumed, refused, with many venomous "Bahs" and sarcastic "Chahs," every offer of an alternative *plat*, expressed his mortification in a growing fury of speech and emphasis, finally snatched up his hat and gloves from the chair beside, and stalked out of the room, followed by the still protesting hôtelier.

And so he disappeared from our lives, never to enter them again. We sat without a word, quiet as mice. Presently I looked at Fifine, my eyes twinkling. She responded, still silent, to the unspoken suggestion, rose, and we went out together.

"Now for the Roman theatre," I said, in a suppressed voice.

And it was not until we had penetrated into that august ruin, and climbed the tiers of seats, and sat ourselves down on the highest, in commanding view of the mighty proscenium and of the distant slopes of Mont Ventoux, that she permitted herself to give way, and broke into a fit of laughter which presently threatened to become hysterical.

"O—O!" she cried—"his libelled waistcoat! and after all I had said about his ideals!"

"Now, gossip," said I, putting my arm about her, for we sat there quite alone. "You must be reasonable, if you please."

She obeyed at once, dear child, and lay panting against me, only crying and laughing together now a little, and whispering words of love and remorse into my ear; and in a very little she was her own sane self once more.

We stayed in Orange only long enough to familiarise ourselves with its two noblest antiquities, the magnificent theatre and the arch that stands on the Lyons road; then went on by Valence to Vienne, where we lay a couple of nights, and visited the fine Cathedral, and the little temple like the Maison Carrée but not near so satisfying, and went to look down on the Rhone from the heights of Pipet—a lovely vision at sunset. Thence another day's journey, by way of the Côte Rôtie, and through the rich deep heart of the vine country, carried us to Dijon, town of cakes and cassis and mustard, where, in Burgundian streets, with the high-pitched tile-patterned roofs rising loftily above us, we seemed to realise, as never yet, the sense of an alien atmosphere, not unromantic yet not Paradise, and chill with the shadow of approaching change. Passed and gone were the tamarisk, and the rosemary, and the wild sweet aspic; passed were the ruby-fruited pomegranates, the fig-trees hung thick with purple pendents, coldly luscious to the thirsty palate, the great cypress rows, packed close to screen the gardens from the mistral; passed were the little brisk black bulls, the teams of slow white oxen ploughing in the fields, the be-ribboned sheep, the ranks of gourds, orange and ivory and palest blue, ripening in the open. They were not for our eyes again; but in their place, and in place of the luxuriant hills, peaceful pastures, and endless plains, and the interminable poplars of northern France stretching everywhere. The phantom roar of Paris already echoed in our hearts; and presently, impatient over its insistence, uneasy but allured, we came to a decision, and entered upon the final stage of our journey.

Fifine was very quiet during that stage. She sat most of the time in her corner by the window, looking out on the flowing landscape; sometimes, when she thought I did not observe her, letting her eyes rest on my face, mute, questioning, pathetic; occasionally rousing to enthusiasm over some picturesque detail of the paysage—a leafy farm; a town built on a gentle eminence, which just lifted it shapely above the levels; a group of poplars, singularly effective in its place. These poplars paid everywhere a largesse to the late season, scattering their gold over a bereaved land, and so freely, that only their royal crowns remained to them of all their profuse sovereignty. One could read into them a score of dreamy fantasies—here a silver stem bursting high overhead into a sparkling constellation, there a misty coppice, streaming ashy purple, and ridged with a running fire of stars. They thronged the subdued landscape, just emphasising with their soft radiance its autumn melancholy. Nowhere did they figure so beautiful as in the neighbourhood of Sens, which we passed at a short distance at twilight. Mirrored in the placid waters of the Yonne, the old town first appeared to us, lifting the velvet umber of its tower and huddled buildings against a lemon sky. A poplar or two hung above the river for foreground; there was hardly a ripple there to shake the pictured rushes; it was as lovely an impression of antique peace as I have ever encountered. Fifine, after we had passed it all, made a little gesture to me, and I came and sat by her side, when she stole her hand into mine. I thought I knew what was in her heart—something emotional, a little piteous, the sense of a loveliness spent and of doubts to come. I pressed the soft palm in reassurance.

And so at last—Paris. The benediction of the season remained with us to the end. As we turned under the archway in the Rue de Fleurus, we left behind us the memory of a quiet little moon rising over the towers of Notre Dame.

Madame Crussol appeared to greet us as we passed the conciergerie.

"Ah! So you are back," she said. "It is a time ill-chosen for those who would seek Paris for its comfort and its safety. You had better have remained with your savages in the south."

Her manner was severe, if her utterance was cryptic. But I was confident in her secret regard for me; and I believe she had always a soft place in her heart for Fifine. Nevertheless I was startled for the moment.

"What is all that?" I said; "and why and with what are we threatened, ma bonne?"

And she told us.

CHAPTER XXII

IT was not very much, after all: just this. Paris, it appeared, was suffering, had been suffering for some weeks, from one of those epidemics of panic which will occasionally seize on an entire populace—especially if of the excitable and impressionable Latin race—and we happened to have alighted on it at the psychologic moment. You will remember, perhaps, that brief plague of motor-dacoitage which for a time kept the whole city in a state of nervous ferment, until it came to culminate in a siege and massacre which were very much a replica of the London Sidney Street affair? Well, that was the occasion; and, according to Madame Crussol, a general condition of terror prevailed; good citizens walking furtively, with looks askance at every petrol-driven vehicle, and bad searching their consciences for past oppressions in any possible way provocative of reprisals. No one knew whose turn it would be next with these murderous miscreants, whom a persistent baffling of the police and long immunity from arrest had rendered absolutely reckless.

The story had left Fifine and me, I may say, virtually unconcerned. Fresh from the sun and the south, serenely ensconced in the impregnable citadel of our love, we felt no tremors but such as arose from the thought of the social reckoning we should have to pay at last, and the possible difficulties in the way of an accommodation. All the trepidations of the outside world were as nothing to us in the shadow of that problem; I do not think that, after we had entered my rooms and shut ourselves in, we once again referred to the subject of the panic, or to Madame Crussol's excited enlarging on it for our benefit.

As I turned up the light and closed the door, Fifine stood and looked around her, with a smile upon her lips. And then she sighed, and turned to me wistfully.

"What am I to call it, Felix?" she said in a low voice.

"Home, Fifine," I answered.

She sighed again, like a very happy thing, and went about the room, renewing her acquaintance with its objects, touching this one lovingly, that reprovingly for its untidiness; and presently, coming to her portrait on the wall, she bent and kissed it—"not for your own sake," she said severely to the beauty, "but for the sake of the hand that flattered you."

It was very touching to me, this sense of sure possession, as illustrated in her pretty joys and confidences. A dimness always comes to my eyes in recalling that night—the last we were ever to spend together. For the cup was nearly drained, and the scroll written—Fifine's whole story, as a woman reads such things; and yet but a paragraph in mine, one brief glowing passage lost in a waste of platitude. Sometimes I wonder how men, having once known a perfect confidence in love, can bear to cloud its memory with later fancies. Gross and imperfect, our souls, I suppose, are not meet for the sublime; but, having gathered and eaten fruit from heaven, we must be for taking the taste of its intolerable sweetness out of our mouths with some coarser earthlier savour. Yet I think I may say that I have that of myself put away, locked into secrecy, jealously excluded from knowledge, which no woman but one has ever shared or shall share. It is hers, and, by so much as it is hers alone, the worthless residue of me lies to what flattering uses the interested can extract from it.

There was store of potted things in the flat, and we had bought some rolls and butter by the way, which, with a bottle of good wine from the cupboard, made us an ample meal. I ate and drank a thought gravely myself, preoccupied with the consideration of something that was inevitable to follow; and Fifine, conscious of herself as of my mood, was little more inclined to talk. She made but a half-hearted meal; and, when we rose at last, I was struck all at once, seeing the breathless parting of her lips and her poor cheek's whiteness, with a realisation of the strain which that long suspense must have been putting upon her. However, it had to be gone through with, and the sooner the more merciful to her.

Without a word I led her into the studio, where, under the light, I took her face between my hands and turned it up so as to look at me.

"Fifine," I said.

She closed her eyes; I could see her lips trembling; but she made no answer.

"Fifine," I said again, very quietly: "You know what it is I have to say; what cannot any longer be evaded, now we are returned. In all this—in this question between us—where does the Marquis de Beaurepaire come in?"

I felt a quiver go through her; and something like the faintest of moans swelled like a pulse in her throat. Overcome with love and pity, I put my lips to hers, and fondled her soft hair, and murmured words of passionate reassurance into her ear.

"Come," I said. "This is no judgment, dear love, but a confession and an absolution. Come and sit with me, and hide your face if you will, and lose all your fear in something I am going to ask you."

I sat down, and she slipped to my feet, where she leaned, her right arm flung over my knees, her cheek resting upon it, so that her face was turned from me.

"I asked you," I said, "where, in this question between us, the Marquis de Beaurepaire came in. Shall I answer, then, for you, Fifine? He does not come in anywhere, does he? If any one's formal consent to our marriage is needed, it is not his, I am sure."

She raised her head quickly.

"Marriage, Felix!" she whispered, in an amazed voice.

"I have thought it all out," I said. "What does the 'guinea stamp' matter one way or the other. Love, we know, is the only bond, by whatever name we call it. Throw this sop to the priests, if, by satisfying them, it secures us our idyll in peace. It makes no difference to the understanding between us. There is only one thing that can tie us, or that we should ever wish to tie. Were it to fray and snap—I think I know you, Fifine—that thread of convention would count for nothing in our severance. Even our knowledge of its existence would count for nothing—only the liberty to be ourselves unchallenged."

"But, what you once said!" she answered, still in the same amazed tone.

"You mean in response to your query about men of genius, and their use for wives?"

"Yes."

"I am not a man of genius, Fifine. Perhaps that is it."

"But I say you are."

"Then, for love of me, you would rather remain my mistress, which is to say my imagination, than become my wife, at the risk of turning my imagination out of doors?"

"I should not do that," she said. "But, whatever I were called, I should stay if you told me, and go if you told me."

"And that is just what I say. The 'stamp' is immaterial any way; at its best a sort of social diploma, entitling one to legal protection in one's daily practice of the virtues. Will you marry me, Fifine?"

"Yes, if you wish it, Felix."

"And do not you wish it?"

"It is only that I am frightened to think of 'the poor Billy tethered to his stake in the backyard.'"

I smiled, recalling my own words so faithfully remembered.

"I promise you I will never submit to the tethering," I said. "Rather, for your sake, I will emulate the golden one, leaping from rock to rock, and always, though pursued, unattainable."

"If you would—ah, I could be so happy in following you," said Fifine, "though my knees were bleeding all the way, and my nails torn from their fingers."

"Poor little fingers! Well, in that case, counting me your assured ideal, what are your prejudices in favour of—the existing or the potential?"

"Then—I am only a woman, Felix—I should, I *should* like my love for you to be given a name—in case——"

She did not end her sentence; but I stooped and gathered her to my heart, and whispered:—

"Perhaps that *is* the ideal, Fifine. O, my sweet, how I am lost in love of you! But here comes in the question—what is immaterial to the bond we know, but there is something material to it, Fifine—the truth."

She stole her arms about my neck; then leaned her head back, and looked at me steadily, passionately.

"Yes, Felix. How did you learn?"

"That Brooking girl, as it happened, had once given lessons in drawing to the Countess Josephine. She did not recognise in you her former pupil?"

"And you enlightened her?"

"Of course I did not. I finessed in the most admirable way."

"So you have known it all the time; and ever since you have been looking upon me as a liar and impostor?"

"No, indeed, my girl. I knew you were bound by a secret not your own; that you were trying to be loyal to a trust."

"Felix—it was that, but not only that. I dreaded horribly that the truth might repel you."

"You thought me no better than a snob, in fact?"

"O, no, no! I thought only that you would despise one who could so lie to you! And then—your own origin—I used to cry to myself over your scorn of the people. Felix——!" her arms tightened, a desperate pain came into her eyes—"*I* am a child of the people myself." She paused an instant— "Doesn't it make you hate me?"

"That is foolish, Fifine," I said gravely; "and very wrong to our understanding. What have I ever said to justify such an assumption in you?"

"O, forgive me, Felix, forgive me, forgive me! You don't know what my mind has suffered."

"I do not scorn the people, child; and, if I did, what has love to do with social differences? And, if there are any such between us here, the credit for the best is yours. I love every individual part of you; your wit, your intelligence, and your manners, as well as your pretty body. Now, what may I ask you and what may I not?"

"Ask, please, Felix."

"Very well. Your particular confidences with my step-sister shall be sacred from me. If you reveal them, you shall reveal them in your own good time."

"When she lets me—if I may."

"But, in this matter of our marriage—well, you know your own laws of fiançailles? If there is a father, his consent must be obtained. Shall I hazard a guess? The violoncellist——?"

"I was always afraid you might suspect."

"Why should you be afraid? Has he been a good father to you, Fifine?"

She sighed a little.

"Pauvre petit! He was not born ever to fight a difficult world. But he is a great musician, Felix."

"That time he came and went—you had been lending him money, I suppose?"

"He is always so poor."

"How did he learn the way to you?"

"He was in the secret, to a certain extent; he had to be. But he should not have come; it was against the agreement."

"And your mother, Fifine?"

"She is long dead. She was an actress. She was in the company of the Comédie Française when they played in that Roman Theatre at Orange the year I was born. A Provençale by birth, my papa had brought her south to prepare for the two events, first the domestic and later the professional. We stayed on in Orange for three years: I don't know how we lived or where; and then one day she ran away from Papa and from me. I think it killed his heart. He could never bear to speak of that time; and so it is all a shadow to me. But it was so strange sitting up there in the theatre, and thinking what it meant to me, both first and last."

"Not the least poetic of the dramas played in it, I'll go bail. Now tell me, Fifine: how is your father called?"

"Fréron, Felix."

"And your yourself?"

"It is truly my own name—mine as well as hers. I am Josephine Fréron."

"So? That is something saved from the wreck—just a plank or a spar as I was going under. You haven't another remnant for me to cling to, I suppose—your age, for instance?"

"I am nineteen."

"As certified? Good! I am getting quite buoyant. Why, what are the eyes opening so tragic about? You soft, foolish, sensitive, covetable goose, when are you going to trust to my passion as something a little stabler and more enduring than a summer's day. Come, we are devoted lovers; it only remains for us to be unreserved friends."

That night—so beautiful—such a perfect consummation! That pause, our journey ended, and the radiant serenity of the stars above, and, beneath, the black unseen gulf, plunging from our feet! I can hardly bear to dwell upon its loveliness, its poignancy. We sat till late, quietly talking together. All that was not Marion's—and of what value to me in the prized context was that brief parenthesis?—was made mine—the story of her young innocuous days. She had been good; she had been chaste, and in circumstances well calculated to trip by the feet one less scrupulous in her self-respect, less cleanly intelligent, less precociously worldly, perhaps, since her self-education had been pursued in sometimes slippery places. For they had been poor; and indeed I gathered so far that the money consideration had been an incentive to this part she had consented to play in an unknown plot. What issue she had conceived of it, as regarded my inclusion in the conspiracy? Why, she had had no time to think: it had all been decided in a moment; and at least she knew that I was of the Marion stock (which I was not, by the way), and, as such, must pass for morally trustworthy. Besides, she had regarded the movement as of only a temporary character; and besides, besides, the actual fun of the adventure had something tickled her young humour—the prospect of experiencing, for however brief a time, the joys of social adulation in her feigned part. That was natural and delicious; but what she could not foresee was the sympathetic nature of the environments to which she was committing herself. She had her own fine aspirations, her own ideals: the danger came when they were allured into interest in a subject who could be coaxed and petted into giving them practical expression. And so grew in her the subordination of flesh to soul. She would consent to surrender the lesser to the greater, to buy our mutual self-realisation at the fullest price I asked.

And so at last I knew my Fifine wholly; the little story of her loves and her perplexities lay bared before me. Ah, why had I not accepted that confidence earlier? When she had hesitated that day on the brink of revelation, what mad perversity had made me reject her? Likely, then, the air cleared, we should have long lingered out our return, until—but that does not bear thinking of.

Presently we took to recalling softly, happily, the golden secrets of our wanderings together. And, so murmuring, she fell asleep in my arms.

CHAPTER XXIII

THERE are those who pet their own misery, who derive pleasure from dwelling upon it; there are those who gather comfort from putting off an inevitable evil day; there are those who can borrow even a brief agonised solace from delaying their own execution. I am not of such. If a tooth worries me I have it out; if a painful thing has to be done, I like to get it over as quickly and as shortly as possible. I do not propose to myself to linger over this last chapter of Fifine's story: all that is essential to its elucidation is soon told.

There was the perfect night; and, then, the dawn! It opened, as I would have had it open, dismally, ominously. A grey drizzle soaked the streets; the shimmering of the silver night was all alloyed into a leaden ruin; a sodden curtain hung over the whole city.

I was bound on an early visit to M. Fréron. He lived, I had learned—*he? they*, when they were together—in a little dingy suite of rooms above a curio-dealer's shop in the Rue de Seine. We kissed, she and I—I am terse, you see—and I left her standing and looking after me—such eyes, my God. Down in the street I shivered; a doleful epilogue this to the sunny story of Provence.

M. Fréron was not at home. He had stated that he would be back, in case anybody should call, at three o'clock or thereabouts. In case any one should call? Whom could he expect, then, this timid, invertebrate old nobody; unless, indeed, it were some one on whom he depended for his little extras, luxuries; some one for whom his love, perhaps, figured a trifle cupboardly. Well, he should not suffer for me.

It was no matter. I would return about that time on the chance of finding him. I had a plenty of small commissions to fill up the interval; and, in fact, I did not return to the Rue de Seine until near four o'clock.

M. Fréron, I was told, was again out. Yes, again. He had come back punctual to his appointment, and had been almost immediately fetched away by a sergent de ville. The man had come, and they had left together, in a great hurry. No one knew what was his errand; it was impossible to say how long the musician would be gone. He had departed without a word, but looking certainly very pale and agitated.

Obviously it was no good my remaining; the interview must be postponed. I was not much concerned over that; at the worst it represented no more than a formal necessity, about whose issue I had not the slightest doubt. Fifine was what she was; not what her father had made her. I knew that much. He would not object to a paying son-in-law, on the strength of whatever irregularities provided. He had been known even to comment a little peevishly on the rigidity of his daughter's code—not rebuking it, but only feebly wondering. The "professional" class is always a little apt to indefiniteness in these matters; and when one is very poor——!

I turned my face for home. That should have been an occasion for joy; yet somehow a dense oppression sat on me. I could not master it; it increased with every step I took. It was the weather, no doubt—or was it that sort of moral dyspepsia, common to those, I had heard, who are realising for the first time their committal to the matrimonial lottery? Were we really wise in throwing this sop to the social Cerberus? And for what? Why, for nothing but that we might penetrate into the dismal regions he guarded. What a fool I had been, maybe! She had given me everything: the law would take away the loveliest part of that gift, its spontaneity. Yet, if *she* wished it; if it would make her happier? And, then, the tender thought she had implied—the promise——!

No, she was right, God bless her! Dismiss that as settled. But the oppression would not lift. Damn that sergent de ville! Somehow he had been there all the time, hurrying and hurrying through the background of my brain; I recognised it now—

I recognized *him*, or his like, in the flesh the next moment. He stood at the entrance to the archway in the Rue de Fleurus, officially barring the way to a crowd of people who pressed and gloated to look in. They hovered there, a vulturine swarm, fulsome and unclean in the soaking twilight. What was the matter? What carrion had attracted them? For some instinctive reason they parted to let me through; but the man challenged me. A thought of the tragedy that I had so often mocked at as a stage illusion had caught at my heart like a physical agony, and it was with a thick gasp that I gave my name. He murmured "Continuez," looking at me curiously, as he moved to let me by, and I went on into the dancing shadows. There were others congregated there—officers, strangers—a confused indefinite group; but only and for all eternity to me the white aghast face of Madame Crussol, hung up in the dim gaslight and staring my way like a stone gargoyle.

"Comment?" I said, with an insane little giggle. "What is all this about; and why do you look at me like that?"

And thereat the gargoyle seemed to detach itself from the wall, and to spring at me with a shriek:—

"Go to her—she is hurt—she is dying—she has called for you!"

Go to her? Where? There was a roaring in my brain: somebody was leading me by the arm: we were in a running cab, and a whirl of mud and water flashed incessantly outside the windows. It was a brief race: the Hospital was somewhere in the Boulevard de Port Royal close by: but if it had extended over hours, I could have found no word to say to my escort—no question to put to him. What was that moment for idle discussion? and he could have nothing essential to tell me that I did not know already. There was a subconscious voice going on in me all the time, whispering of an inviolable hush; a dark soft hand seemed to steal itself over my eyes. I never thought of vengeance. What did the motive or the method concern me? This tragedy was one not of the living hate but of the living love. I thought I kept saying to myself, "But she fell asleep in my arms—but she fell asleep in my arms," over and over again, in a protesting monotonous amazement; but no doubt I uttered nothing articulate.

In a moment the flash and whirr of the mud had ceased; and a muffled throbbing and drumming succeeded. And then suddenly we were in a dimly-lighted vestibule, and as suddenly moving on by cold clean passages, always cold and always clean, yet intricate and eternal, and a soft-stepped woman went eternally with us. Her soundless upspringing had been quite in keeping with the churchlike atmosphere of the place; she might have been the verger especial to its ghosts and tombs. And presently we passed an open doorway from which exhaled an essence thinly sweet and shuddering, and glancing mechanically in I saw the flitting of dusk shapes, and shadows pierced with gleams, and a vortex of wooden forms, going down in concentric rings to a shining altar. But we went by, and did not stop—not until the end came in the little quiet room with its truckle bed.

Then I knew too well; and knew from the first I had never felt one thrill of hope. They were quite gentle with me. She had survived to consciousness, they said—after that ineffectual attempt to extract the bullets—only long enough to make her brief depositions and to give them her father's address. But many times she had whispered my name, imploring them to send for me; and she had died with it on her lips. Died with it on her lips—and I, loitering in the rainy street!

Her face was quite peaceful, they told me—quite peaceful and beautiful. But I would not let them show it me. There were the living eyes to remember; and I could not bear it. What had *this* to do with the vital reality, the hot vivid ecstasy of old confidences?

The father was there—aghast, tremulous, helpless. He recognised me, and, rising from his knees, came to me, weeping:—

"You were her friend, Monsieur: you will continue to be mine for her sake?" And then he threw up his hands—"My child, my little one, with that voice of an angel, that sang so sweetly on the earth, and now goes to mingle with the heavenly choirs! Never, never shall I hear thee sing again! And what hadst thou ever done of harm to mark thee down the prey to these cruel miscreants?"

I regarded him stonily.

"She never sang to me," I said.

He was sobbingly, self-interestedly eager at once to explain and propitiate—

"She would not, indeed, Monsieur, uninvited: she was ever modest as to her own gifts: it was to the realisation of the best there was in those she loved that she devoted her unselfish faculties."

And his plaintive cry pierced into my heart like a knife.

* * * * * * *

"I was under the archway"—so ran those pitiful faint-spoken depositions—"when I saw an automobile stop quickly at the entrance in the dusk and rain. I moved to retreat; and instantly footsteps came following me, and a voice whispered close behind: 'Mademoiselle Fréron, I think?' I turned, and saw a man. His face was masked. I was too frightened to speak. And then suddenly there was a flash and shock, and another flash and shock, and everything went."

Why was she in the archway at all? She had been nervous and restless because her friend, M. Dane, had not returned from a certain expedition, attested Madame Crussol, and had ventured out in her anxiety to look for him. She herself, ensconced in her logement, had not heard the stranger's words: it was the sound of the double shot that had brought her hurrying out. Then she had seen the poor innocent's body prostrate on the stones, and a man walking from it up the yard. He walked, very cool and deliberate, towards a lighted car that stood at the gate. She screamed; whereupon the man had turned, showing a masked face impossible to identify, and had pointed a pistol at her, terrifying her into silence. And in another moment he had jumped into the car and was gone.

But the reason why this girl had been deliberately, as it seemed, marked down for a victim to the prevailing Thuggism? Ah! that did not appear. There was something, said the police, of the nature of a vendetta in the methods of these bandits, and until its complications could be unravelled, its various provocations must be held only problematical. In the meantime all remained confusion and terror and perplexity. For me, I was content to let it rest at that, keeping to myself any theory I might have formulated as to a vengeance wreaked by a half-insane morphiomaniac, through vile emissaries quick to seize on opportunism, on the discovered head of a poor innocent instrument in his outwitting. There had been whispers of suspicious characters seen loafing in the neighbourhood some days before our return; there had been whispers———

But let it all pass. Theories are not evidence; nor was I interested in anything but the staring fact of my own desolation. A new Reign of Terror, and ten thousand decadent aristocrats chopped by the head in the Place de la Concorde, would not mend that inexorable fact. I was suffering only to shake free from all the inquiries, official and magisterial, that ensued—the siftings, the empty evidences, the procès verbals which left things after all precisely where they had started. It was known clearly at the end, and not much more was known, that I had been Mademoiselle Fréron's friend and protector, and that I had been actually on my way to propose a formal emendation to that understanding, when the catastrophe occurred. The exposure, so to speak, was an acutely painful one to me—not because of its moral aspect, which from first to last to the Parisian was quite en règle, but because the inner holiness of our idyll seemed violated in the publicity it brought. But at last they set me free to go and suffer my utter loneliness unvexed; and with that and my memories I shut myself away.

CHAPTER XXIV

ONE day I was pacing my room in the restlessness that now seldom left me, when a knock sounded on my door; and, going irritably to open it, I saw my step-sister Marion. She looked at me and I at her for a full minute before either of us spoke; then "May I come in, Felix?" she said in a low voice.

I shrugged my shoulders. "You may come or you may go," I said. "It is all one to me."

I turned from her, and she closed the door and followed me. In the studio she sat down, while I continued my wild-beast pacing.

"You are not looking well," she said suddenly.

"What does that matter—to you or any one?" I answered, and came to a quick stop before her. "Did you really call to enquire after my health?"

"I came to say good-bye."

"O?"

"I am going back to England."

"Having satisfactorily completed what you came to do here?"

"Yes, in a way. Mademoiselle de Beaurepaire is about to be married."

I stared down on her in amazement.

"Upon my word!" I said. "This to my face?"

"What," she answered, a little frigidly, "is the use of keeping up that fiction, since you and your affairs have become public property?"

"None, for you, perhaps, in default of what we will call a natural remorse or shame."

"I will not have you say that, Felix. Apply it to yourself, rather, remembering the advantage you took of the trust committed to you."

"I took no advantage, as you call it, until I learnt that the trust was a lying one."

"She told you?"

"She did not. You will be careful, if you are wise, how you deal with her name here. She was loyal to her betrayers to the end. It was quite by accident that I learned the truth—the imposture to which we had both been induced to lend ourselves—unconsciously on my part—by a clergyman's moral daughter."

"You may save your sarcasm, Felix: it does not impress me. I had a desperate duty to perform, and I took the only means possible at hand to effect it. It was partly with a view to giving you the explanation which is certainly your due that I came to-day. If you wish to hear, you shall."

I had resumed my tramping, but stopped at that, and faced her.

"O!" I said; "you think it my due, do you? Having robbed and ruined me, you think it just to supply me with the psychologic reasons for your act."

"How can you hold me, directly or indirectly, responsible for this tragedy? Am *I* in collusion with these bandits, do you suppose?"

I stood looking at her—no more; but for all her resolution she found something in that searching inquisition beyond her endurance; and her eyes fell before it, while a faint spot of colour came to her sallow cheek.

"Not you, Marion," I said softly—"no, not you."

She looked up quickly, with a desperate effort to recover her self-command.

"Thank you, at least, Felix," she said, "for that handsome admission."

"Marion," I said, still quite quietly confronting her: "how is your noble employer regarding this desertion of yours?"

"He is not regarding it at all. He has had a paralytic stroke, and if he recovers, which is improbable, he will never regard anything again, in reason. A fortnight ago he was removed from the Hôtel Beaurepaire, and he will not return."

I nodded my head, my eyes a little wide.

"So? You interest me. Well, we know to whom vengeance belongs. It is a comfort to think of the settlement being so near." I went up and down again, and again stopped. "You may as well tell me," I said. "Having it now on my mind, I should be worried, lacking an explanation; and I want to get it all cleared away, all the wickedness and the abomination, that the only memory I care about may be left sweet."

"You speak nearer the truth than you think, Felix. Wickedness and abomination indeed: you will understand, when you know; and perhaps then you will take a less merciless view. You remember what I told you about Monseigneur's discovery, and his mad fury thereon? It was necessary to get the girl away, with all despatch, out of his clutches. That evening things had come to an appalling crisis—and she was ill. The nervous shock and strain had been too much for her, and she was in bed—not in her own room, but in one far remote and secreted—incapable of the least effort—to move her would have been certainly fatal. I had made all arrangements for her transference to the school I told you of; but some one—the house was full of his tools, his panders—had betrayed me. That night the girl Fréron happened to be there. She was said to have an attractive voice—I am no judge of such things myself—and she was used to give Josephine singing lessons. She was quite in the confidence of the Countess, who was greatly attached to her in her way, and she was more or less acquainted with the state of affairs. It was to her was due that sudden inspiration, which did actually save the situation. 'Why not,' she said, 'pretend that I am Mademoiselle, and under her name hurry me away to the school, where I can pass for her until such time as it is safe to acknowledge the deception? If we manage cleverly, Monseigneur will be informed of the escape of his daughter, and will no longer think of looking for her in the house; so that, on your return, you will be able, quietly and unsuspected, to nurse her into convalescence, and thereafter seize your first opportunity to smuggle her away, and carry her into hiding, whether at the school itself or elsewhere?' It was a counsel of desperation; but at least it was a straw on which to seize in a terrible emergency. I seized on it, Felix. Dressed in Josephine's cloak and hat—the two girls were fortunately much of a figure—Fréron left with me, leaving it to be inferred, by those interested in my movements, that I had actually put my plan into execution. It is useless to detail the particulars of our escape; but at least one thing is certain, that Monseigneur actually believed his prey to have eluded him, and that he took instant steps, on the information received, to have us followed and intercepted. In that sink of abomination, however, there existed one or two unequal to the strain of villainy imposed upon them; and it was to one of these we owed the warning which diverted us from our course. You know the rest."

Marion ended; and I regarded her in gloomy cynicism.

"No, not by a great deal," I said. "Why, for instance, did you not confide the truth to me?"

"I believed it possible, Felix, that, in spite of all our cunning, his emissaries might track her down."

"Track whom down? O, I see! And, after disposing of her, report to the Marquis the fulfilment of his vengeance on an unruly daughter?"

Marion was silent.

"You holy devil!" I said. "You astute unconscionable devil!"

She rose in great agitation.

"You do not understand, Felix."

"What am I to understand? That this poor unhappy girl was to be sacrificed to a misapprehension rather than risk the truth which would have saved her, and that, for the sake of that misapprehension, I, who might have righted it, was to remain uninformed?"

"It would not have saved her. When he came to hear it, which he did at last—God knows how!—his fury was implacable against every instrument in his deception."

"Poor ruined child! And this was your return to her for her devoted self-sacrifice? Why did he not kill *you*?"

"I don't know. I had an influence over him: I dared him to his face; and for some reason he respected me."

"I don't doubt it—he recognised in you his superior; his arch-fiend. And you dare to accuse me—*me*, of an abuse of trust. Wasn't that in the reckoning? Didn't you know it was? Her virtue, like her life, was only a pawn in the game you were playing. I can see that clearly enough now. All, everything must be sacrificed to your damned emergency—a child of the people rather than a child of the aristocracy. O, you are the very saint of snobs!"

She was controlling herself. She had made a tremendous effort, and stood facing me, flushed but resolute.

"You may say what you like, Felix," she answered. "I make allowances for your natural grief, however wrong the false interpretation it drives you to put upon my motives. But you do not understand those, I say; and I, who do, cannot at this hour believe that I was misdirected in the course I pursued. It is justified in the result; in an appalling design frustrated; in a rescue accomplished at last through much difficulty and danger. You regard it only as an imperilled life saved."

"What else?"

"Much more and much worse."

"What worse?"

"O, Felix Dane! the worse that was actually perpetrated, and on very much the same provocation, by a mediæval monster called Francesco Cenci. It was to save her from that fate that I did what I had to do."

Marion was gone—and in peace. We parted friends; but I hope I may never see her again. Truly, character is the fruit of circumstance, rich or insipid according to the climate it inhabits. Transplanted straight from a humdrum parsonage into the volcanic soil of passion and insanity, who would have thought that that starchy puritanism could ever have developed the qualities of resource and imagination it came to reveal in the face of almost supernatural difficulties and terrors. She was a great soul, I think—the material of a great commander, rigid and unswerving in the course which her duty, as she conceived it, pointed out to her; prepared, if necessary, to sacrifice the lesser to the greater where the ultimate good demanded an inexorable decision.

But I turned from her at last to my dreams, with a sigh of renunciation of all things in the world that were not of them or for them. I knew at length the whole that was to be known of the story of Fifine, and, for that knowledge, all of new that blossomed from it was the piteous added sense of martyrdom. She had suffered, my darling, that her sister might be spared.

That evening, for the first time since my bereavement, I lifted her portrait from the place where I had laid it with its face to the wall, and we sat and talked together, she and I; and, with the tears dropping unconstrained down my cheeks, I upbraided her tenderly for that, of all her sweetnesses, she had withheld from me one that I should have loved among the best.

Now that night, falling asleep and dreaming, I was all at once on the shining hill-sides of les Baux, climbing and seeking alone, but with a great rapture in my soul; and a thousand butterflies looped about my head, and a scent of warm crushed lavender went with me like incense—only I was alone. But suddenly from amongst the ruins came a voice to me, singing so sweetly that my heart brimmed over to hear it in a very ecstasy of joy, and with blinded eyes I stumbled on and towards the beautiful tones—so strange, yet so familiar. And, lo! my girl, with yearning smiling eyes, and extended arms—

I have heard it, then—I will never believe but that I have heard it. Could she bear to withhold from me, even in death, one charm that had not been mine?

And so ends Fifine's story. No man in all his life has known a sweeter love; no man a bitterer desolation.

Finis